Battle Green Vietnam

Battle Green Vietnam

The 1971 March on Concord, Lexington, and Boston

Elise Lemire

PENN

UNIVERSITY OF PENNSYLVANIA PRESS

PHILADELPHIA

Published by
University of Pennsylvania Press
Philadelphia, Pennsylvania 19104-4112
www.upenn.edu/pennpress

Printed in the United States of America on acid-free paper

10 9 8 7 6 5 4 3 2 1

A catalogue record for this book is available from the Library of Congress.

ISBN 978-0-8122-5297-2

For Eli

CONTENTS

INTRODUCTION

The Power of Place and Performance

On November 12, 1969, in a cable to a small antiwar news agency in Washington, DC, independent investigative journalist Seymour Hersh revealed that the situation in Vietnam was far worse than Americans realized.

"Lt. William L. Calley Jr., 26 years old, is a mild-mannered, boyish-looking Vietnam combat veteran with the nickname 'Rusty,'" Hersh began in an explosive article that thirty-five newspaper editors around the country would decide to run the next day. Young Rusty had committed an unfathomable act of barbarity in a war the world's most powerful military had still not managed to win against a country the size of California. After initially looking the other way, "the Army is completing an investigation of charges that he deliberately murdered at least 109 Vietnamese civilians during a search-and-destroy mission in March 1968."[1]

While the public was stunned to learn what had happened in the residential area the American military mistakenly called My Lai, many of the men who had fought in Southeast Asia were not. In January 1971, a New York City–based antiwar Vietnam veterans' group convened hearings in Detroit about the sickening regularity of American atrocities. Over one hundred Vietnam veterans from across the United States showed up to testify.[2]

"We intend to demonstrate that My Lai was no unusual occurrence, other than, perhaps, the number of victims all killed in one place, all at one time, all by one platoon of us," explained an Ohio veteran who had led a rifle platoon in the same division as Lieutenant Calley. Continuing to read the organizers' opening statement to a packed hotel auditorium, the veteran condemned the entire military for the massacre and for the murder of so many other Vietnamese people on what the gathered antiwar veterans believed was an unprecedented scale. "We intend to show that the policies of Americal Division, which inevitably resulted in My Lai, were the policies of other Army and Marine divisions as well. We intend to show that war crimes in Vietnam did not start in March 1968, or in the village of Son My or with one Lieutenant Calley. We intend to indict those really responsible for My Lai, for Vietnam, for attempted genocide."[3]

The federal government had sold the Vietnam War to the American public at the height of the Cold War as a necessary means of stopping the spread of communism from Vietnam to the rest of Asia and across the world. But American soldiers sent out to find and engage the enemy on what the military callously named "search-and-destroy" missions quickly discovered that instead of encountering the ill-equipped communist enemy they had been told to expect, they were met at every turn by fierce freedom fighters willing to do anything to liberate their homeland from the American invaders. The veterans testified that after months in the field losing GI after GI to sniper attacks and booby traps while under pressure from American military officials to increase the daily "body count," or number of enemies killed, American troops were dangerously on edge and utterly broken in spirit. Often choking back tears, they insisted that murdering civilians, torturing enemy soldiers, and desecrating corpses were regular, if not daily, occurrences. Over the course of three days, the veterans built their case that "My Lai," as the crime came to be called, "was no unusual occurrence."[4]

But while Americans had proven themselves willing to read the extensive press coverage of the horrors unleashed over the course of four hours on March 16, 1968, they were not prepared to hear that war atrocities were, in the veterans' military parlance, standard operating procedure. The same journalists who spent months covering Hersh's revelations ignored what the veterans in Detroit had to say. America seemed to be suffering from what the antiwar veterans' frustrated national spokesman identified as atrocity fatigue.

Battle Green Vietnam: The 1971 March on Concord, Lexington, and Boston tells the story of how America's antiwar Vietnam veterans finally grabbed and held the national spotlight by simultaneously mobilizing two powerful tools: place and performance.[5]

There are numerous examples in American history of citizens utilizing place or performance to great effect. In one of the most celebrated cases of using performance to make a political statement, colonists in Massachusetts darkened their faces and dressed up as Native Americans before dumping a shipment of tea into Boston Harbor. While the protestors' destruction of the tea sent the message to British officials that the colonists would not pay taxes that had been levied by Parliament without their consent, it was the performative nature of the 1773 Boston Tea Party that signaled to officials the true depths of their conviction. While modern Americans can bemoan the colonists' appropriation of Native American culture, especially as it came on the heels of a genocidal war against the continent's original inhabitants, it was the protestors' Native American costumes that asserted they no longer identified as subjects of the Crown. They were Americans.[6]

In a famous example of marshaling the power of place, Dr. Martin Luther King Jr. gave his "I Have a Dream" speech at the 1963 March on Washington for Jobs and Freedom in front of the Lincoln Memorial with its massive statue of the Civil War–era president. This "hallowed spot," as Dr. King termed it, allowed him to bolster his claim that the freedom promised by Abraham Lincoln when he issued the Emancipation Proclamation must finally be extended to the enslaved's descendants. The Great Emancipator was physically standing by Dr. King's side, sharing his dream that white Americans would finally see fit to destroy "the manacles of segregation and the chains of discrimination" that precluded African Americans, King declared, from sharing the Declaration of Independence's promise of "Life, Liberty and the pursuit of Happiness."[7]

In the spring of 1971, four months after the Detroit hearings, a large contingent of antiwar Vietnam veterans in New England drew on both means, of place and performance, when they decided that rather than continuing to merely describe the atrocities carried out by Americans in Vietnam, they would work to end the war by enacting them at the storied locales in Massachusetts where their forefathers had laid down their lives for the cause of freedom. There is a very real difference, they aimed to show, between heroically fighting against a brutal imperialist regime and *being* such a regime.[8]

Long before the antiwar Vietnam veterans arrived on the Commonwealth's Revolutionary War battlefields, the citizenry had set them aside for perpetuity, marked them with monuments to the fallen and their cause, and made them the center of civic life through highly ritualized anniversary observances that by the 1960s included reenacting the battles. Visitors to these sacralized sites are guided back to the hallowed time of the nation's founding and thereby asked to quietly contemplate but also viscerally feel the sacrifices made on their behalf. And thus, when the antiwar veterans announced their intention to bring the horrors of 1971 to these sites where time had been stopped at the sacred birth time of 1775, they were immediately embroiled in a controversy the press could not ignore. For the three days it took the antiwar veterans of New England to carry out their protest, they were on the front page of the region's newspapers and featured prominently in newspapers and television news programs around the country. Their strategy proved effective in drawing the public's attention but also dangerous insofar as many local officials and a good number of their constituents were incensed at the veterans' unorthodox use of Revolutionary War battlefields.[9]

Battle Green Vietnam is based on over one hundred interviews with veterans and civilians who participated in the protest as well as with civilians and officials who were opposed to the protestors' methods. It draws on research at the extensive archives of Vietnam Veterans Against the War, the organization that carried out the protest, and those of the National Park Service, which oversees two of the battlefields the antiwar veterans visited. And it makes use of the extraordinary number of still and moving images recorded over the course of the protest. The aim of the book is to reveal the power of place and performance in oppositional politics, the traditional function of Revolutionary War battlefield memorialization in American life, and the role of Vietnam veterans both in the antiwar movement and in changing American memorialization practices. Beginning on the Friday morning of May 28, 1971, when the protest launched, and ending on the late Monday afternoon of its closing on May 31, 1971, each of the book's six chapters focuses on a veteran, his reasons for joining the military, his experience in Southeast Asia, his role in the 1971 march, and what the march meant to him. Each chapter also explores a part of the memorialized landscape stretching from Concord to Boston. *Battle Green* is thus the story of a highly unusual and breathtakingly creative protest march organized by men and women determined to end the war in Vietnam as well as a meditation on each of the four Massachusetts Revolutionary War battlefields on which their protest unfolded: the Old North Bridge, the Battle Road, the Lexington Battle Green, and Bunker Hill. These sacred sites appear in these pages through a perspective that only war-traumatized soldiers can provide.

CHAPTER 1

Paul Revere's Ride

When the first American combat troops were sent to Vietnam in 1965, Peter Wilson was in high school. Transfixed by the helicopters he watched on the nightly news ferrying troops around Vietnam's lush countryside, he dreamed of going to Warrant Officer Flight School. However, by the time he was eighteen and eligible to enlist, Pete was four inches taller than the Army height limit of six foot four and twenty-five pounds over the 225-pound weight limit. To his dismay, the military classified him as 1-Y: eligible to serve only in times of national emergency.

Over the next four years, as the United States drafted more and more men for military service in Vietnam and spent millions of dollars training them in various specialties, Pete found other ways to fly. He saved what money he earned helping out with his family's landscaping and taxi businesses and looking after their two-and-a-half-acre farm in Newton Centre, Massachusetts, for flying lessons, becoming close friends with his very exacting instructor, the only woman pilot at the small, nearby airport, and her husband. Eventually, he was able to purchase his own Piper Super Cub, but its similarity to the type of small airplanes used in Vietnam for observation and forward artillery only reminded him of lost opportunities. So, in 1968, when his girlfriend read an article in the newspaper announcing that the height limit had been raised, Pete quickly starved off twenty-five pounds and rushed to the recruiter's office. Careful to take off his shoes and socks before scrunching down to be measured, he managed to shrink himself to six feet four and a quarter inches.[1]

"I can get rid of that with an eraser," Pete later recalled the recruiter saying of the quarter inch. "But you're going to take a flight physical and there's a good chance they might throw you out."[2]

Deciding to risk it, Pete enlisted.

"But," he later explained, shaking his head, "the Army said, 'Here, try this rifle on for size.'"

After basic training and advanced infantry training, Pete was en route to Vietnam when he was stopped at Fort Lewis, near Tacoma, Washington.

"Ordinarily you might stay there a couple of days and off you'd go," Pete explained of what became an extended layover. However, in order to be in compliance with President Nixon's orders to draw down the number of ground troops in Vietnam, the military was waiting for a certain number of troops to return before sending more soldiers over. "It was just political skull-duggery," is how Pete described the way in which Nixon was fulfilling his campaign promise to end the war.

As the layover dragged on and more and more troops left Vietnam, Pete grew increasingly anxious about how much support he would have in the field.

"What's it going to be?" he remembered wondering. "Five of us there by ourselves?"

And, indeed, when Pete finally got to the war zone, one of his assignments left him and an engineer guarding a bridge along a main supply route all by themselves.

"There had been a lot more troops the previous couple of years," Pete later explained of why they were mortared so often, including one time by an eighty-pound shell.

"It picked me up and drove me back into the bunker. I couldn't hear anything. It was even a moment or two before I could see anything, it was such a bright flash. The next morning, I looked at the sandbags where I had been standing. There was a piece of shrapnel large enough that if it had hit me, it would have taken my leg completely off."

Five months after arriving back home and unable to stop thinking about the American ground troops still in harm's way, Pete decided to make his experience vividly clear to the public. He removed the six-foot plow frame, hard top, and doors of the olive drab Land Rover his family used for clearing snow, mowing grass, and hauling things. He folded down the windshield. He retrieved the two removable jump seats from the barn and bolted them to the floor. Having transformed the Rover into a military jeep, he used masking tape to create four large capital letters on each side of it: V V A W. Looking around for a means of marking the front of the vehicle, he found a manila file folder, opened it, and used a thick black marker to write VIET-NAM VETS AGAINST THE WAR before affixing the makeshift sign to the Rover's grill.

Figure 1. Peter Wilson in his family's Land Rover.
Photo © Cary Wolinsky, Trillium Studios.

After changing into a set of well-worn Army fatigues and stashing what appeared to be a full-size M16 behind the driver's seat, Pete folded his long legs behind the steering wheel and, with his knees pressed against the dashboard, set off for the peninsula north of the Charles River that overlooks the city of Boston (Figure 1 and Map 6).[3]

Founded in 1967 as a speakers bureau, Vietnam Veterans Against the War was initially committed to working within the political system. Dressed formally in business suits and ties, members spoke at antiwar rallies and sat for interviews with the press. In 1968, when Eugene McCarthy ran for the Democratic presidential ticket on an antiwar platform, many of the members, who by then had stopped shaving and cutting their hair, readily embraced the slogan "Get Clean for Gene" in order to make the best possible impression as they campaigned door-to-door for him. Despite VVAW's best efforts, McCarthy lost the Democratic nomination to Hubert Humphrey at the 1968 Convention, and Republican nominee Richard Nixon won the presidency on a vague platform of "peace with honor," which, as Pete would soon learn, entailed ramping up the American air war in Southeast Asia while only very slowly drawing down ground troops even as more soldiers continued to be sent over.[4]

By the time Nixon took office in January 1969, the majority of Americans had turned against the war, anguished over the number of American casualties and frustrated with the lack of progress as the financial cost of the war rose precipitously. But even after the participation the following October of millions of Americans across the country in a one-day Moratorium to End the War in Vietnam, the war dragged on. When plans to regularly repeat the moratorium petered out, it became clear to VVAW that the two traditional methods of effecting change in America, advocacy and voting, were ineffective means of achieving the organization's goal of ending the war immediately. In the summer of 1970, while guys like Pete were getting killed, the VVAW leadership determined to change the organization's tactics.[5]

VVAW called its first effort Operation RAW. RAW was an acronym for what the veterans were seeking, a Rapid American Withdrawal, as opposed to the slow drawdown Nixon had initiated, as well as an expression of how raw they felt after serving in Vietnam and a symbolic spelling reversal of what the veterans were aiming to stop: the WAR. The military had a history of calling sustained actions "operations," and RAW, VVAW's first sustained action, was a long-distance march in the tradition of Gandhi's month-long Salt

March, which proved to be a powerful first step in India's fight for independence, and the fifty-four-mile civil rights march from Selma to Montgomery, Alabama, in 1965, which influenced President Lyndon B. Johnson's decision to sign the Voting Rights Act. Long distances allow large numbers of people to witness the tremendous amount of energy the marchers are willing to expend as a result of their convictions. In VVAW's demonstration of its members' commitment, two hundred antiwar veterans walked eighty-six miles, from Morristown, New Jersey, to Valley Forge, Pennsylvania, over the course of Labor Day weekend in 1970.[6]

The veterans' attire and posture, however, were nothing like the business suits and Sunday-best dresses that the civil rights activists had worn as they made their way arm in arm to Montgomery in a demonstration of their continuing commitment to nonviolence even after being turned back on their first attempt by state troopers wielding billy clubs and tear gas. Instead, the veterans took a page from New York University theater faculty and students who had protested the massacre by National Guardsmen of college students during an antiwar protest at Kent State. Dressed in their usual college attire, faculty and students reenacted the massacre in the streets of Manhattan using fake blood and animal guts. This kind of spontaneous or "guerrilla" theater, as it had come to be called in the 1960s, was a means of sending a message across multiple senses to a public intent on going about its regular business. Bystanders were forced to see, hear, and smell the carnage carried out in their country's name against innocent young people. To make the war as vividly real as possible, while also establishing their authority to address it, the Labor Day veterans dressed in jungle boots, military fatigues, and boonie hats or camouflage-covered helmet liners (the actual M1 helmet being too heavy to wear comfortably for long periods of time), and they armed themselves with realistic-looking toy M16s that made the sound of loud, automatic gunfire when fired. They performed the war by marching single file in patrol formation and by acting out search-and-destroy missions in every town through which they passed. The VVAW veterans grabbed, searched, and pretended to execute each of the Vietnamese people played by their civilian supporters. Only when the ground was littered with bodies would they break character to explain to visibly shaken onlookers the chain of events that led to these kinds of atrocities.[7]

In 1945, at the end of World War II, they explained, Vietnamese revolutionary Ho Chi Minh had given a speech proclaiming Vietnam independent of the French imperialists who had colonized the region since the mid-nineteenth century. In a bid for support from the United States, he quoted from the American Declaration of Independence. However, France refused to acknowledge Ho's claim, at which point the world's two largest communist countries, the Soviet Union and the People's Republic of China, recognized Ho's Democratic Republic of Vietnam, based in the northern city of Hanoi, as the legitimate government of Vietnam. Immediately thereafter, even despite Ho's invocation of the Declaration of Independence, the United States recognized the French-backed State of Vietnam in the southern city of Saigon instead. China began to arm and train northern guerrillas, turning them into a regular army, while the United States funded the French, sent military advisers to help them, and trained Vietnamese soldiers in the South. When the American-backed French suffered a decisive military defeat at Dien Bien Phu in 1954, the Geneva Agreements created Cambodia, Laos, and Vietnam. However, when the conference also divided Vietnam temporarily into two provisional states until such time as elections could determine who should rule Vietnam, U.S. president Dwight Eisenhower refused to allow the elections to proceed, fearful that Ho Chi Minh would prevail and Vietnam would thus become a communist country.[8]

"You have a row of dominoes set up," was how President Eisenhower famously put it at a 1954 news conference. "You knock over the first one, and what will happen to the last one is the certainty that it will go over very quickly. So you could have a beginning of a disintegration that would have the most profound influences."[9]

The next American president, John F. Kennedy, dramatically increased the number of American advisers in South Vietnam out of concern that North Vietnam would conquer it. After he was assassinated in the fall of 1963, his successor, Vice President Johnson, went even further. By accusing the North Vietnamese of attacking the destroyer USS *Maddox* on two occasions in early August 1964 in the Gulf of Tonkin off the coast of North Vietnam, he convinced Congress to authorize military assistance to any country in Southeast Asia threatened by communist aggression without first formally declaring war. (Only much later did the American public learn that the Department of Defense never bothered to respond to the first so-called attack and that the second one was wholly fabricated by the U.S. government.) A week after President Johnson began a bombing campaign against North Vietnam in early 1965, the Marines landed in South Vietnam. What Americans call the Vietnam War had officially begun.[10]

American and South Vietnamese ground troops were forced to fight not only traditional military forces based in North Vietnam but also the military branch of the National Liberation Front (NLF) in South Vietnam, comprised of lawyers, doctors, school teachers, and other professionals across Vietnam, both communist and noncommunist, who had banded together and developed a ten-point program that included as goals the peaceful reunification of their divided country and an end to all American military advisers and bases. The North Vietnamese Army and the NLF killed almost two thousand American soldiers in the year following the Marines' arrival in Vietnam. Even as the United States unleashed an unprecedented amount of firepower, dropping over the course of the war more than twice the number of bombs dropped in Europe and Asia during World War II, the American death toll rose over the ensuing years. In 1968 alone, after three years of intense effort from both sides, almost seventeen thousand Americans were killed. The number of Vietnamese civilian casualties was many times that. As the veterans participating in Operation RAW explained, because the NLF's guerrilla fighters were often indistinguishable from civilians, American soldiers had to always assume they were in a kill-or-be-killed situation. The veterans used their performances during the Labor Day march to show how American soldiers could run afoul of the Hague and Geneva conventions that are supposed to protect noncombatants in war zones when fear, anger, and grief mix.

Intent as they were on using performance to convince as many Americans as possible that the United States was carrying out an illegal and immoral war, the antiwar veterans also wanted to make clear that their critique of the American government was born of a deep-seated patriotic conviction that the nation should return to its cherished ideals. And thus, for Operation RAW, VVAW charted a march route that took them from Morristown, where the Continental troops had billeted during the bitterly cold winter of 1779–1780, to Valley Forge, the site of the Continental Army's main encampment during the harrowing winter of 1777–1778. The protected status of Valley Forge Park, with its grand triumphal arch and soaring gothic Washington Memorial Chapel, made clear that it was sanctified in the national memory as the place where American loyalty to the cause of liberty had been dramatically tested and, thanks to two of the nation's founding fathers, where it endured. After one thousand of General George Washington's ten thousand men deserted, the future president had successfully rallied the cold and starving men who remained by having his officers read to them the latest pamphlet by political theorist and patriot Thomas Paine.[11]

"These are the times that try men's souls," Paine had acknowledged of that difficult, wartime season, before urging Americans to remember that the future of their new country was at stake. "The summer soldier and the sunshine patriot will, in this crisis, shrink from the service to his country; but he that stands by it now, deserves the love and thanks of man and woman."[12]

The veterans' march route was their means of asserting that, like the soldiers who saw the winters through at Morristown and Valley Forge, they would not be deterred by the arduous nature of the task at hand. Out of love for their country, they had served one and, in some cases, two or even three tours in Vietnam. Now that same devotion compelled them to serve yet another tour before returning to the comforts of civilian life, this one devoted to righting the nation's course by protesting the very war in which they had served, something no other American veterans had ever done before.

When they arrived at Valley Forge State Park, the exhausted veterans had shouldered their toy M16s and lined up in military formation. Instead of practicing the kinds of military maneuvers Washington's men carried out, they proceeded, many crying openly, to break their guns in two. By performing parts of both the Revolutionary War and the Vietnam War simultaneously and thereby making clear their respect for the former and their opposition to the latter, the veterans asked the public to measure the ethical difference between the two wars. It was a rhetorical move as ancient and powerful as the one made in eighteenth-century New England by Protestant theologians intent on recommitting their flocks to the colony's founding religious principles. In fiery sermons packed with vivid images of hell, they preached that all of the calamities afflicting the colonists were the direct result of their present sins. For the veterans who participated in Operation RAW, the nation was also in decline. Their performed renditions of the hell that was the war in Vietnam was an argument for the nation's return to its founding ideals.[13]

Much to the antiwar veterans' frustration, the press largely ignored Operation RAW as well as, several months later, the Winter Soldier Investigation, the atrocity hearings VVAW organized in Detroit and named in a pointed play on Paine's castigation of "sunshine patriots." Then Hugh Hefner donated a free, full-page ad to VVAW in the February 1971 issue of *Playboy* magazine featuring a black-and-white photo of an American flag–draped coffin. "Over 335,000 of our buddies have been killed or wounded," the ad lamented. "We don't think it's worth it." So many veterans and active-duty soldiers decided to join the organization after seeing the ad that regional VVAW chapters were formed. Massachusetts Political Action for Peace, or Mass PAX, offered New England's antiwar veterans a room in their

Cambridge suite of offices just off of Harvard Square, as well as a phone line and an executive secretary whose salary was paid by Mass PAX.[14]

One of the many veterans who rushed to join the New England chapter was Pete Wilson, whose return to civilian life was unsettled by haunting memories of American GIs venting their anger and frustration over the slowly diminishing troop levels that left them vulnerable to attack. On one occasion, instead of providing medical assistance to a critically wounded North Vietnamese soldier they had taken prisoner, as required by the Third Geneva Convention, several soldiers in Pete's unit had propped up the prisoner, put a cigarette between his lips, and started posing for pictures with him.

"Hey, get out of here!" Pete had barked at them, horrified.

"They didn't listen to me at first," he later recounted. "So I put a bullet in the chamber of my rifle."

"Go. Now!" he ordered, raising his loaded weapon.

Pete was left holding the prisoner's hand until he passed away.

Just as heavy as this memory was the large piece of shrapnel Pete also lugged home, a reminder that the war had almost cost him a leg. He shared VVAW's goal of attracting the media's attention and thereby getting the message to the people about the importance of an immediate cessation of the war before more Americans committed atrocities or died needlessly fighting in a war the United States was slowly winding down.

The April after Operation RAW and the Detroit hearings, Pete's chapter decided to join forces with the VVAW chapters that had sprung up across the country after the *Playboy* ad. This time, they paired the theatrical methods they had first employed over Labor Day weekend with another proven technique of nonviolent social struggle: occupying the nation's capital or, in VVAW's parlance, "invading" it. They called their action Operation Dewey Canyon III in a pointed critique of the two illegal American incursions Nixon ordered into Laos, a neutral country bordering Vietnam.[15]

To get a large contingent of veterans to DC, VVAW's New England leaders needed money. Thanks to the Boston area's many universities and the government-funded labs that had spun off from them, the surrounding suburbs were arguably home to many of the country's most educated and wealthy citizens. Having already initiated a host of liberal initiatives, including the Metropolitan Council for Educational Opportunity, Inc. (METCO), a voluntary and one-way school desegregation program started in 1966 that involved busing inter-city African American students to the largely white suburban public schools, and land conservation and historical preservation programs meant to ensure that the former farming communities maintained their rural beauty, these new elites had been organizing against the Vietnam War since the late 1960s. At coffee klatches and cocktail parties organized by Mass PAX and Citizens for Participation in Political Action (CPP), with which it would soon merge, the veterans would show film footage of the Detroit hearings and then pass around a helmet that inevitably returned brimming with money. VVAW-NE had been able to send the largest number of antiwar veterans of any of the VVAW chapters to Operation DCIII, filling two Greyhound buses paid for by their fundraising efforts.[16]

While the 2,300 veterans who had descended on Washington from across the country pursued traditional political opportunities during their stay, including lobbying their congresspeople to end the war, testifying before the Senate Committee on Foreign Relations about American war crimes being committed in Southeast Asia, and demanding that the Supreme Court rule on the constitutionality of the war, they had continued to think in theatrical, RAW-like terms. In addition to performing mock search-and-destroy missions on the steps of the Capitol Building, the veterans marched to Arlington National Cemetery to lay wreaths in memory of both the American and Vietnamese war dead, held a candlelight vigil at the White House, and did a noisy version of the can-can on the steps of the Supreme Court while court was in session. Most dramatically, on the final day, they returned to the steps of the U.S. Capitol Building to throw away their war medals. Photographs of the veterans at these national sites were splashed across the front pages of newspapers across the country with headlines that focused on the Nixon administration's ill treatment of the veterans, many of whom were wounded.[17]

The federal government has allowed citizens to use the landscape of the nation's capital to express their collective will since 1892, when five hundred unemployed workers claimed the National Mall as "the property of the people," an assertion that would be underscored in 1963 by the March on Washington for Jobs and Freedom. And yet, in the spring of 1971, the Nixon administration was determined not to hear from those men who had returned from the war to testify that they had been forced to kill people who wanted the same freedoms Americans had once fought to claim for themselves. At every turn during Operation DCIII, the federal government had moved to block the veterans' efforts, barring their entrance to Arlington, arresting them on the steps of the Supreme Court, erecting a chain-link fence around the Capitol Building, and securing an injunction in an attempt to dislodge them from their campsite on the Mall. Captivated by the veterans' street theater and a rousing address to the Senate Foreign Relations Committee by their spokesman, a former Navy lieutenant named John Kerry, millions of Americans grew incensed that their government would treat so poorly the very men who had risked their lives for their country.[18]

Buoyed by their success, the New England veterans had decided on the bus ride home that now was the time to keep up the pressure to end the war. Memorial Day was coming up, and for the first time, as a result of the Uniform Monday Holiday Act going into effect that year, it would anchor a three-day weekend. They determined to try another RAW-style protest, only this time, instead of marching to the winter encampment at Valley Forge, they would use ground even more sacred than that, the very ground on which men had spilled their blood so their country could be born. They decided, in short, that they would use the battlefields where the Revolutionary War began: Concord, Lexington, and Bunker Hill. And whereas last time the veterans had used Thomas Paine as a means of presenting themselves as the newest incarnation of the nation's most patriotic soldiers, they would now appear in the guise of the man mythologized for rallying the people of New England to fight for their liberty, he whose journey to warn the colonists of a British mobilization connects these most sacred of places into an unfolding narrative of freedom and democracy.[19]

"Vietnam Veterans Against the War are planning a reverse Paul Revere march from Concord to Boston on the May 28 weekend," VVAW-NE announced in a press release shortly after reconvening in the chapter's Cambridge office (Map 1).[20]

In a pointed attempt to counter President Nixon's argument for why he could not immediately end the war, VVAW-NE named the march Operation POW. In 1969, Nixon had insisted that the North Vietnamese account for all of the missing American war dead, even as the United States never would have been able to provide such a list of the Vietnamese killed by American forces. Nixon then proceeded to change the official name of Veterans Day in November 1970 to Prisoner of War Day, after which he directed that soldiers shot down in enemy territory no longer be counted as "Killed in Action—Body Not Recovered" but as "POW/MIAs," a conflation of Prisoners of War and Missing in Action, two categories that had heretofore been separate. Now, those who were most likely dead could be imagined as possible POWs who might be able to return home one day if the United States just kept fighting. In March 1971, Nixon told the press, "As long as there are American POWs

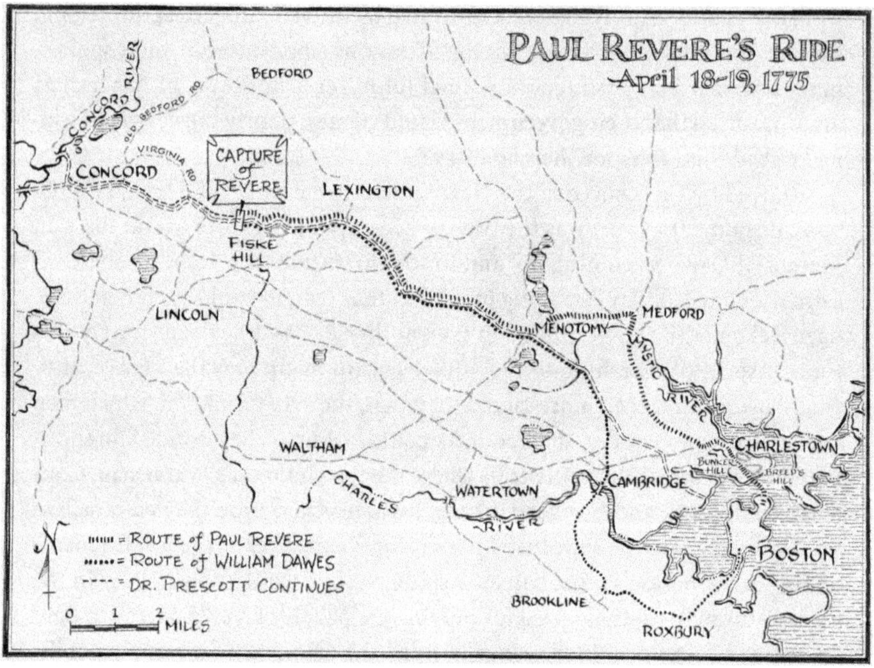

Map 1. Paul Revere's ride, April 18–19, 1775.

in North Vietnam we will have to maintain a residual force in South Vietnam." He made similar remarks at a news conference on April 16, stating that "as long as there is one American prisoner being held prisoner by North Vietnam," he would keep U.S. ground and air forces in Vietnam.[21]

"We Are All," VVAW-NE countered in the flier it distributed inviting veterans to participate, "Prisoners of This War."[22]

While Pete Wilson had participated in other small-scale VVAW-NE protests, both the name and the plans for Operation POW were particularly appealing to him. Here was an opportunity to protest the slow drawdown of the troops, which Pete knew from experience to be deadly, as well as the POW/MIA argument Nixon was using to justify the slow drawdown. Here, too, was the opportunity that had been denied him in Vietnam to finally follow in his father's heroic footsteps.[23]

A longtime farrier for the National Lancers, a volunteer cavalry militia troop based in Massachusetts, Pete's father had served in Germany at the end

Figure 2. Robert Wilson: (right) impersonating Paul Revere on the Lexington Green (c. 1952). Courtesy of Peter Wilson.

of World War II, spending his days helping hungry German soldiers as young as twelve years old make it safely onto military transport trucks ahead of the Russians. Not long after a 1954 American book for children listed Paul Revere's ride as one of "History's 100 Greatest Events" alongside Jesus' crucifixion, the signing of the Magna Carta, and the invention of the printing press, Pete's father was honored for his military service with an invitation to play Revere for the Lancers' annual reenactment of his ride, a local custom the organization has observed since 1914. He proudly wore a tricorn hat, ruffled shirt, and long, colonial-style riding coat for the horseback ride from Charlestown to the Lexington Battle Green (Figure 2).[24]

During the early years of the Vietnam War, Pete's father had considered antiwar protests harmful for troop morale. Whenever protestors had gathered with antiwar placards in Newton Centre, he and Pete's active-duty younger brother, outfitted in his Marine dress blues, would quietly stand nearby in counter-protest.

"But, you know, things changed," Pete noted of the months leading up to the spring of 1971. "My father wasn't too pleased with what the U.S. government was doing."

When Pete had asked his father for permission to use the Land Rover to protest the Vietnam War by retracing Paul Revere's route in a modern military-style vehicle instead of observing it the orthodox way on horseback, his father did not hesitate to support his son.

Paul Revere has not always been the legendary figure known to the Wilson family. Unlike John Singleton Copley's portraits of John Hancock and Samuel Adams, which were proudly displayed in Boston's Faneuil Hall, Copley's now-famous 1768 portrait of a then young silversmith working wigless in his shirtsleeves seems to have languished for decades in the attic of a Revere family member. Its subject only became widely known in 1860 when the already very popular New England poet Henry Wadsworth Longfellow devoted a 130-line narrative poem to celebrating the silversmith's actions on the night of April 18, 1775.[25]

While the poem launches straight into the journey Revere took eight years after Copley painted his portrait, the story of how the ride came about begins earlier that tumultuous spring, when the Massachusetts colonists, determined to protect their natural rights from the army occupying Boston and the imperial government whose rulings it enforced, began secreting military stores in a bustling shire town twenty miles east of the port city. Longfellow imagines Revere giving the colonists a fighting chance to throw off the yoke of tyranny by singlehandedly warning colonists scattered across the countryside of the impending arrival of the over seven hundred British Regulars ordered to find and destroy the materiel the colonists had hidden in Concord. Generations of American schoolchildren have since been required to recite "Paul Revere's Ride," which remains one of the nation's most popular poems on account of how its heroic story about the nation's birth is set to a meter that, while at times quite complex, regularly resolves into the sound of the cantering horse Revere rode into history (dee-dee-DUM, dee-dee-DUM, dee-dee-DUM), while its strong end rhymes make it easy to memorize.[26]

> Listen my children and you shall hear
> Of the midnight ride of Paul Revere,
> On the eighteenth of April, in Seventy-five;
> Hardly a man is now alive
> Who remembers that famous day and year.[27]

The poem argues that the story of Revere's exploits needs to be handed down to each rising generation for two reasons. First, Longfellow's Revere uses an admirable level of creativity in helping secure his country's liberty. The optical semaphore system he devises allows him to carry the warning past the barrier of the army's sentinels and the water surrounding the then peninsular city of Boston.

> He said to his friend, "If the British march
> By land or sea from the town to-night,
> Hang a lantern aloft in the belfry arch
> Of the North Church tower as a signal light,—
> One if by land, and two if by sea;
> And I on the opposite shore will be,
> Ready to ride and spread the alarm
> Through every Middlesex village and farm,
> For the country folk to be up and to arm."

Second, the poem celebrates the tenacity and fleetness of foot required of Revere to carry the warning deep into the countryside. It is organized around regular announcements of the time Revere arrives in each of the towns along his route:

> Then he said "Good-night!" and with muffled oar
> Silently rowed to the Charlestown shore. . . .
> It was twelve by the village clock
> When he crossed the bridge into Medford town. . . .
> It was one by the village clock,
> When he galloped into Lexington. . . .
> It was two by the village clock,
> When he came to the bridge in Concord town.

By using clock time as a demonstration of Revere's alacrity and naming the towns through which Revere passes, the poem creates a road to liberty, which the antiwar veterans adopted for their second long-distance, multiday march route after Operation RAW. They announced in their press release the same route Longfellow laid out but in reverse: "Following a planned campout at the North Bridge, Concord on Friday night, the veterans will march to

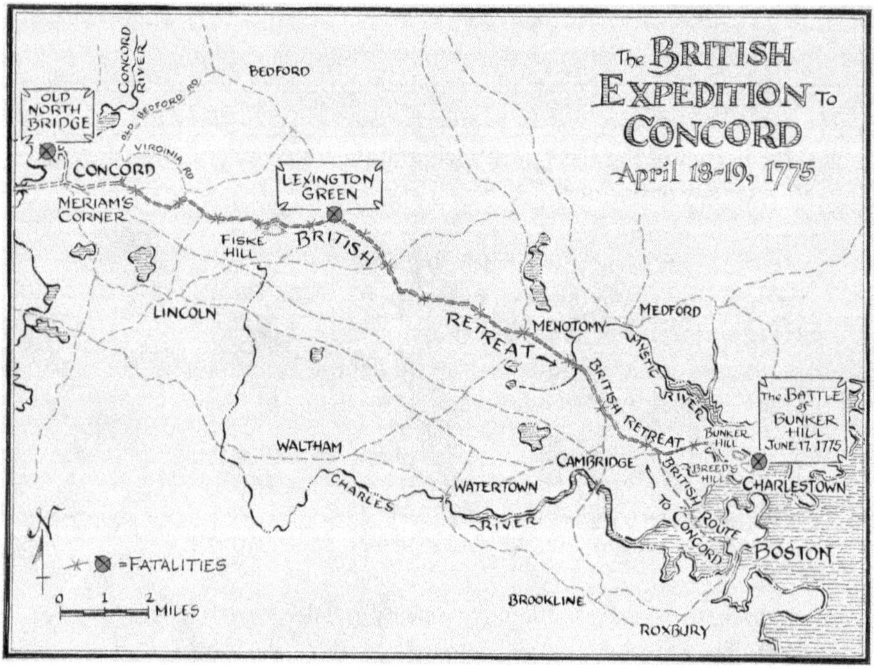

Map 2. The British expedition to Concord, April 18–19, 1775.

Lexington where they propose to camp there on Saturday night and then march to Bunker Hill for a campout Sunday night." Bunker Hill is in Charlestown, and while the battle that took place there on June 17, 1775, had not yet taken place when Revere made his ride, it was just off of his route and thereby solidified the idea of a road to freedom while giving the veterans an opportunity to visit a fourth Revolutionary War battlefield, in addition to Concord's and Lexington's battle sites, and the Battle Road connecting the two towns (Map 2). "About 300 veterans," VVAW-NE asserted, "are expected to march."

The veterans knew that by traversing Revere's route and thus visiting Massachusetts' Revolutionary War battlefields, they could appropriate an even richer array of national symbols than they had been able to access in Valley Forge or Washington, DC. The three battlefields along the route the veterans named and the one they implied (insofar as the road along which the colonists fired at the retreating British Regulars connects Concord to Lexington) are dotted with well-known statues and monuments. The sole difference between Revere's route as mapped in the poem and the veterans' was that the veterans would march the route in reverse for the same symbolic reason VVAW had called its first march Operation RAW: to underscore the point that the United States needed to reverse its course, as well as for the practical reason of wanting to end in Boston on Memorial Day where there would be a lot of people on hand to witness the veterans' fortitude in finishing an over twenty-mile march.

Intent on capitalizing on the Revere myth—namely, the idea that warning the American people is the greatest of patriotic acts—the veterans planned to continue the longstanding tradition of ignoring the poem's many factual errors. To begin with, Revere did not act alone that night; he was part of a vast messengering system that included prearranged signals of church bells, warning shots, and beacon fires, all of which galvanized militiamen from Massachusetts' north and south shores and from its far western towns to set forth for Concord. Within a few hours, news of the Regulars departing Boston radiated outward an astonishing thirty miles, the distance of a daylong horseback ride. Revere's individual heroism is further mythologized in the poem by imagining him as both the inventor and receiver of the signal the poem argues won the day, when, in reality, it was Patriot leader Dr. Joseph Warren, who, having received information from a confidential source near to the British command that the Regulars were heading west, led the way in disseminating this information. For riders, Dr. Warren sent first for William Dawes, who often had business on the other side of Boston Neck and who could thus be assured of getting through the British checkpoint there. Dawes had left Dr. Warren's house by the time Revere arrived there and received his orders to ride to Lexington via Charlestown. Both riders carried written messages from Warren to the effect that the king's troops had left Boston by boat. Contrary to Longfellow's account, Revere thus did not wait in Charlestown to see how many flashes issued from Boston's Old North Church. Those were issued to other Patriots in Charlestown in case he did not make it past the British ships anchored in the river. Longfellow also goes so far as to imagine Revere reaching Concord alone when, in fact, he and William Dawes continued westward together from Lexington with Concord doctor and patriot Samuel Prescott until all three of them were captured in the town of Lincoln by ten British Regulars on patrol. Dr. Prescott managed to escape, and he was the one who eventually completed Revere and Dawes's shared errand, arriving in Concord with the same alarm that was also being transmitted across the colony and even beyond at the significantly faster speeds of light and sound by the prearranged church bells, warning shots, and beacon fires. Even if Revere had made it to Concord, there would have been no need for him to head to the northern part of town. Longfellow seems to have imagined Revere at the North Bridge solely to put the rider's efforts on par with the heroism of the American citizen-soldiers who risked and, in two cases, lost their lives there the next morning.[28]

Indeed, Longfellow's creative use of past events went further still and further than even the most esteemed historians or the antiwar veterans have ever been willing to admit. The poem implies that the colonists triumphed only because Revere's creativity and speed gave the colonists the time they needed to muster in advance of the Regulars' journey over the shorter water route from Boston. In actuality, Revere's efforts proved irrelevant on the night of April 18, 1775. There were not enough boats to ferry all of the king's troops across the Back Bay in one trip. It was two hours before they were all assembled on the other side, only to find they had landed in a swamp. The troops had to wade slowly westward in waist-deep water and then had to wait for their provisions to catch up with them. They were still struggling through the swamp when news of their mission had already traveled far afield by the various means Longfellow omits from his account as part of his efforts to amplify Revere's heroism. It was a total of four hours after the troops' departure from Boston before the order was even given to begin marching. By then, the Regulars had lost the extra time they had tried to buy by traveling across the water under the cover of darkness.[29]

The veterans' keenness to use Longfellow's poem as their script stems from what it offers in the place of historical reality: assurance that the retelling and reenacting of its mythic version of Revere's ride will re-release the same energy that birthed the nation. The poem makes this assurance by shifting verb tenses several times, most notably at its end. The children invoked in the first stanza learn that the sacred moment of the nation's birth is not part of chronological time but rather of an ever unfolding present.

So through the night rode Paul Revere;
And so through the night went his cry of alarm
To every Middlesex village and farm,—
A cry of defiance, and not of fear,
A voice in the darkness, a knock at the door,
And a word that shall echo for evermore!

For, borne on the night-wind of the Past,
Through all our history, to the last,
In the hour of darkness and peril and need,
The people will waken and listen to hear
The hurrying hoof-beats of that steed,
And the midnight message of Paul Revere.

The assertion that, while Revere rode through the night in the past, he will still be out there in the future implies that through recitation of the poem or reenactment of the story it tells, its readers and reenactors can recommit "the people" Longfellow names to the founding document that first imagined them as such, the U.S. Constitution, and thus to the nation whose government it frames. This was the very recommitment New England's antiwar Vietnam veterans sought.[30]

For several years leading up to VVAW-NE's reverse Revere march, Lincoln teenager Jennifer Levin and her local 4-H club had been providing more historically accurate reenactments than Longfellow's account and those of the National Lancers, for whom Pete Wilson's father rode. Whereas reenactors like Pete's father always finish their rides in Lexington, Jen and her fellow riders acknowledged the fact willfully overlooked by both the poet and the Lancers: that Paul Revere, while continuing toward Concord, was captured in Lincoln along with the two other riders accompanying him. If Longfellow seems to have viewed the capture as a less than heroic moment for Revere and thus omitted it, Lincoln residents have been pleased to remind themselves that Revere and two other patriots faced an armed patrol in their town, that Dr. Prescott made a daring escape and continued to Concord, that Revere survived his interrogation, and that, after being released, he returned to Lexington in time to witness British troops fire on the colonists who, having received the warning, had assembled on that town's green. On Patriots' Day, the state holiday that observes the exchange of gunfire between the Regulars and colonists in Concord, in Lexington, and along the Battle Road, Jen would neatly tuck her cream-colored riding britches into a pair of knee-high black boots, slip on a long coat split up the front and back for riding (a surtout in colonial parlance), and carefully secure to her hair with bobby pins a black tricorn hat trimmed with gold-colored ribbon. Being the youngest of the Lincoln riders, she only ever impersonated Dawes and Prescott during the annual reenactment of the midnight ride. But in the spring of 1971, her mother, who was married to the founder of Citizens for Participation in Political Action and who was helping the antiwar veterans organize their Memorial Day weekend march, suggested she play the role of Revere for them.[31]

Despite her young age, Jen was as firmly opposed to the Vietnam War as her parents. When the Lincoln public school required students to make and carry draft cards for a social studies project, Jen and some of her classmates had burned theirs in reenactment of the draft card burnings that had taken place on the steps of South Boston District Court House in March 1966 and in Boston's Arlington Street Church the following year, when over 280 young men ceremoniously turned in or set fire to their draft cards.[32]

"I was at home at night watching how many people died in Vietnam every day," Jen recalled when asked about Operation POW years later. "It was the body count every night. It was footage of people being shot in the head right in front of us."[33]

And thus Jen had readily agreed to help the VVAW-NE veterans by appearing with them on her horse.

"I was making a statement that what happened back then that caused this country to come into being was still real," she explained of her participation in their Memorial Day weekend protest.

Keen to continue spreading the message of the country's fall from the grace bestowed on it in 1775, the veterans had decided to have Jen work in tandem with a modern-day Revere, someone who could carry their warning dressed in fatigues while riding the contemporary equivalent of a horse in a demonstration of the antiwar veterans' commitment to the nation's founding values that would simultaneously show how far the nation had departed from the ideals that had motivated Revere and his compatriots. This was how Pete Wilson, the son of a Revere reenactor and the owner of the perfect modern horse equivalent, came to be asked to help kick off the protest.

"It was a prop," Pete later explained of the Land Rover he had transformed into a military jeep.

And so, with his father's blessing, Pete set out Friday afternoon from his family's farm on a second, very different tour of duty from his first.

"I was saying," he later explained, echoing Jen, "'either support the troops or bring them home right now." Even years later, Pete stressed the "right now," having learned firsthand that Nixon's gradual drawdown was too dangerous for the remaining American troops.

While the rest of the participants would be marching from Concord to Boston over the course of the three-day weekend in reverse of Revere's route, VVAW-NE leaders wanted the two Revere reenactors to kick off the march by traveling in the traditional direction so they could turn back the clock and thereby start the nation's foundational energy flowing again. Using the poem as their script, march organizers directed Pete to drive to a spot in Charlestown overlooking Boston ("I on the opposite shore will be . . .") and wait there for the veterans to signal from the Old North Church. VVAW-NE had announced in a press release that the organization planned to signal "One if by land, two if by sea," as in Longfellow's poem and as reenacted in Boston every Patriots' Day since at least 1961. But they also announced that they would further signal "three if by air" in acknowledgment of the fact that even as President Nixon was drawing down ground troops, leaving men like Pete vulnerable, he was waging an air war not just against Vietnam but against neighboring neutral countries as well. Eschewing the widely available reproductions of what the original signal lanterns are thought to have looked like, VVAW-NE shot off six flares near the same church from which the signal lanterns were hung in 1775. In this way, the veterans both modernized the signal and updated the message: Southeast Asia was being attacked from all directions.[34]

After stopping in Charlestown to watch the veterans' flares shoot high into the Boston sky, Pete turned the Rover westward and proceeded to follow the typed set of directions VVAW-NE organizers had provided him. When he finally arrived at a predesignated field in Concord, he handed off the written warning VVAW-NE was bringing to the people to a costumed and mounted Jen Levin. VVAW-NE's traditional reenactor then cantered off to the site where the antiwar veterans had gathered at the Old North Bridge, clutching between her horse's reins both the warning and a reproduction signal lantern that made clear who she was impersonating, even as the historical Revere did not carry one of the signal lanterns that night. (The lanterns were minimally effective when flashed from a point as high as a church steeple, but they did not emit enough light to make holding one on horseback worthwhile even if it had not been a well-moonlit night.)[35]

In following, albeit in reverse, the route described in the poem, the veterans were beginning their march at what has become a 155-acre memorial landscape in Concord that invites visitors to approach the site of that town's Revolutionary War battle with reverence. Those who do not already conceive of themselves as pilgrims become such when they disembark from their cars, cross the parking lot and the intervening road, and, leaving the modern world behind, make their approach to the battle site on foot via the long gravel allée lined with a double row of trees planted in 1838 (Map 3). Emerging at a quiet, manicured clearing by the slow-flowing Concord River, sojourners come to a reproduction memorial bridge built to mark the site of the actual bridge across which Regulars and colonial militiamen exchanged gunfire in 1775. At either end of the bridge is a memorial. On the side closest to the allée is a granite obelisk raised in 1836. On the other side of the bridge is a bronze statue, dedicated in 1875, of a farmer pivoting away from his plow and his fields, musket in hand, to face the oncoming British Regulars about whom he has just been warned. These memorials, the one funereal in shape, the other representational, ask visitors to give thanks for the service of the farmers who fought and, in some cases, died here so that Americans could be free. While there are no overtly religious structures here as there are at what is now Valley Forge National Historical Park, the absence of modern buildings underscores the fact that this is meant to be a space that exists outside of chronological time. (Just as the parking lot was installed across the road in 1929, the public restroom was discreetly tucked behind some trees when it was added in 1954.) The Old North Bridge area seems to exist in the eternal, fixed time of the sacred.[36]

While the town of Concord continues to own the memorialized battlefield, the National Park Service (NPS) has operated and maintained it since 1959. It was thus to the NPS that the veterans had submitted their request to camp, or bivouac in military parlance, in a field next to the Old North Bridge the first night of their march. The NPS set aside any concerns about desecration in order to avoid the same adverse publicity the federal government had suffered when it obtained an injunction in an effort to displace the antiwar veterans from the National Mall the month before. While careful to remind the public that camping at the battle site is prohibited, the NPS gave the veterans permission to hold an all-night meeting.[37]

The first indication that the veterans were going to encounter obstacles along their march route had come when they sought permission to bivouac the second night of the march in Lexington either on that town's Battle Green or in its Tower Park. Both are on the main thoroughfare of Massachusetts Avenue, but the latter is closer to Boston and thus initially appealed to the veterans who were thinking about how far they would have to walk on Sunday to reach Bunker Hill. NPS has never sought to enter into an agreement with the town of Lexington. And thus, unlike the Old North Bridge battle

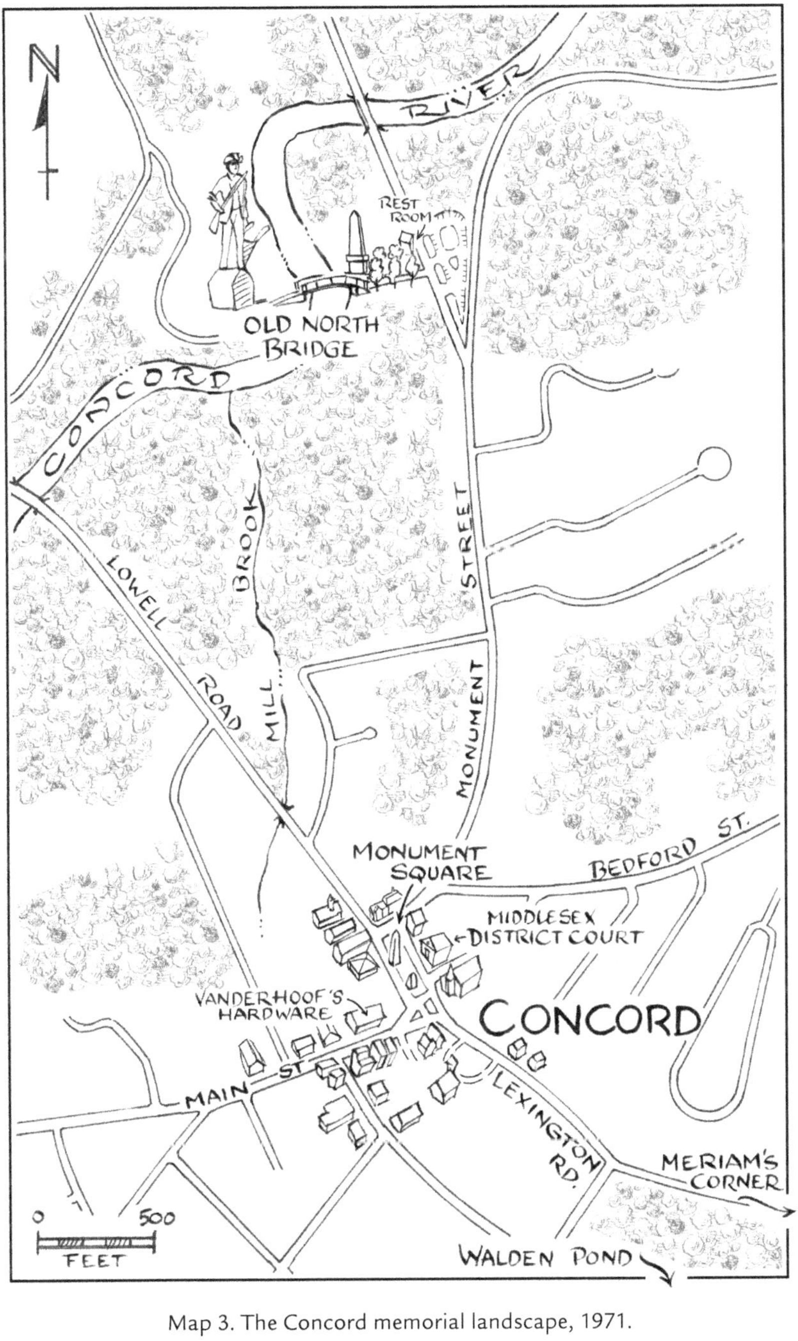

Map 3. The Concord memorial landscape, 1971.

area, the Battle Green is under the jurisdiction of that town's selectmen, whose decisions concerning its use are guided by a local 1923 bylaw that limits the kinds of activities that can take place there:[38]

> No person shall engage or take part in any game, sport, picnic or performance on the Battle Green, without the written permission of the Selectmen or other board having charge and control thereof, and no person shall climb upon, deface, mutilate or otherwise injure any tree, shrubbery, monument, boulder, fence, seat or structure thereon, or behave or conduct himself on the Battle Green otherwise than in a quiet and orderly manner in keeping with a respectful regard and reverence for the memory of the patriotic service and sacrifice so nobly rendered.[39]

Less than a week before the march, at the May 24 meeting at which VVAW-NE's executive secretary, a recent college graduate, had appeared before the Lexington Selectmen to answer their questions about the antiwar veterans' request, the Selectmen had cited numerous concerns about the planned march from the practical to the purely ideological. What would happen to the vehicular traffic in Lexington Center? The executive secretary explained that the veterans would perform their mock search-and-destroy missions on the sidewalk, not in the street. Would the veterans pay for police protection? Yes, and they had already pledged to underwrite the cost in Concord, where they had secured permission from both NPS and that town's selectmen to perform and camp. What if people discarded VVAW's leaflets on the ground? The veterans always "policed" an area before departing, considering cleaning up after themselves "good politics." What would the veterans do for bathrooms? Rent a truck carrying six Port-o-San facilities. What if a resident could not tell the difference between a real invasion and a performance? Designated veterans would be on hand to explain to the people that no one was really being killed. "Will you show the people what the Viet Cong do to our boys?" "What the Viet Cong do is a Vietnamese problem," VVAW-NE's executive secretary replied, "and what the Americans do is an American problem."[40]

The minutes from this and a subsequent Special Selectmen's Meeting called a mere twenty-four hours before the march was to begin, as well as later interviews with the Selectmen, reveal that while the Selectmen briefly considered the veterans' right to free speech, they believed their first responsibility was to protect the Green from defilement.

"The Green is sacred to us, sacred to the country."[41]

"We feel the Green is a national shrine."[42]

It is "historic."[43]

Insofar as "reverence" for the Green is stipulated by the town bylaw, the fact that the veterans were, in the Selectmen's words, asking to "use the Green as a hotel" and a "campground," and further that there might be "drugs and liquor involved," immediately disqualified them. Anything but orthodox usage of the Green, the Selectmen ruled, would be "inappropriate." They decided at the first meeting and confirmed at the second that the veterans could march through town on the sidewalk and distribute leaflets but could not camp either on the Battle Green or in Tower Park, nor could they perform mock search-and-destroy missions anywhere within the town's borders.[44]

Apart from their concern about the cost of police protection, litter, and toilet facilities, each of which the town readily handled on other occasions, the Lexington Selectmen's refusal to allow the antiwar veterans to stay overnight or reenact the violence of the Vietnam War seems to have stemmed from their fear that VVAW-NE would use their storied town as a site to undermine Longfellow's and other mythicized accounts of American values. "Paul Revere's Ride" insists that the colonists prevailed through creativity and alacrity rather than their willingness to fight and use violence. Indeed, Longfellow preferred to insist that the day the nation should forevermore celebrate is "the eighteenth of April," the day of Revere's ingenious signaling and his heroic ride, and not the next day of fighting, which in 1894 became an official state holiday in Massachusetts to honor the forty-nine colonists who gave their lives in defense of the people's natural rights. Longfellow goes so far as to obfuscate the call to violence issued by Revere as he rode through the night. The poem only refers obliquely to "a word that shall echo forevermore," even as the narrative requires Revere to explain that he will be "Ready to ride and spread the alarm. . . . For the country folk *to be up and to arm*" (emphasis added). The point of VVAW-NE's march, in contrast, was to insist that the United States is a militaristic and violent country. Rather than show what the North Vietnamese Army and the National Liberation Front do "to our boys," the veterans would be illustrating how the United States had become the same kind of imperialist aggressor the British had once been in Lexington.[45]

The veterans responded to the Selectmen barring them from camping and performing mock search-and-destroy missions by informing the press that they might camp on the Lexington Green despite the ruling. As veterans, they felt entitled to visit the sites where fellow soldiers had lost their lives. Then, too, they were beginning to think tactically about what their staging on the Green would allow them to say and the interest the public would have as a result. Just two months earlier, in March 1971, when members of VVAW-NE had visited the Massachusetts State House to kick off the regional tour of a semitrailer truck they had filled with informational materials about the war, the lone article about it in the *Boston Globe* had been buried on page 18, even though the governor came down from his office to speak with the dozen veterans on hand and to be photographed with VVAW-NE leaders. But, on the Friday morning of the march, when the *Boston Globe* learned of the possibility of another showdown exactly like the one that took place between the federal government and VVAW the month before in Washington, DC, its editorial board promised to cover Operation POW over the course of the entire holiday weekend. And thus, when Jen Levin arrived at the Old North Bridge to kick off the proceedings, she found numerous reporters not only from the *Globe* but also from several different local and regional newspapers, all taking pictures and conducting interviews with the veterans and the many supportive Concord residents on hand to serve them a dinner assembled from local food donations.[46]

Jen was disappointed, however, to find that there were fewer than a third of the three hundred veterans the VVAW-NE leadership had announced would attend. Still, there were enough of them to create a small sea of olive drab at the top of the allée leading down to the Old North Bridge, and it was exciting to see several people with movie cameras on their shoulders. Hart Perry, a graduate student at Columbia University, had marshaled student and other filmmakers from New York and Boston to help him film the march. A similar group of volunteer filmmakers the fall before had walked with the veterans from Morristown to Valley Forge, eventually producing *Different Sons*, a dynamic, documentary-length film. The new lightweight 16-mm cameras had allowed filmmakers to shoot the veterans walking in patrol formation, performing mock search-and-destroy missions, and encountering a wide range of responses from the public, from being called traitors to being flashed the peace sign. With the tape reel on its back, the Éclair 16 could be carried easily on a cameraperson's shoulder, while the instant-change magazine solved the problem of having to pause to reload the film. VVAW showed *Different Sons* at festivals and fundraisers as a powerful means of spreading the message that while they had been forced to fight an illegal and immoral war, they were still the patriotic descendants of George Washington. Intent on creating another VVAW film that the organization could use to further increase its audience, Hart had struck a deal with a popular political variety show broadcast by the New York member station of the newly established Public Broadcasting Service (PBS). In exchange for providing his film crews with reels of film and audiotape, the show would broadcast the resulting documentary film of the Memorial Day weekend march. Jen noted that, like VVAW-NE's executive secretary and other VVAW-NE civilian supporters, the filmmakers had been careful to come to Concord in jeans and jean jackets, as opposed to something olive green that might make it appear they were stealing the veterans' valor, attempting to swell their ranks, or both. Hart Perry had found a way sartorially to signal his support of the veterans and his leadership of the film crews he had assembled: like Jen, he was wearing a tricorn hat.[47]

Without dismounting from her horse, Jen delivered VVAW-NE's warning to a veteran waiting for her on the back of a flatbed truck the veterans had set up as a speakers' platform at the top of the tree-lined allée. The veteran proceeded to solemnly read to the assembled crowd the same demands VVAW had presented to a congressional delegation during their occupation of the National Mall: unless Congress "enact[s] legislation to necessitate the immediate, unilateral, unconditional withdrawal of all United States Armed Forces and Central Intelligence Agency Personnel from the countries of Vietnam, Cambodia, Laos and Thailand," there will continue to be, the veterans declared, "war crimes committed against the people of Indochina as a result of Official and De Facto United States Military policy in the conducting of the illegal war of aggression."[48]

Pete Wilson arrived at the Old North Bridge area in time to hear the updated "cry of alarm," as Longfellow once put it, which he and Jen had carried to Concord in an attempt to awaken the people. He parked the Land Rover near the veterans' makeshift stage so that this largest of the veterans' props would be readily visible to the filmmakers and the assembled press. Leaning against his modern version of a horse, fashioned out of the plow his family used on their farm, Pete looked down the gravel-paved allée. On the other side of the Concord River, raised high on a massive granite pedestal, was the bronze statue of another farmer who also had his plow by his side. It occurred to Pete that he may have arrived in Concord as Paul Revere, but the looming showdown with the Lexington Selectmen suggested he was also the descendant of the American citizen-soldiers who were not afraid to face British tyranny. After all, VVAW-NE was prepared to face those local officials who, from the veterans' point of view, were in their own tyrannical way intent on not letting them exercise their right to be free. While the press had not yet made this connection, the veterans would soon make it explicit, being very adept at reimagining their relationship to the past and shifting their mobilization of American symbols accordingly in an attempt to end the war in Vietnam.

As the feeling returned to his cramped legs, Pete watched a priest approach the microphone the veterans had set up on the back of the flatbed truck. Recently elected the U.S. representative from Massachusetts on an antiwar platform, Father Robert Drinan urged the press and the public to listen to the men assembled before him.

"The Vietnam Veterans Against the War may be the one group that has more credibility than any other individual or any other collective group of people in this country."[49]

CHAPTER 2

Minute Men Statues

The next morning, after loading their gear into rental trucks, carefully policing their campsite, and eating the generous breakfast provided by local supporters, the antiwar veterans began to gather at the statue of the bronze farmer. In 1873, twenty-two-year-old local sculptor Daniel Chester French, chosen to create a centennial Revolutionary War monument on the strength of a recommendation from Louise May Alcott's artist sister, decided to honor the American men who fought and died here by picking up the story of what happened where Longfellow's poem leaves off. Having received the alarm that British Regulars were marching to Concord to find and destroy the colonists' hidden military stores, French's citizen-soldier steps away from his plow, picks up his musket, and steps toward the direction of the oncoming troops, fully prepared to risk his life protecting what the colonists claimed were their natural rights (Figure 3).[1]

Almost one hundred years after French's statue was dedicated in 1875, the VVAW-NE leadership was thrilled to see more Vietnam veterans arriving at the Old North Bridge prepared to join them in protesting the war. Some were patients at area Veterans Health Administration hospitals and had not been able to camp out Friday night. Others were just hearing about the Selectmen's decision to bar the veterans from the Lexington Battle Green and had dropped everything to join the protest. When all of the veterans were assembled at French's Minute Man Statue, Arthur Bestor Cram, a heavily bearded, redheaded man in jeans and an olive-drab button-down shirt, stepped onto an overturned crate and, using a battery-operated bullhorn, addressed them.[2]

"Just as the Minutemen gathered freely in 1775, we gather freely in 1971."[3]

Holding a clipboard in his other hand, he read from the press release he and other VVAW-NE leaders had written after the veterans voted the night

Figure 3. Daniel Chester French, *Minute Man Statue* (1875). Photographed by and courtesy of Staci Bigelow.

before to proceed onto the Lexington Battle Green without the Selectmen's permission. It revealed the veterans' shift from aligning themselves with Paul Revere to claiming the Minute Men as their forefathers.[4]

Born one month after the United States dropped an atomic bomb on Hiroshima, Japan, Bestor, as he prefers to be called, had been looking forward to his junior year at Denison University, where he was majoring in economics and theater, when President Nixon's predecessor, Lyndon B. Johnson, doubled the monthly draft call. It was immediately clear to Bestor that once he graduated in the spring of 1967 and lost the II-S status that exempted college students from conscription, there was a good chance he would be drafted into the Army and sent to Vietnam. If, however, he enlisted before graduation, he could become an officer, parlaying his college degree into the kind of leadership position held by the men in his family. His maternal grandfather, after whom Bestor was named, had served from 1915 to 1944 as the president of Chautauqua, the famous summer learning community in upstate New York, where a steady stream of national political and cultural figures, from Susan B. Anthony and Franklin Delano Roosevelt to Amelia Earhart and Duke Ellington, has lectured in the years since its founding in 1874. Bestor's father had fought in several Army combat operations against the Japanese during World War II before settling down to a lucrative career as a Wall Street lawyer. Determined to make his own mark on the world, Bestor joined the branch of the military known for demanding the most of its men: the U.S. Marine Corps, the initials of which were stamped on the shirt he saved from that time and wore on Saturday morning at the Old North Bridge.[5]

In Da Nang, South Vietnam, Bestor had been tasked with erecting a thirty-five-mile-long barbed-wire fence equipped with sensors to keep Vietnam's guerrilla fighters off the massive American air base there. The difficulties associated with executing such a big assignment were compounded by the fact that the 160 Marines assigned to him had either proven themselves unprepared for war or had already been traumatized by it. One day, when their work took them through a swamp and they emerged covered with leeches, Bestor's beleaguered troops dropped their guns, screaming. Stripping off their fatigues, they thought only of using their cigarette lighters to remove the blood-sucking creatures, not about the fact that they had blown their cover. When they returned to the same area a few days later with a convoy of trucks carrying the equipment they would need to put up the fencing, there was a landmine waiting for them. It exploded, overturning two trucks behind Bestor's jeep and severely injuring some of his men. Bestor called in the coordinates, and soon American air support was on the scene dropping bombs. By then, however, the guerrilla fighters who had placed the landmine were already long gone.[6]

The effect on the American soldiers was immediate. "Some soldiers went off the deep end," Bestor later explained. "They took the safety off their guns and started to shoot at just anybody."[7]

Eventually, Bestor was able to direct the completion of the perimeter fence only to learn his Marines had risked their lives installing sensors that were never able to tell the difference between humans and wild boars.

When Bestor's tour of duty in Vietnam ended and he was given the job of training new soldiers, he decided to become the first officer in the Marines' history to file a conscientious objector claim. He was released at the "Convenience of the Government" in April 1970. Rather than use his return to civilian life to escape the war, Bestor started working at the Legal In-Service Project, counseling soldiers at Fort Devens and other military installations in Massachusetts on how they too could get out of the military before they were forced to serve under the direction of military officials who believed American technological innovation could trump the Vietnamese people's determination to be independent.

Bestor had first learned of Vietnam Veterans Against the War when he saw a flier advertising Operation RAW. In his response to a survey the national VVAW office sent out after he and the other veterans completed the eighty-six-mile march, Bestor gave his reasons for why someone already supporting GI resistance had decided to walk from Morristown to Valley Forge.

"I felt disgusted and repulsed by the US involvement in the War in Vietnam," Bestor reported, "and felt that going directly to the people of New Jersey and Pennsylvania would be a positive declaration of my shame and intolerance for the Vietnam War and a positive and responsible manner in educating and confronting people with their feelings about a situation they and we are equally responsible for."[8]

Bestor's explanation captured the two sides of VVAW's message since Nixon's election: on the one hand, the organization's members insisted that the United States was committing atrocities in Vietnam while, on the other, they expressed a desire to be "positive" in addressing "the people" who, when referenced as such, are imagined to share an abiding love for their country. Several months after completing the march to Valley Forge, when Bestor and another Vietnam veteran were approached by VVAW leader John Kerry about heading up a chapter based in Cambridge, Bestor jumped at the chance to address the people of New England while finally exercising the kind of morally impactful leadership the Marines had denied him. He became one of VVAW-NE's two coordinators and, as such, was the one who read the chapter's latest press release to the veterans gathered at the Minute Man Statue on what was proving to be a beautiful and unseasonably warm Saturday morning for late May.[9]

"Just as the British judged the Minutemen's act illegal," Bestor continued, before referring to the veterans' decision Friday evening to proceed onto the Green, "some may judge ours to be illegal."

The prior evening's deliberation about what to do in the wake of the Lexington Selectmen's decision not to allow the veterans to bivouac on the Battle Green or to perform guerrilla theater within the town's bounds had essentially been a repetition of the same conversation the veterans had had the month before when the federal government secured an injunction from the Justice Department barring them from the National Mall. In April, the veterans had carried out their deliberations and then their vote on the Mall in full view of the public as a means of rebuking the federal government for its lack of transparency. They knew that, having already served in the military, they were unable to impact the military's ability to carry out the war by burning their draft cards or escaping to Canada. And thus they decided that peacefully breaking a minor law unrelated to the war and accepting the punishment would be their best chance of drawing positive public attention to their antiwar views. And indeed, the result of their decision to continue sleeping on the National Mall was massive amounts of sympathetic media coverage, particularly after several political luminaries came down to the Mall to join them.[10]

"If the country can find a place for you to stay in Vietnam," Massachusetts senator Edward Kennedy told Bestor and the other veterans with whom he sat down on the Mall, "they can find a place for you to stay here."[11]

The federal government eventually decided not to arrest the veterans for camping on the Mall if only because the veterans had proven, by the third day of their occupation, that while their hearts were anguished, their methods were peaceful. Then, too, the Nixon administration was keenly aware that the veterans had attracted large segments of the public to their side.

On Friday night in Concord, the veterans once again held their conversation in front of the public. This was part of what they had come out to Concord to do: demonstrate the kind of democratic decision making they believed the Nixon administration, with its secret military operations, was not allowing.[12]

"If there was a meeting, everybody got to speak, and they didn't care if it took us twenty-four hours to make a five-minute decision, by God, everybody got their chance to speak," one of the VVAW-NE veterans recalled of the Memorial Day weekend march years later. Inclusive discussions were important to the veterans, he explained, "after watching people die from following stupid orders."[13]

As the deliberations got under way, one veteran noted that even as disobeying the Lexington bylaw would normally be punishable only with a ticket, there was a good chance the Selectmen would come up with a reason to order their arrest.

"Trespassing," another veteran had speculated as to a possible charge.[14]

After agreeing that arrest was a real possibility, Bestor repeated the suggestion made in DC that purposefully breaking a law was a necessary counter to the state's own illegal activity. The United States had sent troops to Vietnam and begun a war without a formal declaration, which was a violation of the U.S. Constitution. Furthermore, because the war was not undertaken in self-defense, it was also arguably in violation of Chapter VII of the United Nations Charter.

"The only place we have slept illegally," Bestor declared, perhaps recalling Senator Kennedy's assertion on the Mall, "is in Vietnam."[15]

When the knowing laughter that met this observation had subsided, Bestor called for any final comments. A somewhat older veteran who had served in Taiwan prior to the Vietnam War argued that being arrested in the middle of night would not result in the same heightened press coverage the veterans had garnered in DC.

"It seems to me that they could come in at four in the morning, when everybody else is asleep and the newsmen are in the sack and just round us up and cart us away. No one will see it!"[16]

The concern echoed that of Concord son Henry David Thoreau, who also believed that deliberately breaking a law in political protest can only enlighten the citizenry if the public's attention is drawn to the lawbreaking act. When he went to jail in 1846 rather than pay his poll tax and thereby support a government seeking to expand slavery, only a few of the locals knew about it. That all changed when Thoreau started to give the lecture about the necessity of finding ways to meet the state face-to-face, which in 1849 became his influential essay later published under the title "Civil Disobedience."[17]

"Did the people who were marching on this trail two hundred years ago ask permission of the British if they could do it?" one of the veterans countered, angry at the idea that publicity should be the paramount concern.

Fueled by this idea that they were following in the footsteps of their patriot forefathers, most of the veterans stood up and cheered.

"All those who are voting for civil disobedience in Lexington," Bestor directed, using the title of Thoreau's essay and sensing it was time to end the discussion, "raise your hand."[18]

All but four veterans were willing to risk arrest after the press was in bed if it meant emulating the action that helped bring the nation into existence and that therefore might, by releasing the same energy, right its present course. VVAW operated under majority rule as part of its rejection of the military's strict chain of command. Thus, it was decided that the veterans would become the Minute Men and take a stand on the Lexington Battle Green.[19]

All of the veterans gathered on Saturday morning at the Minute Man Statue, both those who had been told in advance by VVAW-NE what to wear and those who showed up after reading in the newspapers about the impending showdown in Lexington, were dressed in something that made clear they had served in the military, even if it was just a boonie hat. Most, like Bestor, had stopped shaving and were growing out their hair as a means of signaling their rejection of the military's rationale and its methods. Six weeks earlier, the press covering Operation DCIII had commented extensively on the still unusual sight of fatigue-clad American soldiers with hair long enough to cover their ears and, in many cases, long enough to reach their shoulders. A correspondent for the *Christian Science Monitor* remarked that the antiwar veterans in DC "broke forever that clear distinction, made often if not accurately before, between those 'clean-cut young men willing to serve their country' and 'filthy hippies' who won't. . . . Many were rather unkempt, indeed. But they had fought hard, many of them, for their country." The message behind how the antiwar veterans presented themselves was that they could be patriots willing to die for their country and antiwar activists at the same time. When it came to the Vietnam War, these were not, in the antiwar veterans' minds, contradictory positions.[20]

For Bestor, no longer cutting his hair and shaving was also a means of reversing the military's attempts, begun when he first arrived for summer officers training at Quantico, to strip him of his individuality and free thought.

"We found ourselves, heads shaved, in front of someone yelling in our faces," he would later recall of his first few hours at the Marines' base in Virginia. "We had lost part of our identity. We all felt very vulnerable."[21]

Bestor's subsequent military experiences transformed him from the eager Marine who dutifully kept his hair a quarter of an inch long into an antiwar activist who looked every bit the "hippy" identified by the press as one of VVAW's inspirations (Figures 4 and 5).

"The new American soldier," Bestor asserted by way of an explanation in a collection of antiwar statements published by VVAW, "is a person who has

Figure 4. Bestor Cram in uniform at Denison University (c. 1967). Courtesy of Bestor Cram.

come to a point in his life where he's rejected violence—he's seen too much of it. He's been so much a part of it. He's learned about how and to what extent human beings can really torture one another." He went on to describe without any hesitation his new, very non-Marine-like emotions. "He's cried a lot in shame, for the year, maybe two years of his life in which he killed, in which he raped the countryside." What the new American soldier most wants, Bestor continued, is to make sure that no one has to ever again "go through what he's been through."[22]

Figure 5. Bestor Cram at VVAW-NE's Cambridge, MA, office in the spring of 1971. Photographed by and courtesy of Rand E. Martin.

If short-haired Marines "raped the countryside," the long-haired, fatigue-clad veterans waiting to set out for Lexington from Concord's Old North Bridge wanted to present themselves as men very much in the tradition of the bronze Minute Man next to whom they stood during Bestor's remarks. While sculptor Daniel Chester French would go on to carve the nineteen-foot-tall statue of Abraham Lincoln featured in the Washington, DC, memorial to the slain Civil War president, his first indelible mark on the nation's imagination was to imagine the nation's liberators as self-sufficient farmers. In Concord, he presented the American Revolution as a popular movement fueled by the people, not one planned and carried out by wealthy elites and slaveholders, as so many of the founding fathers were. French ensured that his statue conformed to the popular myths of the nation's founding by taking up the story where Longfellow left off, deviating from it only to push forward the arrival time of the warning from 2 a.m., when Dr. Prescott actually arrived in Concord, to several hours after sunrise so that he could depict a farmer in his fields, already warm enough from the labor of making spring furrows that he needed to remove his coat and roll up his sleeves. In thereby conveying that Americans are a people who engage in peaceable pursuits unless driven by circumstance to fight, French was in essence modeling his farmer after the mythic George Washington, celebrated nowhere more enthusiastically than in the oft-reprinted biography authored by Mason Locke Weems in 1800: "in the midst of his favourite labours, of the plough and the pruning-hook . . . [Washington] was suddenly called on by his *country*, to turn his plough-share into a sword, and go forth to meet a torrent of evils which threatened her. . . . [Then] having won the great prize for which he contended, he returns to his plough." For the American citizenry, Washington was their Cincinnatus. Like the Roman statesman and farmer, he would only leave his fields under the moral imperative of answering his country's call and would promptly return to his preferred peaceful farming pursuits when the need to assert force was past. French's farmer will also only leave his fields when called by his country, and like Washington, he intends to return to his fields when his military work is done, as the lingering of his hand on his plow indicates. If pilgrims to the Old North Bridge are prompted, on the one hand, to feel outrage and grief that such peaceable men were killed by imperialist forces at the very spot where the statue stands, they are also invited, on the other, to consider that while the United States was born through war, it is not a war-making country. This latter point helps explain why a line drawing of the statue appeared during World War II on U.S. government war bonds as well as on war bond flags and posters and still appears on the seal of the Army National Guard. The name of French's statue is a nod to the quarter of the colonial militia charged with being ready at a minute's notice and thereby works alongside Longfellow's poem as a celebration of preparedness, which is particularly fitting for the National Guard, but his statue also suggests that war violence is an aberration from the peaceable American norm. The United

States might have had a massive military that could be employed on multiple fronts during World War II, but it was not, the statue and government uses of it insist, militaristic. French's liberties with the timing of Revere's warning, in other words, allow the nation to imagine that it only momentarily and of dire necessity reverses the Old Testament exhortation, also invoked by Washington's biographer, that the people will "beat their swords into plowshares, and their spears into pruning hooks." The Vietnam veterans' Saturday morning gathering place was an assertion that they too were turning from their preferred peaceable pursuits as civilians only out of dire necessity. It was also a means of underscoring that, in proceeding onto the Lexington Battle Green, they were adjusting the focus of Operation POW. They had set out as so many Paul Reveres bringing a warning about the Vietnam War to the people. But they had become the modern incarnation of the Minute Men. They too were prepared to defend their freedom, in this case the freedom to speak out against the war.[23]

Having declared the veterans' intention to follow in the Minute Men's footsteps by engaging in action "some may regard as illegal," Bestor proceeded to direct the veterans into two single-file ranks in a reenactment of the approach the colonial militia made to the Old North Bridge on the morning of April 19, 1775. After receiving the warning that Regulars were on their way, over four hundred armed colonial militiamen gathered on the hill above the bridge in hopes that by amassing outside of town, they would avoid any appearance of inciting violence as British troops searched for secreted military stores. The colonists only approached the bridge, which was being guarded by one hundred of the king's troops while their fellow soldiers engaged in searching a distant farm, when it appeared that those troops still searching the town had set fire to its buildings. The colonists later claimed that their sole aim was to cross the bridge and regain access to their imperiled town. Nevertheless, they primed and loaded their weapons before advancing in formation and possibly, if local legend is correct, to the accompanying tune, played by their fifers, of "The White Cockade," a longstanding British symbol of rebellion. Seeing the armed colonists approach, the captain of the British troops began organizing his men into the formation used for street fighting even as there were none of the protective buildings such a formation required to be successful. Sensing their vulnerability as the American militiamen drew nearer, the Regulars felt compelled to fire a warning shot. When the colonists realized one of their men had been hit and was wounded, they returned fire and a skirmish ensued. In a matter of minutes, two American colonists and two British soldiers were dead, and many more were wounded on both sides. It was the first exchange of gunfire in what became the American Revolution.[24]

Bestor Cram had already instructed the media to wait on the opposite side of the replica memorial bridge with the intention of orchestrating photographs in which French's Minute Man would appear to march alongside the new Minute Men of VVAW-NE and thereby lend the latter the same aura of heroic patriotism the veterans had sought at Valley Forge and the night before as so many modern Paul Reveres. However, as part of VVAW-NE's strategy to make clear how far the nation had fallen from its founding ideals, Bestor simultaneously began to undermine the messages of American peaceableness encoded in Longfellow's poem and French's statue. He put two war wounded veterans at the front of one of the two lines of demonstrators and a flag, pregnant with meaning, brought by thirteen veterans representing VVAW's Rhode Island chapter, at the head of the other.

On the one hand, Bestor's intention with the flag was to reenact the mythic moment described by the famous lines carved into the Minute Man Statue's massive granite base that were taken from the first verse of "Concord Hymn," written by Concord resident and nationally revered philosopher Ralph Waldo Emerson and sung in 1837 at the dedication of the earlier monument on the other side of the river in the town's first step in sacralizing the site.

> By the rude bridge that
> Arched the flood,
> Their flag to April's
> Breeze unfurled,
> Here once the embattled
> Farmers stood,
> And fired the shot heard
> Round the world.[25]

The colonists used many different flags in the Revolutionary War era, from the red and white striped flags flown on top of New England's liberty poles to flags featuring rattlesnakes ("Don't tread on me"), among others, each of which signified resistance. Emerson does not specify which flag the colonists were using, in part because no one knows if there really was one on display that morning. Emerson's vagueness on this front allows the mythic flag to stand, albeit obliquely and anachronistically, for the national flag, which was not adopted until 1777. Emerson imagines a new, spring-like beginning born of the patriotism the American flag would come to signal while simultaneously tempering his poem's celebration of militarized defiance. He imagines the first shot fired not as a deadly projectile but as a message about the benefits of democracy. Because a musket shot cannot literally be heard around the globe, the shot functions in his hymn as pure metaphor. The statue of a farmer preparing the soil for spring planting and the verse on the base supporting him imagine democracy as so many seeds spreading peacefully, not just across America but around the world.[26]

On the other hand, even as the veterans presented themselves as orthodox reenactors and thereby patriotic citizens, the regimental flag Bestor put at the front of one of the lines of march asserted that the United States has a long history of waging violent war and thus that the Concord Hymn and the Minute Man Statue are more myth than reality. Framed by the name of their organization and chapter in all capital letters, VVAW-RI's white flag featured at its center VVAW's insignia, which was a direct rebuttal to the military insignia some of the antiwar veterans were still wearing in the form of a bright red patch on their olive drab fatigue jackets.[27]

The modern U.S. military's insignia used in Vietnam tells the government's very romanticized version of why America was willing to sacrifice so many of its young men's lives there. Eight years after President Eisenhower explained his domino theory, the United States created "U.S. Military Assistance Command, Vietnam," in preparation for significantly increasing its presence in South Vietnam. The MACV insignia depicts a white sword and a yellow crenellated wall or a row of yellow dominos on a red field. The insignia thereby explains that the United States was trying to stop (red) communism from spreading past the Great Wall of China and knocking over a succession of countries like so many dominoes. The specific red and yellow shades chosen by the U.S. military match the colors of the flag of the Democratic Republic of Vietnam (or North Vietnam) and thereby designate that country as the particular focus of American military efforts. The upright sword thrusting through a break in the wall represents U.S. actions as purely defensive. Americans are depicted as pushing back communist aggression. In other words, the MACV insignia offers visual representation of the moral imperative for American citizens to leave their farms, metaphorically speaking, for the field of battle. Their duty was to save Vietnam and, by extension, the world for freedom and democracy.

VVAW's bold red, yellow, and white insignia, reproduced on its flags, as well as on the pins members wore and those they distributed along the march route to supporters, was in the same shape and color as the MACV insignia (see Figures 12 and 15). However, VVAW replaced the American sword that depicts the United States chivalrously defending Vietnam and the world with an upside-down version of the actual weapon given to American GIs in Vietnam. Bayoneted into the ground and topped with a dead soldier's helmet, the M16 becomes, and is depicted in VVAW's insignia as, a Fallen Soldier Battle Cross.

Prior to the installation of refrigeration on ships and aircraft, soldiers had to be buried where they died, and funeral services were thus held in the field around these makeshift crosses. Even during the Vietnam War, the Fallen Soldier Battle Cross was used for a brief ceremony in the field before the removal of the dead soldier's body for transport back to the United States. That so many American soldiers had to be honored in this way was, from VVAW's point of view, a testament to how much the Vietnamese wanted to expel them from their country. And thus, whereas French's statue and the words on its base suggest that Americans prefer peaceable pursuits, the flag brought to the march by the Rhode Island chapter of VVAW and positioned by Bestor at the head of one of the veterans' two lines of march countered that the United States was now waging deadly war in order to exert its control over people who wanted the right of self-government.[28]

Bestor further undermined the messages cultivated at the Old North Bridge area when he decided not to send at the head of the veterans' line of march the kind of steely soldier French imagines. Although French had modeled his statue after Acton Captain Isaac Davis, who tirelessly trained and carefully outfitted his local militia in the weeks leading up to the encounter at the bridge and who then, after volunteering to lead the approach to it, was shot and killed, the sculptor presents the thirty-year-old as an inviolate bronze body. Only those visitors steeped in local history are prompted by the statue to mourn the loss of this patriot. With his sleeves rolled up to reveal well-muscled forearms, French's Minute Man is frozen in time well before he or anyone else ever dies. Nowhere is there reference to the private anguish of Davis's wife, their four young children, or his other relatives. The Minute Man Statue and other memorial efforts at the Old North Bridge area ultimately risk erasing the Revolutionary War's violence and suffering. The antiwar veterans, in contrast, were intent on writing that violence and the ensuing agony of wounded young men and their families back into the nation's most sacred landscape. Bestor directed to the front of the line of march a wounded Vietnam veteran with metal leg braces as well as a war-paralyzed Vietnam veteran confined to a wheelchair. The veteran in braces was in obvious pain and using the wheelchair he insisted on pushing to keep his balance.[29]

At the end of the march to Valley Forge, war-injured men had also decided to display their bodies as a reminder of war's cost. They had allowed themselves to be lifted onto a stage fashioned out of a flatbed truck and presented to an indignant crowd that had swelled to 1,500 family members, friends, and antiwar protestors. VVAW had successfully used a photograph of that moment to recruit veterans for the organization's occupation of Washington, DC, where Bestor had once again seen wounded members eagerly put themselves on display for an increasingly sympathetic public. Twenty-year-old Bill Wyman of Boston, who lost both his legs when his jeep ran over a landmine toward the end of his tour, ended up being photographed more than any other of the veterans who journeyed to DC with the exception of VVAW's national spokesman John Kerry. One United Press International photograph that ran in newspapers around the country shows Wyman sitting on the ground of the veterans' encampment, his stumps prominently sticking out toward the viewer. In another UPI photograph, Wyman is being wheeled at the front of a procession of veterans as they pass the Lincoln Memorial en route to pay their respects to their fallen brothers at Arlington National Cemetery. And in another, his comrades are carrying him down the steps of the Supreme Court after demanding a ruling on the constitutionality of the war. Indeed, the story of the Vietnam War was often told by VVAW through the point of view of the wounded. John Kerry closed his speech to the Senate Foreign Relations Committee by asking the senators to imagine a time "thirty years from now" when "our brothers go down the street without a leg, without an arm, or a face, and small boys ask why." This display of the wounded was another tactic VVAW borrowed from the civil rights movement. Film footage and photographs of state troopers and police officers beating well-dressed, peaceable citizens attempting only to march to Montgomery in pursuit of black voting rights were featured on every TV news program and in every newspaper across the country. The broken bodies at the front of the march at the Old North Bridge asserted that the veterans had been similarly beaten up by the military. Bestor and the other veterans reasoned that if footage of protestors being mauled in Alabama led to President Johnson passing the federal Voting Rights Act, then putting their own wounds on display might prod the federal government to end the Vietnam War.[30]

Finally arranged in two lines, the veterans were ready to begin their reenactment of the colonists' approach to the Old North Bridge. When the two wounded men crested the arched bridge, one of the photojournalists waiting on the eastern side took a photograph of the scene Bestor had so carefully staged (Figure 6). Its power is evidenced by the fact that the *Boston Globe* selected it for its front page the following morning and placed it above the fold. In the foreground are the march's war-injured lead figures. Although blurred, the Minute Man Statue, being widely known, is still clearly legible. By showing the Minute Man seemingly walking in the same procession, the veterans appear patriotic. But the Minute Man's presence also reveals the significant contrast between the veterans' wartime experiences and the statue's promise. While a farmer, rendered in indestructible bronze, with forearms well muscled from the plowing to which he will return, creates the illusion that American soldiers are simultaneously inviolate and peaceable, the VVAW soldiers in the photograph have suffered irreversible injury serving in an unjust war. In other words, even as the veterans meant to stand with the mythical farmer on behalf of the peaceable and limitless future his image promises, they were also restoring to the statue the heartbreaking story of the young father, shot in the chest by an imperial army, on whom it was modeled. Their message about the war in Vietnam meant they had to dramatically and forcefully deconstruct some of the United States' most fundamental myths, first among them that Americans are the descendants of Cincinnatus and that, as such, they only go to war for a short period of time before returning to their fields and that, because the United States is a country with a righteous cause, its soldiers are never physically hurt or emotionally traumatized by war.

VVAW-NE's unorthodox use of Massachusetts' Revolutionary War battlefields was why this particular protest was already proving significantly different from those at Valley Forge and on the National Mall. Valley Forge was a military encampment. The National Mall has a long history of being used for protests. Massachusetts' Revolutionary War battlefields, in contrast, are places watered with the blood of men the nation regards as martyrs even as the language of memorialization often seems to erase that bloodshed. As Bestor Cram was starting to realize, the stakes for this march were going to be high. Looking ahead to the veterans' arrival at Lexington's own very similar statue of a citizen-soldier facing eastward on the morning of April 19, 1775, erected on the edge of the Lexington Green twenty-five years after

Figure 6. Vietnam veterans begin march at Old North Bridge.
Boston Public Library/United Press International.

Concord's, Bestor was prompted to remember the anonymous phone call he had received on Thursday night, after the press reported the possibility of the veterans proceeding onto that sacred space without the Selectmen's permission.

"You're the one leading this group over the weekend?" the caller had asked.

"Yes," Bestor replied.

"Bullets to meet you," the caller threatened before abruptly hanging up.[31]

CHAPTER 3

Memorial War Obelisks

That same morning, less than a mile from the Old North Bridge, small groups of young people wearing colorful short-sleeved shirts and carefree smiles strolled between the colonial-era white clapboard and nineteenth-century brick buildings that ring Monument Square. Ever since residents voted in 1960 to designate this central part of town a historic district, the illustrious Concord past has become a vividly real part of its present. A series of plaques and other markers explain that the first English inland settlers in North America erected tiny, one-room homes under the glacier ridge that shelters the square's eastern side; that, a century and a half later, in the town meeting house, the first autonomous government of the American colonies met with John Hancock as its president; and that, steps away, in 1846, Thoreau opened a new path of political resistance when he protested the Mexican-American War by spending a night in the town's jail, since torn down, rather than pay a poll tax that would contribute to the expansion of slavery. The town of Concord celebrates these moments as evidence that its residents helped birth the nation, not only by settling it and then establishing its independence but also by playing a role in the invention and practice of the mechanisms such as town meeting and civil disobedience by which the United States remains a strong democracy.[1]

The town's decision at the height of the Cold War between the United States and the Soviet Union to use memorialization as a means of making a series of local events into the story of the nation was a repetition of an earlier town gesture made in the face of another war. Several of the people milling about on the morning of May 29, 1971, stopped to read an iron plaque on the thirty-foot-tall memorial obelisk erected in the center of the square that lists the names of forty-eight local "brave men" who "died for their country" in the Civil War. By dedicating the 1867 obelisk on April 19, the anniversary date of the battle at the town's Old North Bridge, and by building its foundation out of a large granite block that formerly served as one of the bridge's abutments, the town linked the Civil War to the Revolution in an assertion that the fight to end slavery was another release of the same energy in Concord that resulted in the nation's founding. By implication, and as the New England antiwar veterans' march route indicated they well understood, every threat to the nation can be battled through memorialization's re-release of the foundational energy that birthed it.[2]

Not long after the veterans were photographed cresting the Old North Bridge as the newest incarnation of the Minute Men, the illusion that time stands still in Concord and that the nation's future will thus always be a return to a glorious past was shattered when a dozen fatigue-clad men ran onto Monument Square yelling and brandishing automatic weapons.

"Di di mao! Di di mao!"[3]

Unfazed by the screams of surprise and terror that met them, the soldiers began to grab and forcibly search Monument Square's early morning visitors.

A few of the soldiers ran down Main Street toward the town's sixty-seven-year-old hardware store. Window shoppers cowered behind the lawnmowers and garbage cans lined up under the store's brightly striped awning.

"Someone grabs me," a young woman later recalled, slipping into the present tense to describe what remained a vivid memory. "They're pushing and prodding me with their rifles."[4]

Even though she had volunteered to participate in this mock search-and-destroy mission, the young woman found herself sobbing as soldiers forced her and her friends up Main Street at gunpoint and shoved them face down onto the grassy expanse at the base of the silent obelisk (Figure 7). She had thought she would be able to tell that the veterans were acting. Now she was not so sure. Cars full of Saturday-morning shoppers and weekend tourists began pulling over. She heard doors slam. Out of the corner of her eye, she could see people gaping at the unexpected violence in this bucolic New England town. While it dawned on the adults that they were seeing a repetition of the kind of performance VVAW had staged in Washington, DC, the children only understood that violent men were hurting people and no one was doing anything to stop them. Hart Perry filmed a shaken little girl try to console her sobbing younger sister.[5]

Figure 7. VVAW mock search-and-destroy mission in Monument Square. Photographed by Ted Polumbaum. Courtesy of the Newseum Collection.

One of the soldiers barking out orders used to have a well-paying job in the hotel and restaurant business.

"But all of my friends were going off and I'm hearing about this war," Donald Carrico later said, explaining why, in 1967, he had suddenly decided to enlist in the Marines. "I had always felt the patriotic duty to serve," he continued, noting that his uncle had fought in World War II and that his father, a mechanical engineer with a medical deferment, also contributed to the war effort by designing pumps for naval ships.[6]

"We were going to fight to save our country from communism," Don recalled thinking en route to Vietnam. "I was," he noted of that time in his life, "very gung-ho."

Don's attitude started to change after a mountaintop battle near the sacred city of Hue. The South Vietnamese troops who were supposed to be fighting alongside the Americans left the field rather than fulfill their assignment of providing a necessary blocking force against what they knew well before the Americans would be a massive deployment from the North's army. Don and a sergeant in his company had been unable to rescue the American soldiers who were left pinned down.

"Every time we made an attempt to move closer to help the wounded, heavy automatic weapons fire would stop us," Don later recalled. "We could hear the Marines dying only 20 feet away."[7]

The United States was supposed to be fighting for the preservation of a democratic South Vietnam (or the Republic of Vietnam), but it seemed that the South Vietnamese did not want the Americans in their country any more than their Northern countrymen did.

"I think it was on the order of sixty dead and over 120 wounded," Don recalled of his unit's loses that day, adding that his own shrapnel wounds resulted in a month-long stay at a military hospital at Cam Ranh Bay.

After he recovered, Don was assigned to another unit where he became convinced that the South Vietnamese wanted nothing more than for the Americans to leave.

"Our enemy was all around us," Don explained of his time in Da Nang. "It was the mamma-san, as we called the ladies who washed our laundry, and our hooch man, or hooch boy as we called the guy that cleaned our hooch" or living space. "On a number of occasions, we ended up finding them having tried to infiltrate our lines at night with explosives to destroy our base camp. A lot of these people turned out to actually be Viet Cong and we thought they were our friends."

Like the Lexington Selectmen who had questioned VVAW-NE's executive secretary about the march ("Will you show the people what the Viet Cong do to our boys?"), Don was referring to the guerrilla forces of the National Liberation Front, using the name given to them in the mid-1950s by Ngo Dinh Diem, the prime minister of Vietnam, who, after the country's forced division, became the first president of the Republic of Vietnam. The Vietnamese equivalent of "Commies," the name "Viet Cong" helped Diem's American handlers obscure the truth that the NLF existed solely to win independence from the United States.

"VC?" the soldiers asked repeatedly as they swept across Monument Square taking captives.

Ignoring everyone's pleading insistence that they were not Viet Cong, the soldiers threw one of their victims up against a large bronze tablet attached to an even bigger granite bolder that serves as Concord's World War I memorial. Like the Minute Man Statue, the tablet contains a verse penned by local philosopher Ralph Waldo Emerson, this one repurposed to commend the twenty-five local men who died in that conflict for fulfilling what Emerson deems a sacred calling:

So nigh is grandeur to our dust
So near is God to Man
When duty whispers low thou must
The youth replies I can.[8]

The soldiers' brutal treatment of the innocent morning strollers called into question the sacred nature of that calling when it came to the Vietnam War.

As the interrogations continued, the American soldiers became more agitated, threatening to kill the women taken captive at the hardware store and whose hands they had finished binding in what likely was a stark reminder for bystanders of William Calley's 1970 court-martial testimony about his and his men's actions in My Lai:

Q: What were they firing at?
A: At the enemy, sir.
Q: At people?
A: At the enemy, sir.
Q: They weren't human beings?
A: Yes, sir.
Q: They were men?
A: I don't know, sir. I would imagine they were, sir.
Q: Didn't you see them?
A: I wasn't discriminating.
Q: Did you see women?
A: I don't know, sir.
Q: What do you mean, you weren't discriminating?
A: I didn't discriminate between individuals in the village, sir. They were all the enemy, they were all to be destroyed, sir.[9]

VVAW-NE's aim was to act out what Calley had reported—namely, that American troops were so fearful of an enemy that appeared to be everywhere, they illegally opened fire on people who were not in uniform or obviously carrying weapons. (While Calley's interrogator succeeds in revealing the indiscriminate violence that Calley unleashed, he fails to acknowledge that thousands of Vietnamese women fought for their country.)[10]

Almost two hundred years earlier, when the British approached the Lexington Green, they were also on edge having been on their feet for hours marching through hostile territory filled with the sound of distant gunshots sounding out the colonists' alarm. When they saw armed colonists on the Green, they did not listen for a command but proceeded to open fire even though the colonists were already in the act of dispersing. British officers later admitted that their men went, as one of the psychologists working with VVAW's war-traumatized members later called it, "berserk."[11]

"On our route home," one British officer reported of what happened next, "we found every house full of people, and the fences lined as before. Every house from which they fired was immediately forced, and EVERY SOUL IN THEM PUT TO DEATH. Horrible carnage! O Englishmen, to what brutal degeneracy are ye fallen!"[12]

"They were so enraged at suffering from the unseen enemy," another British officer similarly reported of his troops, "that they forced open many of the houses . . . and put to death all those found in them."[13]

In reenacting these same kinds of atrocities, the Vietnam veterans were shape-shifting for a third time. Thus far, they had presented themselves as Paul Revere and then the Minute Men. Now, in reenacting an American search-and-destroy mission in Vietnam, they were drawing a comparison between their actions as GIs and those of the British in 1775. One of the fliers they distributed during Operation POW made this point loudly and clearly. "With an ironic twist," it explained, "our presence in Indochina as viewed by a native of an occupied village easily coincides with the British army in America in 1776." (That the year referenced was the signing of the Declaration of Independence and not the one when Concord and Lexington were besieged is a testament to how politically connected the two events were imagined to be.) While as antiwar activists the veterans aligned themselves with the Patriots, they were willing to also present themselves as the modern incarnation of the British Regulars acting on behalf of an imperialist regime in order to make the point that the United States had become exactly what its eighteenth-century forefathers had once died to vanquish.

"It was pretty brutal," was all Don would later say of his own missions in Da Nang. By the time he was discharged and attending Boston's Graham Junior College in the fall of 1970, he had been deeply depressed about what he had seen and done.

"I had no desire to do anything."

Only when he found out that VVAW was using performance instead of just words to convey the brutality of their government's military tactics did he find a purpose.

The first step had been to find fatigues and realistic-looking weaponry. While some of the veterans, including Pete Wilson, whose height made it difficult to find clothes that fit, had kept their government-issue clothing, many of the veterans had thrown away theirs the minute they were discharged from the military. In Concord, they were wearing whatever fatigues the Boston-area army surplus stores had donated to VVAW-NE in support of its antiwar performance work. A man wearing a set of Army pattern duck hunter camouflage fatigues was tying up captives next to another man wearing tiger stripe pattern jungle fatigues and yet another wearing standard-issue OG 107 fatigues, while another veteran was dressed head to toe as a member of Special Forces, known as the Green Berets. While the Special Forces performer was carrying a pump-action shotgun, another veteran carried a Thompson submachine gun. The veterans' gear and weaponry did not match, as it would have if they were all in the same unit, but they still managed to create the illusion that a real search-and-destroy mission was being carried out.[14]

"I had a Mattel M16," Don, who had borrowed his roommate's camouflage fatigues for the weekend, later recalled, noting that it was the weapon most of the participating veterans carried that weekend.

According to a 1967 article in *Popular Mechanics* whose title asked, "VC Firepower: Can We Match It?" the U.S. military had adopted this new automatic rifle, which was "accurate beyond description" and "pure murder," not because of the straight trajectory of their bullets but because they could fire hundreds of rounds per minute. The article explained how the M16 "makes a man a crowd": a "soldier 300 yards away can get an endless grouping in a foot-square target." *Popular Mechanics* was also pleased to report that the M16's bullets are "the most destructive made to date." Each one "tumbles after it hits the target," causing "massive wounds." The magazine was equally enthusiastic about the materials out of which the M16 was made, noting, "The only thing that will stop this baby is the wearing of its parts."[15]

It had proven easy to find a replica of the M16 in preparing for Operation RAW, VVAW's first concerted use of guerrilla theater. The American toy company Mattel had been manufacturing "the M-16 Marauder," an almost full-sized reproduction of an actual M16, since 1964. In a print advertisement, an enthusiastic blond boy fires one from a crouched position as text reproduces the sound.

"BRAAP BRRAAAAP BRAP BRAP!"

"WOW!" exclaims the ad copy, "Keep cocking the fantastic M-16 Marauder and you can cut loose with a solid blast almost a whole minute long! Over 50 rounds! And all with the loud, realistic sound of the actual M-16 rifle!"[16]

The national VVAW office had spent $702.50 supplying Operation RAW participants with 100 Mattel M16s. It was a considerable expense for an event costing $13,488.50, but the M16 was standard issue in Vietnam, and a realistic version was thus considered essential in carrying out mock search-and-destroy missions that looked like the real thing.[17]

Don watched Pete Wilson train his Mattel Marauder on the captives in Monument Square from the seat of another theatrical prop, the Wilson family Land Rover that Pete had transformed the day before into a military jeep. Scaled-down olive-drab vehicles had also recently become war toys. The toy company Hasbro made a nearly foot-tall doll (or "poseable action figure for boys," in their terms) called G.I. Joe who came accessorized with, in addition to a "ten-inch bazooka that really works" and a "beachhead flame thrower," an "authentically detailed replica" of a U.S. Army jeep.[18]

By using toy guns and the Rover, the veterans were critiquing, in addition to the war in Vietnam itself, the American culture of boyhood that had convinced Don, Pete, Bestor, and so many other young men that going off to war would be the exhilarating experience the young boy in the Mattel ad enjoys ("Wow!"). But as much as the veterans wanted to make clear how horrible war is, it was proving difficult not to play into the hands of Hollywood and the toy industry. VVAW-NE's announcement at the start of the reverse Revere march that Vietnam was being attacked from multiple directions, while an extension of Longfellow's "one if by land, two if by sea," was also a refrain of the song that accompanied the ubiquitous television ads for G.I. Joe: "G.I. Joe, G.I. Joe, fighting man from head to toe, on the land, on the sea, in the air." At Valley Forge, the veterans had watched with dismay as young boys crowded around the veterans' discarded toy weapons, eager to play with them even despite the presence of so many anguished amputees and other wounded men protesting the war that had cost them so much. Each of the veterans in Monument Square on Saturday morning knew their task was to reveal the cost of romanticizing war and acted accordingly, terrorizing the young men and women who moments before had been going about the business of enjoying a beautiful Saturday morning.[19]

The fear of those performing as Vietnamese was always so palpable at VVAW's performances that some combat veterans, however, had been finding it necessary to bow out of mock search-and-destroy missions, which could trigger flashbacks not just of the Vietnam War but also of the violence sold to them as children.

"Since childhood, it was slingshots, zip guns, switchblades, nylon stocking bolos, high powered pellet guns, and things of that nature," one member of VVAW explained in a letter announcing that his emotional pain precluded him from further antiwar work. "I'm not just a Vietnam veteran and a combat veteran of one battle, but a person who lived with many wars all my life."[20]

"I did not enjoy it," Don later explained after noting that some veterans found guerrilla theater too difficult, "but I was able to do it." It helped that those performing had agreed to a prearranged signal. If someone touched a performing veteran on the shoulder and said, "Okay, brother,"' that meant the veteran appeared to think he was back in Vietnam and that, for safety's sake, he needed to back away before going berserk and hurting himself or someone else.[21]

One of the elements of American search-and-destroy missions that the antiwar veterans were determined to make clear to the public, no matter how painful it was to reprise, was the racist foundation on which the American invasion of Vietnam was built. When the young woman yanked from the hardware store up Main Street and onto the grassy expanse in front of the memorial obelisk was too afraid to immediately respond to the command "*di di mao*," pigeon Vietnamese for "get down," one of the veterans did not hesitate to use his M16 to make clear that he did not view her as a human being.

"Sit down, you dumb slope," she would later recall being ordered as he forced the barrel of his weapon between her lips.

She crouched awkwardly on the grass, trying not to choke.

"Boy, these gooks can't even follow orders," he said loudly to another.

American servicemen were using the term "goo-goo" during the late nineteenth-century Philippine-American War to describe Filipinos as infantile while simultaneously mocking Filipino speech. The modified "gook" first appeared when the Marines occupying Haiti used it as a means of showing their contempt for the Haitians. And while "goo-goo" and "gook" have been used since then to describe Hawaiians, Nicaraguans, Italians, Turks, Arabs in North Africa, and other groups facing America's aggression, it has mainly been used by Americans along with "slopes" to describe Asians. There were reports during the Vietnam War that officers employed these racial epithets during basic training, and even that they appeared in written materials in an attempt to desensitize American soldiers who might otherwise have balked at being ordered to kill people.[22]

"When you shot someone," one Vietnam veteran had testified at the VVAW Winter Soldier hearings in Detroit three months prior to VVAW-NE's Memorial Day weekend march, "you didn't think you were shooting at a human. They were a 'gook' or a Commie and it was okay."[23]

Even the MACV insignia on several of the soldiers' sleeves served to perpetuate the same racial hubris the veterans were attempting to reveal in Monument Square. The yellow wall and the white sword seemed to imply that people "white" Americans imagined as "yellow" ("gooks") were unable to determine their own best destinies, even as North Vietnamese leader Ho Chi Minh had clearly embraced the same anti-imperialist stance taken by American colonists in 1775.

"All men are created equal," Ho had insisted in a rousing speech to the people of Vietnam within hours of the Japanese surrender that ended World War II. "They are endowed by their Creator with certain inalienable rights, among them are Life, Liberty, and the pursuit of Happiness." He quoted verbatim from the second paragraph of the Declaration of Independence, after which, just as the American colonists had listed Britain's crimes against them, Ho listed the crimes committed by the French against the people of Vietnam, concluding that the history of the United States would not allow them to "refuse to acknowledge the independence of Vietnam." Ho's attempt to appeal to America's sacred history was no match, however, for the United States' imperialist ambitions, bolstered as they were by convictions of white superiority. Under the guise of saving the world from communism, the United States had followed the French in insisting on the right to govern Vietnam.[24]

But while the veterans meant to critique American imperialism and the racism used to justify it in Southeast Asia, as well as American consumer culture for boys, they also ended up once again revealing the darker side of the American war memorials they were using to establish their patriotism, including the four war memorials in the shape of obelisks along their march route: the one erected at the Old North Bridge thirty-nine years before the Minute Man Statue in honor of the "embattled farmers" who took a stand there on April 19, 1775; the one under the shadow of which they were taking prisoners on Saturday morning, which was erected in 1866 to honor Concord's Civil War dead; another established in 1799 on the Lexington Green to honor "the memory" of those eight "Fellow Citizens" who were killed there by British soldiers; and finally the massive one built in Charlestown between 1825, when the cornerstone was laid, and 1842, when it was finally completed, at the site of the June 17, 1775, Battle of Bunker Hill.

As New England's cemeteries make clear, obelisks are used to acknowledge death. The 1855 guidebook to Forest Hills Cemetery, established in the Boston area in 1844, explained that these Egyptian forms were considered "the architecture of the grave." When used as a war memorial, the obelisk shape serves this funereal function by marking the passing of the soldiers it recalls. The war memorial obelisk also, however, serves as a shrine to the nation. This is perhaps most evident in Lexington, where, after the massacre that took place on its Green in 1775, townspeople initially thought only of marking the barren mass grave in the nearby cemetery of the fathers, husbands, sons, and brothers killed by British soldiers. But when nothing came of a suggestion at town meeting in February 1777 that the burial site be marked with "a suitable and decent monument," the idea was forgotten until after the U.S. Constitution went into effect and the first presidential election had been held. In 1791, the town successfully petitioned the state legislature to fund a monument that would establish Lexington's role in the new nation's birth. By then, interest had shifted from marking the burial site itself to memorializing the place where, as explained by the General Court, "the first efforts [were] made by the people of America for the establishment of freedom & independence," a reference to the deadly stand taken by Lexington's militiamen after receiving Paul Revere's warning. The Lexington obelisk erected on the Green in 1799 opens up quotidian time to the eternal time of perpetual remembrance, transforming death into the everlasting life of the nation, with text carved into it insisting that the "Nineteenth of April, An. Dom. 1775" is "ever memorable" because the efforts made by the colonists it names were by "Righteous Heaven approved." The Lexington obelisk imagines that the actions taken in 1775 released a powerful energy that transformed men into citizens:

> The Blood of these Martyrs,
> In the cause of God & their Country,
> Was the Cement of the Union to these States, then
> Colonies; & gave the spring to the spirit, Firmness
> And resolution of their Fellow Citizens.
> They rose as one man, to revenge their brethren's
> Blood and at the point of the sword to assert &
> Defend their native Rights.

Like Longfellow, who would later imagine a "spark," the Revolutionary War serves here as a "spring" that allows previously individual people to become what the poet imagines as "the people," and the Lexington obelisk similarly imagines rising as "one man." Unlike civilians, whose burial sites are as separate as their gravestones, the Lexington fallen shared a grave and later this marker as an outward sign of this loss of their individuality as they became the body of the nation. The result is mirrored in the transformation from individual colonies to "the Union of these States." In other words, the Lexington obelisk insists that the United States itself is continuously born out of the perpetual remembrance of the Revolutionary War dead who live again in the nation. This is why the Lexington obelisk calls for what the town's 1923 bylaw and the town's Selectmen formally protect: namely, that "a respectful regard and reverence for the memory of the patriotic services and sacrifice so nobly rendered" is required on the Green. Used as a war memorial, the obelisk shape helps make it possible for the nation to exist.[25]

Of course, obelisks have also played a very visible role in the history of imperialism. Taken as trophies, they have been a means for conquerors to mark their expanding power. In 10 BC, the Emperor Augustus erected in the Circus Maximus in Rome an obelisk originally installed by Ramesses II in Heliopolis. And after Napoleon's excursion to Egypt in 1798, the French took and installed in Paris a 3,000-year-old obelisk originally situated outside of Luxor Temple. The Bunker Hill Association seems to have chosen the obelisk shape precisely because it conferred everlasting life on those who were killed there and remade the battlefield into a national shrine but also because of this long history of using the obelisk form to stake a claim to the title of world's greatest civilization. Addressing a crowd of 100,000 at the laying of the cornerstone for the ultimately 221-foot-tall Bunker Hill obelisk, Senator Daniel Webster made clear that Americans were also using the obelisk form to make a claim for their own greatness.[26]

"We wish," he intoned, "that the last object to the sight of him who leaves his native shore, and the first to gladden his who revisits it, may be something which shall remind him of the liberty and the glory of his country."[27]

The two Concord obelisks VVAW-NE visited at the start of its march arguably participate in this imperialist tradition even if only tangentially. Rather than seek aid from the state legislature for a memorial at the Old North Bridge, the town backed the Bunker Hill Association's request for $10,000 in return for $600 of those funds and a promise to erect a smaller version of the design chosen for the Charlestown site. And while naming in stone the local war dead and thereby making visible each family's pain, the Concord Civil War obelisk does so with the same kind of assumption of white exceptionalism

Figure 8. Vietnam veteran fires on the Concord Civil War Monument. Screenshot from *Veterans Against the War* (1971), directed by Hart Perry. Courtesy of Hart Perry.

that would be displayed a century later by America's imperialist foreign policy in Southeast Asia; it leaves off the name of George Washington Dugan, a black patriot from Concord who also died fighting in the Civil War.[28]

Watching the veterans perform in the shadow of the second obelisk along the march route, filmmaker Hart Perry decided that in his film of Operation POW, he would superimpose film footage of one of the veterans firing his M16 over an enlargement of the directive carved in massive letters into the obelisk's side to be "faithful unto death" (Figure 8). Originally a religious value celebrated in Revelation 2:10 where God promises "the crown of life" in exchange for faithfulness, the United States had mobilized this pledge for civic ends, if not for the same imperialist ends of Augustus and Napoleon. Before pointing his Éclair at a veteran with his weapon trained on a captured civilian, Hart directed a film crewmember to be ready to audiotape Mattel's "realistic sound" when the veteran pulled back the cocking lever on his gun. He planned to dub it over the superimposed image and thereby make clear the aim of the VVAW-NE protest: to shoot down the obelisk's assertion that "faithfulness unto death" is the highest means of serving one's country, particularly when one's country is still motivated by a sense of white exceptionalism to conquer other countries. What Hart did not yet know, however, was that when his film of the march was completed, its suggestion that there is a possible link between war memorialization and ongoing atrocities would be deemed by PBS executives as too "one-sided" and they thus would decline to broadcast it.[29]

The Lexington Selectmen were already well aware that the veterans and their supporters were intent on starting uncomfortable conversations about violence that could entail highlighting the role war memorialization in their town played in the nation's foreign aims. In VVAW-NE's May 20, 1971, letter to the Lexington Board of Selectmen seeking permission to bivouac in Lexington, the veterans had explained that their protest would entail using multiple means of sharing their message that atrocities were being committed in America's name, including acting out the war in the town's memorialized space.

"We will be talking to townspeople, leafleting, and staging guerilla theatre as part of our general informational effort."[30]

In using the name for shocking, revolutionary theater that was coined by the San Francisco Mime Troupe in 1966 in homage to a passage in a 1961 Che Guevara essay, the veterans made clear their radical intent: "The guerrilla fighter," as Guevara explained, "has the intention of destroying an unjust order."[31]

The request to perform guerilla theater had sparked the most discussion at the Selectmen meeting attended by VVAW-NE's executive secretary. While the Selectmen had voiced their concern that the town would be burdened with discarded leaflets and their fear that surprised and shocked Lexington residents might suffer heart attacks on the spot, they were most worried that enacting atrocities was not in keeping with the quiet reverence for the sacred Battle Green that its own memorial obelisk and the town's bylaw require. The only performed atrocities they sanctioned were those of the British, enacted every Patriots' Day by townsmen wearing the red coats after which the Regulars are colloquially named and which made an obvious distinction between the imperial oppressors and the plainclothes American farmers standing up to them. As Hart Perry had so quickly recognized on Saturday morning, VVAW-NE's guerrilla theater had the potential to reframe memorial obelisks, raising the possibility that as much as these memorials were reminders of the past, they had also helped justify a distinctly militaristic and imperialist future for the United States. And thus, at the same time as the veterans were performing their mock search-and-destroy mission in Concord in an assertion that modern America had become the imperial Britain of old, the Lexington Selectmen were looking for a more effective means than a ticket to keep the antiwar veterans off their town's Battle Green.

The Selectmen's first two meetings regarding VVAW-NE's request to perform guerrilla theater and camp on the Battle Green or in Tower Park had been conducted in compliance with the Massachusetts Open Meeting Law (first enacted in 1958). After the regularly scheduled Selectmen's public meeting on Monday, May 24, 1971, at which the Selectmen voted to deny VVAW-NE the right to both bivouac and perform in town, two of the Selectmen, under pressure from VVAW-NE's local supporters, requested a special meeting to reconsider the matter. At that special meeting, also in compliance with Open Meeting Law and held on Thursday, May 27, alternative locations were considered but ultimately rejected. A Saturday morning meeting, however, was not announced in advance, nor were any minutes taken at it. Asked later if that meeting was "an open meeting, or a closed meeting," the then chairman of the Board of Selectmen dodged the question of the meeting's legality.[32]

"You could call it open," he asserted, "because anybody could have come, but nobody wanted to talk to us."[33]

And yet when the person interviewing him called it a "private meeting," the former chairman did not correct him. Another Selectman at that time was later asked if "meetings at this time [were] open to the public," if they were "supposed to be announced in advance," and whether "the Public Meeting Law [was] in effect at this particular time." That Selectman conceded that "usually our meetings were posted and public, and there would be a stenographer or someone there to take minutes." The Saturday meeting, however, followed none of those protocols being "in response to what we felt was a threat."[34]

With Lexington's town counsel away for the long holiday weekend, the Selectmen called around until they found a local lawyer willing to meet and strategize with them. At the illegal Saturday morning meeting, while the veterans were taking captives in Concord, the lawyer was explaining that, worded properly, an injunction would make the veterans' use of the Lexington Battle Green an arrestable offense. The four Selectmen in attendance (the fifth one, the only woman, was also away for the long weekend) voted unanimously to secure such an injunction just as the veterans were performing the American military's treatment of the Vietnamese in a demonstration against the racist and imperialist attitude instilled in them during basic training and embodied by the four obelisks to which their route was taking them.

BRAAP BRRA-A-A-AP BRAP BRAP!

A single spray of bullets from the veterans' automatic firearms was all it took to kill all of the civilians taken captive in Monument Square. Stone faced, the soldiers picked up the dead by their arms and legs and, with no regard for their humanity, slung them into a pile at the base of the Civil War memorial obelisk.[35]

"This is something the Vietnamese experience every day—absolute repression, an infringement on all civil liberties," a veteran explained to the growing crowd as other veterans distributed leaflets explaining the horrible things American soldiers were doing in Vietnam. "They're murdered and butchered by guys like us who are carrying out the policy of this government."[36]

From VVAW's perspective, because American soldiers were killing civilians or at least nonprofessional soldiers out of uniform, their deaths were "murder" and thus a violation of international law.

"If it doesn't bother you that American soldiers do these things every day to other human beings because they are 'gooks,'" the leaflet the veterans distributed instructed, "then picture yourself as one of these silent victims."[37]

The volunteers playing the veterans' now dead victims had worn their everyday clothes precisely to force the audience to ask themselves how they would feel if they were going about their lives, as these young people seemed to have been doing on a regular Saturday morning and as Vietnamese civilians would have been doing, only to be gunned down.

"Move out!" the veteran dressed as a Green Beret barked once the leafleting was completed. When he raised his sawed-off shotgun over his head and pointed it toward Lexington, the veterans lined up on the sidewalk.

Concord's police chief had allowed the veterans to perform guerrilla theater in Concord on the stipulation that no residents be grabbed and that VVAW-NE's volunteer civilian collaborators wear upside-down VVAW buttons so they would be identifiable to the veterans. VVAW-NE representatives had met with the chief on three consecutive days prior to the march to hash out this and other details, such as agreeing to march through town on the sidewalks so as not to block traffic. VVAW-NE had also designated marshals who checked that the men dressed in fatigues had honorable discharge papers proving they were veterans and that no unsuspecting bystander wander into harm's way. The resulting performance was so seamless that when the civilian volunteers finally stood up, rubbed their sore wrists, and brushed the grass from their hair and clothes, it was the first time some onlookers were assured of what many had started to doubt: this was indeed theater. Deeply moved by what they had seen and by the obviously considerable energy involved in coordinating such an effort and knowing that the Lexington Selectmen were not inclined to welcome these antiwar activists, a number of spectators decided on the spur of the moment to follow the veterans to Lexington on foot.[38]

Marveling at this unexpected show of support, Don Carrico thought back to the prior fall when he was finding it increasingly difficult to function under the weight of his depression. He had found VVAW only because a young woman at the college where he was studying happened to tell him about the new Cambridge office the organization had opened.

Years later, Don chuckled when he recalled coming through VVAW-NE's office door and seeing Bestor Cram for the first time.

"I thought I saw Jesus Christ."

The analogy was sparked not only by Bestor's long hair and beard but also by the warm words Don had not heard since returning from Vietnam.

"Welcome home, Marine," Bestor said to him, grinning.

Don had decided then and there to drop out of school and work full-time with VVAW. On account of his hotel and restaurant experience, Bestor had put him in charge of planning all of the meals for Operation POW. This had required coordinating with local supporters in each of the towns through which the veterans would march, soliciting and coordinating donations from companies of everything from drinks to plastic utensils, and keeping track of developments as the veterans decided how to handle the Lexington Selectmen's denial of their request to camp and perform in that town.[39]

"I seem to be alive again," Don explained to a reporter who asked about the massive amount of energy he was expending in trying to stop the war.[40]

On this sunny May morning, Don celebrated the success of the veterans' ongoing performance as measured by how many civilians set off for Lexington with them. Meanwhile, just a few miles away, the chairman of the Lexington Board of Selectman and a second Lexington selectman were driving to the private Bedford home of the chief justice of Middlesex Superior Court in pursuit of an injunction that could send every one of the protestors to jail.

CHAPTER 4

Battle Roads and Fields

The site the Lexington Selectmen were so intent on protecting from antiwar protestors has not always been considered a sacred space. In the years immediately following the massacre by British Regulars of eight colonial militiamen on the Lexington Green, it remained the bustling center of Lexington life. Citizens were still called to worship in the meeting house located in the middle of the Green by the large bell hanging in a stand-alone belfry behind it, and children attended classes in the schoolhouse located next to it. The events of April 19, 1775, were hardly forgotten, but it was the date, not the place, that the town's minister made sacred when he observed its first anniversary with a sermon.[1]

"From this *remarkable day*," proclaimed Reverend Jonas Clarke, "will an important *era* begin for both *America* and *Britain*."[2]

Sixteen years after the end of the American Revolution, when Reverend Clarke was invited by the town to author the prompt to remember the fallen that would be carved into the nation's first obelisk erected in memory of common soldiers, he continued to sacralize the date. After naming each of the colonists who was killed, Clarke described the date of the massacre and not the place where it occurred as "ever memorable." Even after the war dead were reinterred next to the obelisk in 1835, thereby completing their transformation into martyrs and making the obelisk a national shrine, the Green itself continued to be used for such mundane activities as haying, camping, and baseball games. No one felt it was necessary to underscore the obelisk's bold assertion that what happened on the Green led to "The Peace, Liberty & Independence of the United States of America" by making the entire two-and-a-half-acre Green into a sacred space.[3]

It was not until the latter years of the nineteenth century, when the townspeople of Lexington decided to add additional markers and monuments, that

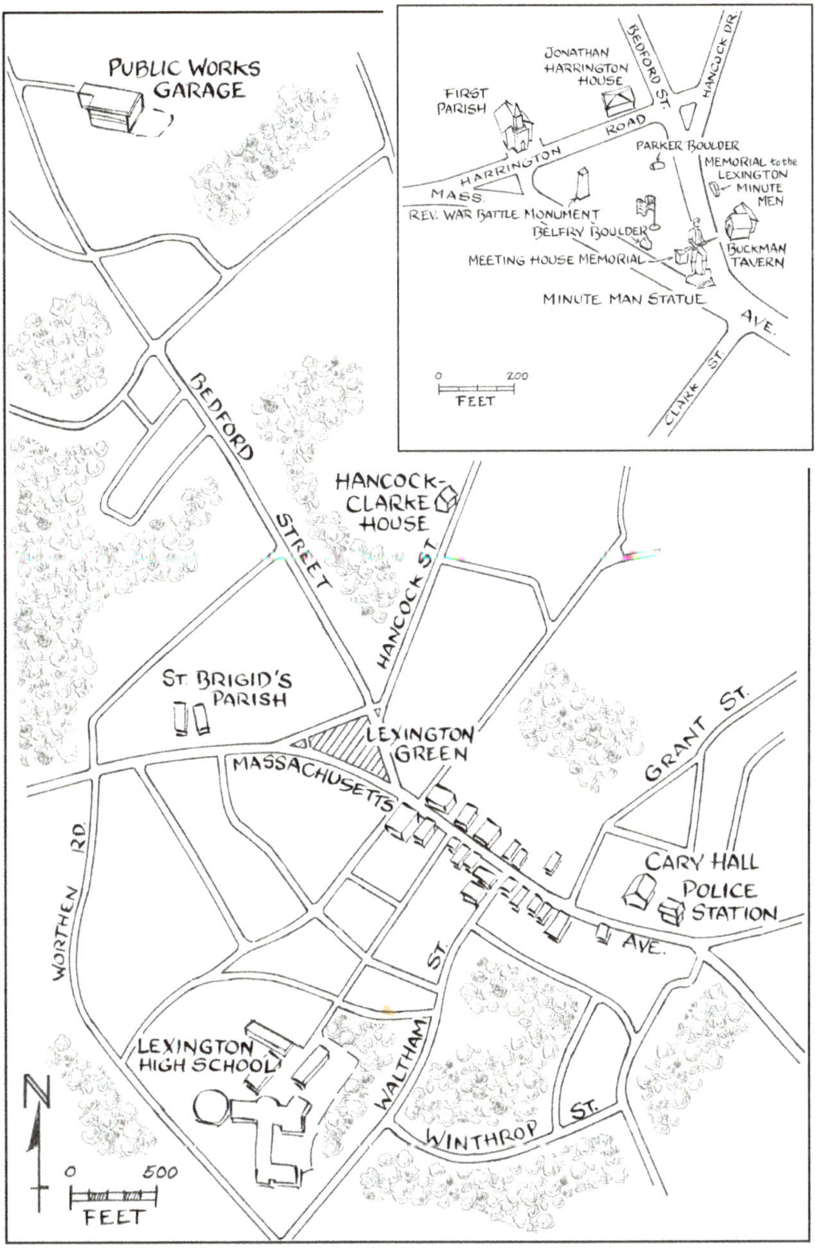

Map 4. The Lexington memorial landscape, 1971.

the place became as sacred as the anniversary date (Map 4). Instead of the obelisk's lone prompt to hold the Lexington fallen forever in the nation's collective memory without dictating how the entire Green should be used, the new additions, spread across the Green, call for the singular activity there of recalling the historical events that gave birth to the nation. Any emotion expressed or activity undertaken on the Green without proper recognition of the Revolutionary events that transpired there verges on the sacrilegious.[4]

Designed by the Lexington Historical Society, the markers champion a very particular version of the town's role in the nation's birth and of the kind of country that is perpetually coming into being at the place where it is forever April 19, 1775. A large granite boulder affixed with an iron plaque designates its location "The Site of the Old Belfry from which the alarm was rung," an assertion like Longfellow's that the colonists' ingenuity was the key to their military success. A marker that shows exactly where forty or so of the local militiamen who had responded to the alarm lined up to face the hundreds of oncoming British Regulars imagines their captain ordering them to "stand your ground" but to refrain from violence unless provoked. "Don't fire," the boulder quotes him as saying, "unless fired upon. But if they mean to have war, let it begin here." Marked thus with what historians have since proven is an entirely fanciful version of what was actually said that day, this boulder underscores, much like French's Minute Man Statue in Concord, the idea that even though Americans are fearless, they are opposed to violence and war. They will fight, but only if attacked, their willingness to defend themselves and their rights underscored by a bas relief of a musket and powder horn hanging prominently over the captain's words. Lexington's own seven-foot-tall bronze statue of a colonial militiaman looking eastward toward the oncoming British troops, his musket down by his side, helps visitors people the 1775 landscape with these determined but reluctantly violent farmers. Yet another marker, in the form of a granite pulpit with a Bible on it, shows where, before it was moved across the street in later years, the Lexington meeting house stood in 1775 while reminding visitors that the armed colonists were a godly if not chosen people.

The federal government lent its approval to the mythicized version of history told on the Green by its memorials when, in 1965, it ruled that the large white flagpole erected there sometime before 1905 could fly the nation's flag under illumination twenty-four hours per day. Noting that the by then well-memorialized Battle Green was protected by both the 1923 local bylaw and the town's 1956 designation of the space and its surrounding streets as the Battle Green Historic District, National Park Service officials decided it would not be necessary to include it in Minute Man National Historical Park, which was created in 1959. The Battle Green's version of the nation's origin story, about the purposefully brutal victimization of a peaceable community of godly farmers intent only on defending themselves and their rights, was already preserved for perpetuity.[5]

While most of the Vietnam veterans marching defiantly toward the memorialized Lexington Green on May 29, 1971, were wearing boonie hats or helmet liners in order to make clear that they were protesting a war in which they had fought, one of them had paired what looked like a cowboy hat with the short-sleeved fatigue shirt to which his name, branch, and rank tapes were still affixed: FENTON, U.S. Army, Specialist 5th Class. Ross Fenton's shirt proclaimed his love for the country he had served, while his hat made the point that, like any of the cowboys played in Hollywood westerns by Audie Murphy, the most decorated soldier in American history, or John Wayne, he was intent on employing his masculine powers in the pursuit of justice, even if it meant having to break the law. As Ross strode toward a nationally sacred space into which he did not have permission to step foot despite his veteran status, his hat was a pointed reminder that, in American mythology, the cowboy's moral compass is truer than any lawman's.

Ross first came to the realization that the Americans were not welcome in South Vietnam in early 1968 when he was serving at a petroleum supply depot at Tan Son Nhut Air Force Base outside of Saigon. He had been driving back to the base when he saw a group of American and South Vietnamese military police stop a small Renault taxi in front of him. Ross learned later that the three Americans in the taxi were AWOL, or absent without leave. When they drew their handguns in an attempt to avoid arrest, they accidentally shot one of the South Vietnamese MPs in the foot. Within minutes, a truck full of outraged South Vietnamese soldiers had pulled over. Only by calling in support was Ross able to prevent a gunfight.

"There was an underlying anger at the Americans," Ross later recalled realizing, "far greater than just the fact of their comrade having a minor wound."[6]

When Ross returned to Brown University to resume his studies after completing his military service, he discovered that most people did not want to hear that the South Vietnamese, with and for whom the Americans were supposedly fighting, wanted to expel what they regarded as imperialist invaders. It was a pleasant surprise when his English professor asked him to write about the war.

"I wrote about a soldier in his trench at night not understanding why the Vietnamese weren't supporting him, why he saw fear and anguish in their eyes."

It was a piece based very much on Ross's own experiences, he later explained, even as he was still unable at that point to use the first person.

"He felt he was duty bound to be there for his country," Ross wrote, "So he lay there at night going 'Why? What for?'"

To his dismay, the professor dismissed his piece.

"This is all hogwash," she retorted, having fully accepted the federal government's insistence that Vietnam must be saved by the Americans from the communists. "It can't be like that."

After meeting a few other veterans as disillusioned as he was, Ross formed the veterans' group that by April 1971 had become the Rhode Island chapter of VVAW. Its first newsletter invited members to drive up from Providence to attend the Memorial Day weekend march organized by VVAW-NE. Eleven Rhode Island veterans made the trip, two accompanied by their wives, along with eighteen veterans from VVAW's Connecticut chapter, one of whom also brought his wife and another his girlfriend. Bestor and the other members of the New England chapter had gratefully made use of the Rhode Island chapter flag that morning, not having yet made one of their own for the Cambridge-based New England chapter. (Each of the three chapters that participated in Operation POW was equally autonomous under the VVAW umbrella.)[7]

A little over a mile from Monument Square, Ross and the other veterans marching toward Lexington passed a marker erected by the town of Concord in 1885 explaining what happened where several roads converge in front of what was the Meriam family's property to trigger the third deadly clash of April 19, 1775 (Map 5).

"The British troops retreating from the Old North Bridge were here attacked in flanks by the men of Concord and neighboring towns," the marker asserts, its granite durability a prompt that will survive for generations to never forget that the Regulars were, it adds, "driven under a hot fire to Charlestown."

Immediately after the skirmish at the North Bridge, the colonial militiamen had been so relieved to see that the center of Concord was not on fire that

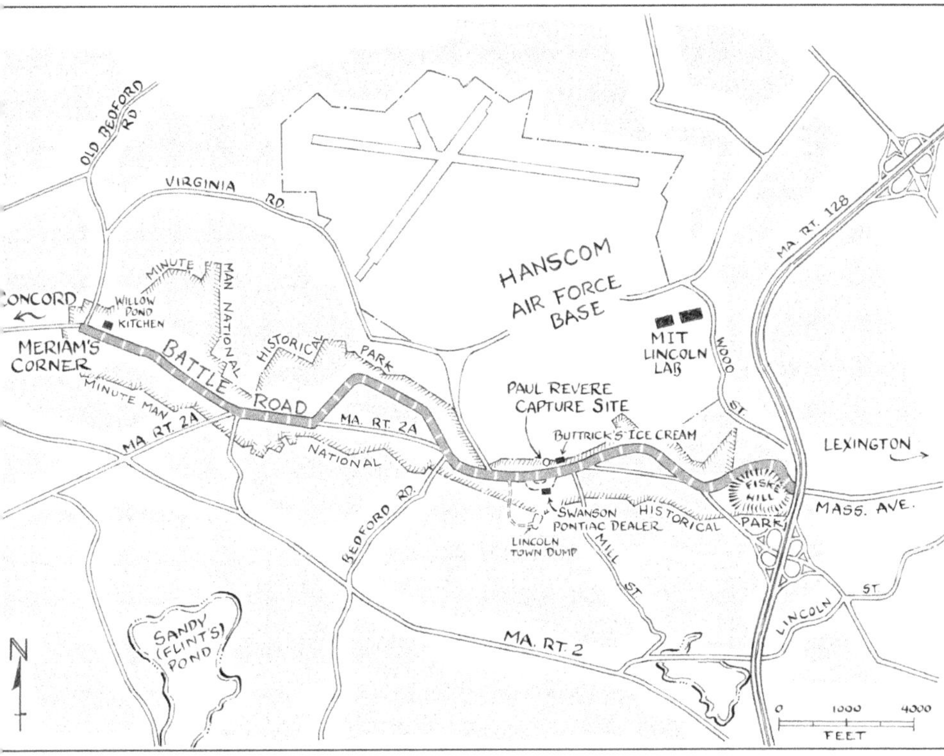

Map 5. Minute Man National Historical Park: The Battle Road, 1971.

they did not take any further action against the occupying troops. The shaken Regulars stayed in Concord until noon waiting for reinforcements that never showed up. By then, colonists as far as thirty miles away had received the news of the massacre of local militiamen on Lexington Green. Forty towns called out their own militias, sending them speeding toward the Lexington and Concord area. They converged at Meriam's Corner, where they watched the retreating Regulars, many of them wounded, bunch together to cross a bridge. When someone shot off his musket, from which side remains unknown, the Regulars turned, presented, and fired off a volley. No one was hit, but the American colonists on the scene proceeded to open fire, killing a half dozen British soldiers before the British column hurried out of range.

The marker may describe the confrontation at Meriam's Corner as a contest of mutual injuring insofar as gunfire is acknowledged even if none of the deaths are, but it is far more invested in celebrating the idea of the road both as a literal place to be remembered and as a metaphor for the American Revolution. Here is the road down which the colonists must travel to arrive at Charlestown but also to arrive at the freedom implied by marking the troops as "British" and therefore a distinct entity from the colonists who were still at that point legally British themselves. This idea that war is a road to freedom was picked up by the National Park Service, which erected the sign just east of the marker announcing the beginning of the "Battle Road." When, in 1957, the Boston National Historic Sites Commission to the Congress of the United States first recommended the creation of a national historical park where fighting had taken place on April 19, 1775, it envisioned "two principal units." The smaller would include the Old North Bridge area that had already been set aside as sacred space by the town of Concord. The larger would comprise the first four of the seventeen miles along which the British retreated, from Meriam's Corner in Concord to Fiske Hill in Lexington, the rest having been lost to urban sprawl.[8]

One of the best-known accounts of the running battle is in "Paul Revere's Ride," where it is recounted by Longfellow's narrator after he imagines the midnight rider arriving in Concord:

> You know the rest. In the books you have read
> How the British Regulars fired and fled,—
> How the farmers gave them ball for ball,
> From behind each fence and farmyard wall,
> Chasing the redcoats down the lane,
> Then crossing the fields to emerge again
> Under the trees at the turn of the road,
> And only pausing to fire and load.

In making their written recommendation for a national park, the Boston Commission cited this stanza, noting that it "does not fail to kindle the dullest of imaginations or to stir the most sluggish sentiments of patriotism," even as Longfellow treats the running battle only tangentially, referring his readers to their history books and without ever mentioning the fact that forty-nine colonists and seventy-three Regulars were killed. What seems to have made the Commission describe this oblique reference to the running battle as stirring is the fact that readers are invited by the narrator to imagine mere "farmers" as prevailing solely on the strength of being deeply familiar with "each fence and farmyard wall" on the land where they subsisted, not because they had weapons and shot and killed people. Indeed, Longfellow obscures the reality of flesh torn by projectiles, instead using the metaphor of farmers "giving" musket balls to the Regulars. Here, as throughout the rest of Longfellow's poem, the Revolutionary War is recalled not as a violent contest but as a display of an intimate acquaintance with a place that seems naturally to confer both nourishment and protection to its inhabitants. (This insistence has the added benefit of disguising the fact that places are not themselves inherently sacred but rather are sacralized retroactively through memorialization practices.) Longfellow evokes violence (there seem to be guns, bullets, and the act of firing) but then erases it (no one is hit or killed), thereby asking readers to consider that American ingenuity and American places such as Meriam's Corner are more powerful forces than violence.[9]

The Boston Commission recommended that the federal government purchase and raze the suburban homes and businesses along this then still leafy portion of the British Regulars' retreat route and thereby return it to its colonial-era appearance. Henceforth, the road would be called variously "the Lexington-Concord Battle Road," "the historic Battle Road," and the "Battle Road of the Revolution." While the name signifies that this was the road where men killed each other in battle, it also asserts, as did Longfellow and the Meriam Corner marker, that the beginning of the American Revolution took place along a literal road, to Boston's east, and along a figurative one toward the nation's birth. Similarly, and also like Longfellow's poem, the name of the new park, Minute Man National Historical Park, dedicated in 1959, avoids directly referencing the violence of the American Revolution by focusing on preparedness, even as only a small percentage of Massachusetts colonial militiamen was charged with mustering in a "minute."[10]

The National Park Service was never able to close all of the Battle Road to traffic and thereby create as much of a colonial-era landscape as its officials would have liked. The colonists had chased the British down the same road that by the 1950s served as the main entry point for Hanscom Air Force Base, where, in 1951, the Massachusetts Institute of Technology (MIT) had decided to locate Lincoln Laboratory, its federally funded military research lab. Six years later, when the Soviets demonstrated their missile capability by launching the *Sputnik* 1 satellite, a dismayed federal government started to increase expenditures on research and development from 2.5 percent of the total U.S. budget to an eventual high of 12.6 percent in 1965. Virtually all of the recipients of these funds were elite institutions such as MIT that already had the capacity to conduct significant scientific research. It and other Boston-area universities quickly became powerful engines of economic development near the Air Force base and along Route 128, Boston's new ring road, especially as, in a bid to attract the best scientists, engineers, mathematicians, and economists to Lincoln Laboratory and other government-funded laboratories at MIT and Harvard, the federal and state government built roads and other infrastructure while creating the financial mechanisms and tax shelters necessary for home ownership and business development. Soon everything from computer memory, radar transmitting tubes, satellite antennas, and telecommunications to missile nose-cones and guidance systems was being designed and manufactured by the thousands of well-educated newcomers who were delighted to work at what developers called industrial parks, in reference to the bucolic nature of the landscapes cultivated around modern glass and steel buildings, and to live in the new housing developments that also went up at a rapid pace. Traffic along Route 128, which was made the eastern terminus of Minute Man National Historical Park by the Boston Commission, and Route 2A, the feeder road along which part of the Battle Road runs, was heavy on weekdays with commuter traffic.[11]

In 1971, the antiwar veterans knew they could expect traffic along the Battle Road to be heavy on the weekends as well. NPS had not finished relocating all of the bustling businesses on the park's land. Willow Pond Kitchen Restaurant, Swanson's Pontiac car dealership, and a Buttrick's ice cream stand ensured that the veterans had a sizable audience for their Saturday march to Lexington. They were careful to make it easy for the many passersby to understand what they were doing. Upon breaking camp in Concord, they had stowed their camping and other gear in the rental trucks trailing them. Wearing their fatigues, they walked in two single-file lines, one on each side of the Battle Road, carrying nothing but their weapons.[12]

"They were on patrol in the jungle," a local reporter following the march later recalled surmising. "They weren't walking in twos or threes or fours. It was a straight line, all spread out."[13]

"It kind of reminded me of my Army days when you'd go out on the road for maneuvers," one Korean War veteran, a Lexington resident, remembered thinking as he watched the veterans go past. "They'd have you walk single file on each side of the road in case you got strafed or something."[14]

Even as the veterans in their olive drab fatigues were acting out a Vietnam War patrol, they were traveling along the same route and in the same direction as their colonial forefathers when in pursuit of the retreating British. As the wounded pair leading the march demonstrated, soldiers in both time frames were vulnerable to sniper attacks. This doubling of the time frame allowed the veterans to show that war is only metaphorically a road to more and more freedom. In actuality, war is by definition a road toward more and more fatalities.

"You would go from the tedium and boredom that is your normal routine, your normal walk through the jungle," one veteran was recalling of Vietnam as he walked along behind Ross, "to being right in the very thick of it, going into an ambush, having a booby trap go off, that type of thing."[15]

"The country roads were real pretty," another veteran was thinking as he marched past the fields lined with stone walls that NPS had claimed. But rather than enjoy the picturesque landscape, he was prompted to remember a 1945 movie about World War II he had seen as a boy called *A Walk in the Sun*. "It's this story about a patrol, and I think everybody dies."[16]

Ross was also thinking about the dangers of patrolling, recalling the twelve months he spent on burial detail at Massachusetts' Fort Devens after his tour in Vietnam. He and six other soldiers comprised an Honor Guard that fired a twenty-one-gun salute at the close of every military funeral in northern New England.

"We'd go to the graveyard, find out what was happening, pre-scout it," he later explained, refusing to leave out any of the details seared in his memory.

The Honor Guard needed a spot at a slight distance from the burial site, preferably on elevated ground. After a short prayer, the sergeant in charge would present the American flag that had been draped over the coffin to the nearest surviving woman, usually the dead man's mother or wife. Then the Honor Guard would get the command.

"Ready, fire. Ready, fire. Ready, fire."

Finally, the bugler would sound Taps.

"Mothers, sisters and wives wailed." Decades later, Ross trembled with emotion at the memory. "Some threw themselves on the caskets, unwilling to let go of their loved ones."[17]

Bestor Cram had his own recollections about war's cost. One of his responsibilities as an officer in Vietnam had been to identify the bodies of American soldiers killed in action. They were stored in a refrigerated barracks on his base prior to being shipped back to the United States. One day, when the corporal in charge of the morgue had opened the door for him so that he could compare a corpse to the official photograph he had been given of the deceased, Bestor could see that the corporal was storing Coca-Cola cans in the midst of the refrigerated cadavers. He had casually offered Bestor a can, as if the loss of so much life was the most normal thing in the world. Now, while Ross and the others made their way eastward on foot, Bestor passed their patrol in a car en route to the Lexington Police Station. Having recently taken a course offered by the Committee on Nonviolent Action in Voluntown, Connecticut, he knew the best way for the veterans to avoid police violence on the Lexington Battle Green would be to keep that town's police chief apprised of the veterans' plans.[18]

Also on his way toward Lexington by car was Don Carrico. He was heading toward Fiske Hill, the designated lunch spot, to make sure there would be enough food for the hungry marchers. Like Ross, Bestor, and the other veterans, he too was prompted by the patrol to recall the dead. So many soldiers were killed on that day near Hue, the vast majority of them just eighteen years of age, that there were no longer enough of them to field his unit. The unit's colors had been sent back to the United States.[19]

Those proceeding on foot had blisters by the time they passed the sign marking the turn off for Hanscom Air Force Base, the possible expansion of which had been what initially compelled the Boston Commission to recommend a park as a permanent means of preserving "for posterity" the "boulders and stone walls behind which the Minute Men fired and [the] pastures they overran in hurried pursuit of the retreating Redcoats."[20]

Amedio (Al) Armenti, one of the Concord residents who had decided along with his draft-age son to walk behind the veterans to Lexington, had started working at the Hanscom-based Lincoln Laboratory in 1961 on an enterprise called the Command and Control Information Project. He continued to work there during the Vietnam War.

"I worked in a laboratory that was funded by the government," he later explained, "whose major charter was developing systems of defense against a threatening enemy."[21]

If Al never saw any possible contradiction between his career and his opposition to the war, that may have been because at the height of the Cold War, the federal government's creation of Minute Man National Historical Park helped Americans see themselves as part of a long tradition of patriots defending American freedom. Just as the federal government had disguised its ongoing military excursions around the world when it renamed the War Department the Department of Defense in 1949, so did NPS ideologically screen the American violence, weaponry, and militarism that Hanscom Air

Force Base and Lincoln Laboratory might otherwise represent by picking a name for the park that stressed the colonists' preparedness and by revisioning war as a road to freedom. For while Al was right about there being a "threatening enemy" in the form of the Soviet Union, it was also the case that at least since the Philippine-American War of 1899 to 1902, the United States had used its might to impose its will around the globe.

A journalist intent on describing why scientists and technicians like Al wanted to live and work in the area was quick to note their investment in the myth of America that Longfellow cultivated in his poem by downplaying the violence of April 19, 1775, in favor of focusing on defense initiatives in the form of preparedness (arranging a means of communication), ingenuity (the signal lanterns), and fleetness (riding quickly along the road to Lexington and Concord).

"The prestige of Lexington and Concord, as of Cambridge, is a big factor in the development here," the journalist concluded five years after Minute Man National Historical Park was founded, adding of the addresses scientists, technicians, and their firms enjoyed putting on their letterhead that "they favor them because of their history—Paul Revere and so on."[22]

A VVAW supporter living in Lexington in 1971 later concurred with the journalist's assessment, adding that the storied town had made "all of us . . . aware that things happened in certain places." Her and Al's comments make clear that the monuments dotting the Revolutionary War–era landscape had convinced everyone that specific locations have the power to create patriotic citizens. "We are passing them every day and can stop to remember what happened there."[23]

Still another resident asserted of living in Lexington in 1971 that he liked "to live in a fine, historic town," one with "wonderful symbolism and meaning."[24]

If the vast majority of the scientists and technicians who flocked to the Concord and Lexington area during the Cold War boom were highly educated white elites, so too were the VVAW leaders involved in the Operation POW. Bestor and his co–executive director were college graduates and Ross was attending Brown, an Ivy League university, while John Kerry was famous for being a Yale graduate. In deciding to stage their protest in the symbolic landscape of Concord and Lexington, the VVAW-NE leadership was engaging a demographic similar to its own. Indeed, four years after VVAW-NE's reverse Revere march, the Massachusetts Advisory Committee to the U.S. Commission on Civil Rights and the Massachusetts Commission Against

Discrimination would issue a joint report on the effects of high-tech development along Route 128 that was subtitled "Boston's Road to Segregation." Boston's ring road divided the greater Boston area into the haves, with their jobs in the swiftly expanding and highly lucrative industries supported by the Department of Defense, and the have-nots, who resided in an inner city gutted by the flight of business and industry to the suburbs.[25]

Minute Man National Historical Park was part of the engine driving the exclusivity of the suburbs along Route 128. The Battle Road runs through the northern part of Lincoln, which, prior to the park's founding, was home to working-class people and small farmers, people whose annual incomes were a far cry from those of the scientists and technicians who worked in MIT and Harvard laboratories and who could thus afford to live in one of the many new developments in South Lincoln, Concord, and Lexington. The federal government's determination to remake the epicenter of the academic-military-industrial complex into a landscape celebrating the American commitment to freedom and peaceable pursuits dovetailed with the elites' desire to replace a working-class area with a green sward that would also ideologically screen them from the Air Force base. When NPS went so far as to threaten with eminent domain those who lived along the Battle Road, park officials found little to no resistance from area selectmen.[26]

"They were absolutely ruthless and they had no conscience," Jen Levin's mother Betty always said of NPS officials determined to create Minute Man National Historical Park at any cost and the elected Lincoln officials who supported their efforts. Her husband, the founder of CPP, which would later merge with VVAW-NE's sponsor Mass PAX, had been left a quadriplegic after contracting polio not long after building his family's house near the Battle Road. The family had gone to great expense to outfit the house for the wheelchair to which he was confined for the rest of his life, but NPS refused to allow the family to stay there beyond the extra two years they were granted to find a suitable replacement home. "It was government robbery" was how Betty put it, still indignant years later about the loss of her family's home.[27]

After watching so many of their friends in the area suffer the same displacement, the Levin family assiduously avoided visiting the park.

"Is it all right? Is it okay?" Betty later remembered Jen asking every time she wanted to ride her horse in the Patriots' Day reenactment of the three midnight riders' capture along the Battle Road, which for Betty would forever be "enemy territory."[28]

But when there was an opportunity to assist VVAW-NE in using the park to protest the Vietnam War, Betty encouraged her daughter to assist the veterans as a Revere reenactor and went with chapter leaders to the local NPS office inside the park to help them secure permission to use the site. This and her other efforts over the course of Memorial Day weekend both within and outside the park were so prodigious and so instrumental to their success that the veterans took to affectionately referring to her as their "den mother." Having learned its lesson after the debacle of trying to oust VVAW from the National Mall, NPS granted the veterans' request.[29]

The Lexington Selectmen, who were charged with policing how one of the nation's most sacred places is used, had far less experience in public relations than NPS. In denying the veterans' request to camp and perform guerrilla theater, they had already attracted negative publicity for themselves. A *Boston Globe* editorial on the Friday morning of the march's kickoff chastised them for being, "as the young people put it, a little uptight about all of this. There is more loitering and littering every evening in Lexington Depot Sq. (to say nothing of the town's Patriots' Day parade) than the veterans could dream up in a month of Sundays." But while the Lexington Selectmen had voiced concerns about the veterans littering, they were far more worried about the rewriting of American mythology the veterans' mere presence would promote along the march route. Even as the veterans were presenting themselves as patriots in the tradition of the farmers who chased the Regulars "down the lane," they could not help but continue to reframe the Revolutionary War monuments in ways that were revealing the mythic nature of the story told within the park.[30]

One such memorial the veterans would end up reframing had been erected at their lunch stop long before NPS purchased and removed the turkey farm and several other modern buildings that stood on Fiske Hill. In addition to installing picnic tables and an information kiosk that welcomes visitors into the park at this, its easternmost point along the edge of Route 128, NPS cleared a path designed to draw pilgrims to this memorial and the astounding narrative authored by the Lexington Historical Society in 1885.

At this well
April 19, 1775
James Hayward of Acton
Met a British soldier
Who raising his gun said

You are a dead man.
And so are you replied Hayward
Both fired. The soldier
Was instantly killed
& Hayward mortally wounded.[31]

By suggesting that Hayward was the real victim of the deadly encounter on the grounds that he was targeted first, the marker heroicizes the American colonists for winning a war in which they were the underdogs. They triumphed, according to the marker, not because they were inherently violent but because they were steady in their determination to sacrifice themselves for American independence, the larger cause that the marker need not even mention.[32]

The Vietnam veterans reframed this marker and the events it memorialized after arriving at Fiske Hill with their rental trucks and portable toilets and discovering a large crowd of Lexington supporters waiting to greet them in a recently mown field next to the kiosk. After selecting a sandwich and a piece of fruit from the long, groaning tables set up by the local church groups Don and Betty had approached, the veterans ate lunch and then carefully stacked their arms before settling in for a brief nap. Knowing how to place rifles in a pyramid and thereby keep them together in a uniform and protected manner has long been a sign of a soldier's readiness and experience and thus allowed the veterans to establish that they had in fact served in Vietnam, that their views about the war should thus be regarded as highly credible, and that they shared a bond with their military forefathers as far back as James Hayward of Acton. Through this performance, the veterans turned back time on Fiske Hill to 1775, even as in their usual hybridizing fashion they also turned Fiske Hill into the present day by stacking M16s instead of muskets. Then, in a gesture meant to remind everyone that, having experienced the kind of situation in which James Hayward had found himself, the veterans rejected war violence, they broke off sprigs of the lilac bushes that continued to bloom where private yards had dotted the hillside prior to the park's creation and placed the flowers, whose heart-shaped leaves signify love, into the barrels of their stacked M16s (Figure 9).

Poet and social activist Allen Ginsberg had first recommended the use of flowers as an antiwar tactic in a response to the Hell's Angels' avowal in 1965 to beat up any demonstrators at a peace march planned in Berkeley, California. Ginsberg proposed that protestors bring "Masses of flowers" that

Figure 9. The Vietnam veterans stack flower-bedecked arms at Fiske Hill. Photo © Cary Wolinsky, Trillium Studios.

"can be used to set up barricades, to present to Hell's Angels, police, and press and spectators whenever needed or at parade's end." His idea was that protestors could "change war psychology" by demonstrating "peaceable health which is the reverse of fighting back blindly." In May 1967, Abbie Hoffman, also a social activist, followed suit. Wearing capes with the word "Freedom" on them, he and a group of antiwar activists showed up at a parade in New York City honoring American soldiers in Vietnam and began waving American flags to demonstrate their patriotism while also carrying flowers to show their rejection of the war. Newspaper photos showing prowar demonstrators punching and kicking what Hoffman dubbed "the Flower Brigade" and grabbing and ripping to shreds their American flags made the point that war only fuels hatred and intolerance. Hoffman and Jerry Rubin went on to organize the 1967 March on the Pentagon, during which protestors held out flowers to the 2,500 Army National Guardsmen sent to control them, in some cases placing them in the guardsmen's rifle barrels. In one photo of that encounter, a young female high school student holds out a daisy to a guardsman with a bayonet, the photo's instant fame evidence of the power in using flowers symbolically and performatively.[33]

On Saturday afternoon at Fiske Hill, the veterans were amplifying the power of flower symbolism by presenting themselves as allied with both the nation's soldiers *and* the protestors who chose love over war. This mixture of two historically separate identities was what made VVAW a radically new organization. If the soldiers who fought in the Vietnam War were also rejecting that war, then the "us-versus-them" dichotomy that structured those earlier photographs of Flower Power had been eradicated. Not surprisingly, of the over one hundred photographs one freelance photographer took of the Memorial Day weekend march, the one of a veteran resting next to flower-bedecked stacked arms was the one the *Boston Globe* purchased and then published in the next morning's edition as emblematic of who the veterans were.[34]

As word of the impending showdown continued to spread, more veterans, including more of the wounded from area Veterans Affairs hospitals, joined the marchers resting at Fiske Hill. The presence of men who needed crutches and wheelchairs to move around prompted many of the veterans to thread sprigs of lilac through the buttonholes of their helmet covers in preparation for their final approach to Lexington and as another transportable sign of their rejection of a war that had harmed so many. In this way, the veterans made clear what NPS would not: that the faceoff that the Fiske Hill marker glorifies had proven effective only in injuring and killing both

Heyward and his opponent. The result of their gunfight was not freedom but, quite literally, a dead end for both.[35]

One Lexington woman who had driven out to Fiske Hill to meet the veterans was a stay-at-home mother to a young handicapped son. Walking among the wounded veterans as they ate lunch, she was struck by evidence of the same harmfulness the Fiske Hill memorial recalls even as it masks it. She broke down completely a few weeks later when she tried to explain to a friend living in Canada what she had seen.

"I remember telling him about the antiwar vets coming into Lexington and seeing them paraplegic, in wheelchairs, with missing limbs. I remember just being absolutely hysterical. I was crying, I was shaking. I must have gone on like that, just about totally out of control for about twenty minutes, and I couldn't stop."[36]

Despite her obligations at home, she decided then and there that the veterans had a right if not an obligation to reframe the Lexington Battle Green as a reminder of war's harmfulness to the young men charged with fighting. Returning home, she set to work making spaghetti to contribute to their upcoming evening meal on the Green.

Gathered together on Fiske Hill with their growing number of supporters, the veterans performed for a second time their belief that democratic decision making is far preferable to war violence as a means of moving forward. As in Concord the night before, they took a vote in full view of their now substantial audience (Figure 10). Nothing had changed: the veterans were still in favor of proceeding unto the Lexington Battle Green even without the Selectmen's permission. They resumed their march, stopping only when the Lexington chief of police met them at the town's border.

"As their group approaches Lexington Center," the chief told the veterans over his cruiser's loudspeaker, his use of the third person making clear he was reading orders the Selectmen had issued to him, "they will remain on the sidewalk. There will be no guerrilla activity permitted."[37]

As the veterans had already proven in Concord's Monument Square, guerrilla theater was one of their chief means of superimposing their own time frame onto the Revolutionary War battlefields and memorials so that the public could see how far the nation had fallen from its founding ideals. The challenge for the veterans in the face of the Selectmen's ban was going to be finding means other than guerrilla theater of making the Lexington landscape speak to the necessity of the United States withdrawing from Southeast Asia. Emboldened by the many residents who had come out to Fiske Hill

Figure 10. Veteran marchers gather with civilian supporters at Fiske Hill. Photo © Cary Wolinsky, Trillium Studios.

to greet and feed them, the veterans decided to bring their warning to even more people than they had initially planned. Hearing the chief's announcement, they swerved to the right and proceeded to take a detour that, as tired and blistered as they already were, extended their march by an additional two miles. Moving south, away from the Battle Green, on Worthen Road, they passed a playground, where they were seen by young parents, and then the town tennis courts, where players stopped to watch them march past. Turning onto Waltham and then Winthrop streets, both tree lined and residential, the veterans' detour put them back on Massachusetts Avenue, approaching the Battle Green from the east instead of the west. This allowed them to pass the Lexington police station, at which they flashed the peace sign in an assertion that, while town officials had decided not to welcome the veterans, many of whom were wounded, the veterans were dedicated to peace and love. Next, they proceeded through the bustling town center. With its gray-shingled Muffin House, white-shuttered House of Deanne hair salon, and many other colonial-styled commercial buildings, there were ample opportunities for the veterans to be seen.[38]

"We wanted to go through the commercial area. We wanted to organize the town," one of the veterans later explained of the detour. "We went into the shops, talked to people on the streets. We told them, 'Hey, this is wrong.'"[39]

Over one hundred of the residents who saw the veterans march past, read the leaflets they began distributing, or spoke with them that afternoon immediately felt a sense of outrage about the Lexington Selectmen's ruling, which, like Al Armenti, they expressed by dropping what they were doing and following the veterans to the Battle Green on foot.[40]

"Behind us, we drew the countryside!" was how another veteran described the growing crowd following the veterans. Years later, he still beamed at the memory. "The Korean War veterans, the WWII veterans, the mothers, the wives, the children!"[41]

The police chief immediately deployed prowl cars to keep an eye on the growing parade. Determined not to flinch at this assertion that he and the other veterans did not have the right to speak from their own experiences about the war's immorality, Ross Fenton looked straight ahead as he marched past one of them trailed by a group of teenaged Lexington boys on their bicycles. It was a warm day for marching, and he and several other veterans had unbuttoned their shirts all the way. But, as unseasonably warm as it was, Ross kept the strap of his hat stretched tightly under his bottom lip as an outward sign of the toughness he had already proven in Vietnam and that he was now intent on using to protest the war no matter what the Lexington Selectmen said or did (see Figures 14 and 27). From remarks made later by one of the teenagers following him, it seems this very masculine version of the antiwar movement offered them a way to reject the war and perhaps later even the draft without losing the credibility that Mattel and Hasbro's G.I. Joe linked exclusively to soldiering.[42]

Little did the Lexington teens know that Ross's tightly affixed hat was also as a reminder to himself of the toll the war had taken on the buddy who gave it to him. His friend had swapped his own hat with one of the seven thousand Australian soldiers serving alongside the Americans in Vietnam.

"He was in the armored division and had run into some pretty ugly action," Ross later explained of why this other veteran had decided he could not perform in or even attend Operation POW. "He was carrying a lot of scars from that time."

After receiving some much-needed counseling from Ross, the veteran had decided to give him the Australian Army slouch hat, a cherished symbol in Australia of the tough soldiers that country had fielded in World Wars I and II.

"This seems to suit you more," he had said to Ross. "You wear it."

Up ahead, Ross could see that the veteran being wheeled at the front of the line of march by the wounded veteran in leg braces had finally reached Lexington's Minuteman Statue. Immediately behind them was one of several veterans distributing bifold leaflets to the public that featured a photo of the same statue on its cover in an assertion of the veterans' brotherhood with this iconic image of preparedness, bravery, and self-sacrifice. The inside pages of the leaflet stated what the veterans would have preferred to teach using one of their multisensory performances. They had reprinted on the verso side the words of a 1775 broadside announcing "8 killed! An Atrocity! Lexington, April 19, 1775," while on the recto, they made the case that "Lexington Green in 1775 could be a South Vietnamese or Laotian village in 1971." Taking a leaflet, one of the many photographers trailing the protestors in anticipation of the impending showdown with the Selectmen decided to photograph the lead veterans from behind the statue, capturing the same stark contrast Bestor had staged at the Old North Bridge between the dynamic contrapposto stance of the statue and the now useless legs of the wheelchair-bound veteran (Figure 11).[43]

Thrilled to have finally arrived at the place where their forefathers took a stand in 1775, the veterans clapped and raised their fists triumphantly as they flowed onto the triangular expanse of grass behind the statue that is the Lexington Battle Green. The newspaper photographers who swarmed after them focused on capturing that same confluence of soldier and hippy that had so entranced the nation the month before when the veterans occupied the National Mall in DC. Veterans with long hair and beards were framed so that the Purple Hearts and other medals they had not already angrily discarded were clearly visible next to the VVAW pins featuring the Fallen Soldier Battle Cross (Figure 12).

Ross's pleasure at reaching the Green and being a role model to the town's boys and young men was tempered when he discovered that the Lexington police had encircled it with "No Parking" signs. The ban on parking was clearly intended to make it difficult for the veterans to move their camping gear, audio equipment, and other supplies from the trucks they had rented onto the Green while making it easier for the police to access the protestors. Then Ross recalled that congregants at what had been Reverend Clarke's church in 1775, since moved from the location marked by the granite pulpit

Figure 11. The veterans pass Lexington's Minuteman Statue.
Photo © Cary Wolinsky, Trillium Studios.

Figure 12. A veteran with a Purple Heart arriving on the Lexington Battle Green. Photo © Cary Wolinsky, Trillium Studios.

to the side of the Green, had volunteered to support the veterans during their stay in town. In addition to the meals they had already told Don and Betty they would provide, they offered access to the church's bathroom facilities and, importantly, its ample parking lot, which conveniently fronted the Green. Church officials were already directing the veterans to park their many trucks and vans as closely together as possible in front of the white steepled building. Looking to the left of the church, Ross saw that a large welcome banner festooned with a giant peace sign had been affixed to the front of the colonial-era clapboarded parsonage. Made by the church's youth group, the sign formed a powerful contrast with another sign long affixed next to the parsonage's front door that romanticized the final moments of its most famous inhabitant: "Wounded on the common April 19 1775 Jonathan Harrington dragged himself to the door and died at his wife's feet." As the Lexington Selectmen must have feared, the veterans' presence made it harder to see this story as solely one of abiding love for family and country and easier to see its gruesome details and a wife's grief. Indeed, the chief's warning, the prowl cars, and now the "No Parking" signs made evident that while many residents

Figure 13. Vietnam veterans encircle the ivy-covered Lexington Revolutionary War Monument. Photo © Cary Wolinsky, Trillium Studios.

supported and welcomed the veterans, town officials had not changed their minds on the question of whether the veterans should have access to the town's memorialized battlefield and the preserved buildings surrounding it.[44]

Well aware that they and the Selectmen were battling in the court of public opinion, the veterans immediately moved to establish their patriotism by following the 1790 Revolutionary War Monument's prompt to honor the war dead. Linking arms, the fatigue-clad veterans encircled the granite obelisk into which Clarke's words and the names of the dead are carved (Figure 13). In doing so, they demonstrated their respect for the soldiers who had died so that the rising generations of Americans could be free, just as they had at Arlington National Cemetery near Washington, DC the month before. But as they would do repeatedly over the weekend, the veterans also repurposed the obelisk, using it to issue a reproach. With the obelisk as their backdrop, they sang the refrain from a John Lennon song over and over: "all we are saying, is give peace a chance." Written as the U.S. military was escalating its violent efforts to conquer Vietnam, the 1969 song begins with the

Figure 14. Bestor Cram, Arthur Johnson, Ross Fenton, and Don Carrico (far right) embrace each other on the Lexington Battle Green. Photographed by Ted Polumbaum. Courtesy of the Newseum Collection.

barking out of words made up by adding "ism" and, in subsequent verses, "sters" and "tion," illustrating the ridiculousness of the government's pretensions. ("Ev'rybody's talking 'bout Bagism, Shagism, Dragism, Madism, Ragism, Tagism, This-ism, that-ism, is'm, is'm.") The refrain asserts that faux-scientific gibberish is escalating a war that could be stopped if people would only commit themselves to trying peace. Lennon stripped away the political details of the Vietnam War in order to ask a basic question: would you rather be alive or dead?

While the obelisk on the Battle Green and other war memorials along the veterans' planned route assert that death on the battlefield results in glorious everlasting life, the presence of the veterans, many of them wounded and all of them imploring the public to "give peace a chance," called the desirability of war-making into question. Bestor, Ross, Don, and the other veterans stood shoulder to shoulder, hip to hip, their arms around each other's shoulders in a counter-expression of love for each other and their cause that rejected their fathers' model of militarized toughness (Figure 14). They were showing the people what they had learned so well in VVAW: that there is far more purpose to be found in political activism, brotherhood, and being alive than in killing and dying, even taking into consideration the ample honors American war memorialization bestows on the dead.[45]

Upon seeing the veterans arrive in town, many of the young parents, tennis players, and shoppers had gone home to make use of their own modern messengering system: the phone chain, prearranged lists of people who are each assigned to call a list of other people so that each single call is multiplied into many more telephone calls. Word of the impending showdown between the veterans and the Selectmen thus spread through town quickly. Many people who were called came to the Green to show their support, some with signs they made referencing Lexington's role in the nation's birth. ("If they mean to have peace, let it begin here.") Grateful for such a large and supportive audience and still thinking in terms of the political power of theater, the veterans followed up their circle around the obelisk with a modified version of the ceremony they were planning for their Memorial Day arrival on Boston Common. They formed a new, larger circle, this time around the flat open space in the middle of the Green. Then, one by one, the veterans danced with great jubilation into the middle of the circle. Raising their toy M16s over their heads for everyone to see, they threw their guns down on the ground in a symbol of their rejection of war violence as the other veterans stamped their feet and cheered.[46]

This dance, according to one veteran's memory, "went on for a while," so pleased were the veterans with the level of support and the chance to demonstrate to their followers and each other how good it felt to disburden themselves of their weaponry and all that it stood for. When all of the veterans were done demonstrating their rejection of war violence, the middle of the Battle Green was littered with discarded weaponry.[47]

What happened next would change the course of the protest.

"The vets sensed that they had made themselves into an exclusive group, so everyone in the circle took a step back," one of the veterans later recalled of how the veterans changed their script on the fly in order to include the growing number of civilian supporters and thereby build more energy on the Green. "As the distances became too great to hold each other in our arms, we grasped the other people behind us. Pretty soon there was a circle of all the people, which reached all the way out to the perimeter of the Lexington Green, and they were all swaying and singing 'Give Peace a Chance.'"[48]

Figure 15. The veterans begin their occupation of the Lexington Battle Green.
Photo © Cary Wolinsky, Trillium Studios.

Years later, the veterans still talked enthusiastically about the amount of energy born of so many people joining them in making a statement against the Vietnam War.

"The en masse thing creates immense energy," one veteran explained. "You're involved in it and all of a sudden your group of twenty-five becomes a group of one hundred and hundreds more added in. It's some kind of affirmation. It's very, very powerful, very elevating."[49]

Having been made such an intimate part of the march, the civilians began to confer with one another about what they could do to help the veterans bring their antiwar message to the people of Massachusetts. One idea was to pressure the Selectmen, who served three-year terms at the will of the people, to change their minds and permit the veterans to stay. Another was to occupy the Battle Green with the veterans and make it politically dangerous for the Selectmen to do anything but allow all of them to stay on the Green lest they not be reelected.

While the townspeople were deliberating, the veterans quietly proceeded to set up the sound system they had rented and unfurl their two chapter flags, the one from Rhode Island and another that had arrived with veterans from Connecticut, after which they took a seat on the Green in a signal that their occupation had begun (Figure 15). They and their supporters were as yet unaware that the Selectmen had succeeded in obtaining an injunction from the chief justice of Middlesex Superior Court and were themselves energized. Back at the Lexington police station, the chief of police proceeded to call in his entire police force, as well as the Lexington Fire Department, more police from neighboring towns, and state police as well. Finally, he and the Selectmen ordered the Lexington Public Works Department to clear the town garage of all trucks and equipment so that it could be repurposed as a makeshift jail.

CHAPTER 5

Historical Reenactment

Henry Wadsworth Longfellow asks readers of "Paul Revere's Ride" to imagine the midnight rider heading straight to the Old North Bridge without stopping, as if Revere knew from the start that the Regulars were heading to that particular part of Concord to begin a war. In actuality, when the historical Revere set out from Charlestown, he was heading to Lexington with the aim of warning John Hancock and Samuel Adams. In October 1774, the military royal governor of Massachusetts, General Thomas Gage, had dissolved the provincial assembly, thereby stripping the colony of its historical right to self-government. Outraged members declared themselves the Provincial Congress and took charge of governing those parts of the colony not occupied by the British Army. On April 14, 1775, six months after John Hancock was elected its president, Gage was ordered to arrest him, along with Adams, for being "the principal abettors in the Provincial Congress," which had just met in Concord three days before. Thirty minutes after Revere dismounted at the Lexington parsonage where the two Patriot leaders were hiding a half mile from that town's green, alarm rider William Dawes arrived via Boston Neck and the Patriots conferred. The sheer number of soldiers moving eastward, they deduced, must mean Hancock and Adams were not their object but rather the military stores the colonists had secreted further west along the same road the Regulars were traveling toward Lexington. As Revere and Dawes set off together to warn the people of Concord, the bell on Lexington's green began to toll a warning for area residents to rouse themselves.[1]

The name given to the Lexington Minuteman Statue notwithstanding, the town never followed the Provincial Congress's suggestion of designating the quarter of its militia composed of the most able-bodied and well-armed men a "minute company" charged with being ready at a moment's notice. Lexington's militia was a single "training band" comprising 130 members ranging in age from sixteen to sixty-two, many of whom, like their captain, forty-six-year-old farmer John Parker, were experienced combat veterans. During the French and Indian War, Parker and his Lexington peers had proven their loyalty to Britain by risking their lives to secure its expansion in North America. But the British government's subsequent attempts to make the colonists pay for that war by levying taxes had led many of them to question whether their continued loyalty was warranted. By the time Lexington's bell began to toll, the relations between the American colonists and the Crown had deteriorated to such an extent that upon hearing the news from Revere and Dawes, Lexington's militiamen were prepared to make a show of their resistance. Arming themselves, they rushed to the Green.[2]

Almost two hundred years later, the first warning that reached that same Green came in the form of a report from a young Lexington lawyer who had volunteered to assist the antiwar Vietnam veterans while they were in town. Having heard about the Selectmen's renewed commitment at their hurriedly assembled Thursday night meeting to bar the veterans from camping and performing, he had stopped by Middlesex District Court in Concord's Monument Square on Friday to see what he could learn from the judge, a personal friend.[3]

"There was the clerk of the court and a sergeant and a lieutenant of the Lexington police force making out criminal complaints," he informed the veterans, as congregants of the same East Lexington church where Ralph Waldo Emerson once served as the minister prepared to serve them a picnic supper on the Green. "The criminal complaints," the lawyer continued, "were for violating the town ordinance and being disorderly persons."[4]

Violating the town ordinance regarding what can take place on the Lexington Battle Green could only result in a ticket and a fine. But a disorderly charge was a criminal citation and thus cause for arrest followed by a trial in Middlesex District Court, which serves Concord and Lexington.

Years later, the lawyer was still angry.

"The police decided what these people were going to be charged when they didn't know what they were going to do," he exclaimed.[5]

Having already assumed they would be arrested for trespassing, the veterans proceeded to eat their supper in defiance of the bylaw. Then, just as they were starting on coffee and dessert, they received a second, more dire warning in the form of the Selectmen's injunction, which was served to them right on the Green. It spelled out in the convoluted syntax typical of legal documents that the Selectmen had a restraining order calling on the veterans and "and all other persons acting with them" to "desist and refrain from being on after 10 p.m. or bivouacking, camping, or staying overnight on Lexington Battle Green or Tower Park, or any public property in Lexington without permission of the Selectmen."[6]

While a disorderly charge would warrant arrest and a trial in county court, an injunction, if enforced, would elevate the veterans' occupation of the Green to an even more serious criminal offense that would have to be tried in Massachusetts Superior Court.

Now that they were facing charges of a different order than the one they had anticipated Friday night, the veterans gathered in front of the 1799 obelisk for a third and, as always, deliberately very public conversation on how to proceed. Should they still commit civil disobedience under these circumstances? A disorderly charge would be an official assertion that the veterans were dangerous, and Betty Levin, who continued to be on hand to help with food and other logistics, was worried they might be treated accordingly by the police. She had vivid memories of the 1968 Democratic National Convention, which she had attended with her husband, a Massachusetts delegate-at-large working with the Massachusetts McCarthy for President Committee. When the police cracked down on the ten thousand people there to protest the Vietnam War, she had watched a woman plead fruitlessly with an officer that she had a right to be there in her capacity as a physician.

"The policeman had his club and raced over," Betty later recalled. "He smashed it down on her."

She also watched a graduate student she knew get his arm closed in a door by a policeman. "He broke his arm."

Recalling the police's actions years later, she sighed. "They were egregiously brutal."[7]

"You didn't ever know how the police were going to react," was how Bestor put it to the assembled veterans.[8]

One of the combat veterans dismissed Bestor's concern.

"Given the level of violence," he replied in reference to what he had experienced in Vietnam, "I wasn't afraid of the police. What are they going to do? Break my head?"[9]

The VVAW leadership then asked the veterans to consider how such serious charges might impact their future plans. In many cases, these young men still had college, perhaps graduate school, and their careers ahead of them. Then, too, a few of them were still on active duty. Appearing at a political event in uniform or otherwise announcing that they were soldiers was a punishable offense. As the conversation continued, this and every other possible outcome of staying on the Lexington Battle Green was considered as local supporters looked on from the periphery of the veterans' circle.[10]

Two hundred years earlier, the Lexington militiamen had also deliberated carefully after receiving their warning, as noted famously by Lexington's militia captain in a sworn statement.

"I, John Parker, of lawful age, and commander of the Militia in Lexington," he testified, "ordered our militia to meet on the common in said Lexington, to consult what to do, and concluded not to be discovered, nor meddle or make with said Regular Troops (if they should approach) unless they should insult us."[11]

In the wake of the deaths inflicted by the colonists over the course of that day, Parker and the other Patriots were anxious for the public to know that they had decided in the democratic fashion denied them by the Crown to be nonviolent and that a battle had ensued only because the Regulars started it.

After also "consulting what to do," the Vietnam veterans proceeded to take their third vote of that weekend and as publicly as they had the first two. Filmmaker Hart Perry, still wearing his tricorn hat, sat amid them so that he could film the deliberations close up. This time, the vote to stay on the Lexington Battle Green was unanimous (Figure 16). The four veterans who had voted against civil disobedience on Friday night had changed their minds.

"I always sort of persuaded myself that I couldn't really end the war if I went to prison," Joseph Baratta explained when approached by one of the film crews regarding his earlier stance that being arrested in the middle of the night would be a fruitless gesture.[12]

At thirty, Joseph was older than most of the other VVAW members, but like them, he had paired a beard with a set of fatigues to signify his rejection of the very military in which he had served (Figure 17).

"Now I think that's wrong," he continued. "I think that kind of reasoning just gets us in deeper and deeper."

In 1964, two years after joining the Marines, Joseph had been sent to Taiwan for six weeks on military exercises to defend the Taiwanese against an unnamed aggressor that could only be communist China. After participating in a dramatic World War II–style beachhead landing as jets and helicopters provided coverage, he spent two days on leave, or R&R in military

Figure 16. The veterans vote for a third time to commit civil disobedience. Photographed by and courtesy of Richard Robbat.

parlance, in Taiwan's second largest city. Kaohsiung was crisscrossed with dirt roads lined with little wooden houses packed full of people.

"I couldn't help but wonder as I walked along the streets with all these people, what would happen if somebody lit a match to it?" He knew how much firepower the Marines had and he knew his nation's history. "This is the kind of city that in Japan we bombed with incendiaries during WWII."[13]

"I'm in the wrong outfit," he decided then and there. "I don't want to be part of an organization that's prepared to kill millions of people."

Joseph left the military and, after converting to his wife's religion, moved with her to Israel. However, his hopes of living a more spiritually meaningful life there were soon dashed.

"I saw that the Israelis were using American equipment everywhere you looked. The airplanes were F-4 Phantoms or A3D Skyhawks. I realized that Israel is a client state of the United States," he later explained. "While we were over there, the trial of Lieutenant Calley broke and I felt just as responsible for this massacre at My Lai as was Calley because I had prepared the way. I had served and done my part. We decided to return to the United States to struggle against the war in Vietnam."

Figure 17. Joseph Baratta being interviewed on the Lexington Battle Green. Screenshot from *Veterans Against the War* (1971), directed by Hart Perry. Courtesy of Hart Perry.

Joseph took an entry-level job at a high-tech company that he was falsely assured had no military contracts. He began devoting his weekends to VVAW-NE's efforts. His wife often joined him and was one of several spouses and romantic partners marching alongside the veterans to Lexington.[14]

"I was a Vietnam-era veteran. I had been to the Far East and I was part of that whole process of war in Asia," Joseph lamented, referring to the over seventy years of continuous American wars waged there, starting in 1899 when the United States took the Philippines from Spain after the Spanish-American War. "I hadn't actually been ordered to Vietnam and I hadn't killed anybody and I hadn't collected a lot of medals for bravery, but I just felt that I was a veteran, I was part of it, I wasn't lacking in responsibility."[15]

As veterans and civilians swirled around Joseph on the Green, the film crew asked if he was now willing to go to jail.

"Yes," Joseph asserted without hesitation.

In modern life, it is difficult to tell if individual actions matter or to see coherent connections between events. Joseph had participated in war exercises in Taiwan, and he had lived in what he had come to see as a U.S. client state. While he figured this made him culpable in the American war in Vietnam, he did not have the confidence Friday night to believe his actions on the Lexington Battle Green would make an impact. What finally gave him that confidence was historical reenactment. By Saturday afternoon, he had experienced the way in which reenacting Revere's ride and the American militia's march across the North Bridge and down the Battle Road released an incredible amount of patriotic energy in both the participants and those observing them. These particular historical reenactments were of events that had already proven highly effective and thus gave the distinct impression that the veterans' actions would be effective as well, prompting bystanders to drop what they were doing and join the veterans' protest. In Joseph's mind, taking a stand on the Lexington Green should thus generate even more participation and energy. It would be a reenactment of the Lexington militia's stand as well as of yet another moment that changed American history: the moment when Thoreau discovered a new means for people to shape their nation's future.[16]

"Thoreau went to jail for the same issues. There was a war on with Mexico in those days. The United States had invaded that country," Joseph explained to the film crew, focusing on the parallels to the Vietnam War, even as what worried Thoreau was the expansion of American slavery. "Thoreau wouldn't pay his tax. They put him in jail. You remember what Emerson said, don't you?"

Joseph could assume the filmmakers remembered because the encounter had recently been dramatized in a widely performed new play, *The Night Thoreau Spent in Jail*, by Jerome Lawrence and Robert E. Lee.

"Emerson came into the jail and here's his good friend Henry David Thoreau," Joseph explained of the interchange the play imagines. (In actuality, Emerson did not know that Thoreau was in jail until the next day, after Thoreau had been released.)

"Henry! Henry! What are you doing in jail?" the playwrights imagine Emerson asking Thoreau.

"Waldo! What are you doing *out* of jail?" Thoreau replies in the play, chastising his friend for paying his taxes and thereby supporting what Thoreau regarded as an immoral government. Even in jail, Thoreau insisted, he was the freer of the two men. "Under a government which imprisons any unjustly,"

Thoreau wrote of slavery in his influential essay on civil disobedience, "the true place for a just man is also a prison."[17]

Joseph had not mentioned Thoreau on Friday night when he argued against civil disobedience on the grounds that no one would see the veterans get arrested in the middle of the night. However, since then, he had passed the plaque in Monument Square marking where the Concord local was incarcerated for "refusing to recognize the right of the state to collect taxes from him in support of slavery." Locals had been quick to point out that the veterans had an opportunity to commit civil disobedience not far from where Thoreau had done so all those years before.

"This is the only chance in my life I'll have to imitate Thoreau and take this dare to be civilly disobedient," one local woman later recalled thinking.[18]

"If dissent in of all places Lexington, right next to the birthplace of Thoreau, was going to be snuffed out, then everybody was going to suffer," was how another resident explained the need to get arrested. "We would all lose our freedom."[19]

And thus, during the day on Saturday, the veterans made yet another adjustment to their march. They expanded their performance of the past to include not only Revere's warning and the showdown between colonial militiamen and British Regulars but also Thoreau's successful search to find a way to tell the state face-to-face that they were refusing to support its immoral actions. While the veterans were planning on breaking a law unrelated to the war they opposed, doing so would nevertheless create, as Thoreau's refusal to pay his tax had, an opportunity to speak to the public about their motivation. And insofar as the veterans' act of civil disobedience would take place in Thoreau's backyard and thereby serve as a repetition of the Concord philosopher's own historic efforts, it had additional emotional resonance for Joseph and gave him confidence that his actions would produce the same outcome Thoreau's eventually had when slavery was abolished in the United States. And thus, even though Joseph had just walked eight miles on a warm day, he appeared the opposite of tired. He was on his feet, facing the camera, beaming, having learned that the energy of the past can be rereleased in the present through reenactment.

This conviction that reenacting the heroic American past might actually change the future was a newly popular one in 1971. The first reenactment of the encounter on Lexington Green between British Regulars and local militiamen, in 1822, was solely to celebrate the twenty participating survivors. In 1875, when seven thousand people gathered on the Green to remember the actions of the local militia and the loss of the eight who died one hundred years before, there was no reenactment. There was a second reenactment in 1911 but exclusively for the purpose of making a film about the American Revolution. Scripted and costumed annual reenactments for area residents and tourists only started locally in 1962. It was then that the town of Concord called for the "mustering of a new company of militia to be known as the Concord Minute Men" with Lexington doing the same. At the first Concord muster, in 1963, one hundred local men turned out. Within a year, members were outfitted in colonial-era outfits and could play the fife and drum. With the nation's bicentennial fast approaching, these reenactments were a way to showcase the important role these towns had played in the nation's founding while insisting that so long as reenactment helps ensure that time stands still at certain sacred spots, the energy of 1775 will continue to be ready for release, whether in the fight against communism, a cause still very dear to the country in the early sixties, or some other threat.[20]

The veterans' unorthodox use of this recently established pastime of historical reenactment was a main point of contention for the Selectmen, who otherwise permitted battle reenactments every Patriots' Day and even allowed antiwar protests on the Green, later claiming to have opposed the Vietnam War themselves. In 1966, the Selectmen had allowed Voice of Women–New England and the local chapter of the Women's International League for Peace and Freedom to hold silent, hourlong vigils every week on the Green. Appearing in skirts and heels, often with children in tow, the women protestors were the very picture of middle-class respectability. More recently, on October 15, 1969, the Selectmen had permitted a besuited governor of Massachusetts to also speak out against the war on the Battle Green. In these cases, while the Green served as a symbol of American freedom and was thereby used as a means of reproaching the federal government, its users had not also repurposed the Green by turning it into Vietnam in order to show that America had become the kind of imperialist country its forefathers had once fought to the death. The physical and emotional wounds of war that the new, twentieth-century "Minute Men" of VVAW made visible with their own injuries while acting out the murderous treatment of Vietnamese civilians risked debunking the beloved American myths, perpetuated at the Old North Bridge and on the Lexington Battle Green, that Americans are peaceable people and that any wars undertaken are undertaken because war is the road to freedom.[21]

Ever since the veterans had expanded their afternoon circle to include the people who had followed them onto the Green, the tension building in town had become palpable. When the circle on the Green broke up, over one hundred locals had marched to the Selectmen's office, then a temporary trailer on account of a building renovation that was under way, where the chairman of the Board of Selectmen and one other Selectman were meeting. When the two Selectmen declined to appear, the crowd grew increasingly angry and frustrated, and the Selectmen requested police protection. Finally, with officers standing by, the two Selectmen came outside and momentarily defused the situation by offering residents a Special Selectmen's Meeting at 8 p.m. that evening, at which they hoped those residents who agreed with their position would be on hand to lend political support. That meeting, in the auditorium of Cary Hall, next to the Lexington police station, was attended by a crowd of between five and seven hundred locals, far more than typically attended town meeting. The chief of police felt it necessary to have a large police presence at what proved to be a raucous gathering. While there were plenty of residents who supported the Selectmen's view that the Green must be kept sacrosanct, they were outnumbered by residents in support of the veterans. As the VVAW-NE leadership had anticipated, their excursion into the liberal suburbs of Boston put them in contact with likeminded citizens with a demographic similar to their members. As several Lexington residents reported later, the local VVAW supporters tended to be relative newcomers, people who were highly educated, worked in technological fields, and supported liberal endeavors. While many of their causes proved to be self-serving insofar as they resulted in attractive, green, and highly exclusive enclaves, suburban liberals, like the veterans, were driven by a belief in the power of grassroots activism and the conviction that federal resources should be used for scientific and educational purposes, not for war. Those who, conversely, supported the Selectmen's decision to bar the veterans from the Green tended to be from the dwindling number of Lexington families that had moved to town around the turn of the past century to farm and who had more conservative political views.[22]

When the VVAW supporters' impassioned speeches failed to move the Selectmen, they queued at the Cary Hall pay phone in order to urge even more people to come show the veterans their support. At that point, concerned local religious leaders stepped in to try to avert the mass arrest the Selectmen were threatening by hosting an executive session of the Selectmen with the VVAW leadership at St. Brigid's, the Catholic church near the Green. By then it was 10 p.m. and as many as a thousand civilian supporters were occupying the Green alongside a still growing number of veterans. While that was a small percentage of the total number of people living in Lexington at the time (almost 32,000 were counted in the 1970 census), the outpouring of support from hundreds of concerned citizens intent on welcoming and standing with the veterans was a radical departure from what the veterans had first experienced upon arriving back home from Vietnam.[23]

"My parents and people I knew, nobody ever really asked me about what it was like," one veteran lamented. "Nobody was interested."[24]

"When I started complaining about my experience in Vietnam," another veteran recalled of finally talking to his career military brother, "he took me to the floor and beat the crap out of me."[25]

And thus, even as they were angry and frustrated with the Selectmen for not giving them permission to camp on the Green, the veterans basked in the warm embrace they were receiving from so many others.

"Everybody was happy and singing, or drinking beer, kissing and hugging each other," one recalled of the surge of energy on the Green. "It was terrific."[26]

"It gave us a lot of hope," another veteran still remembered years later.[27]

As they had all weekend, the veterans continued to focus on cultivating the idea that they and the other protestors with them on the Green were repeating the actions that had birthed the nation. At the Special Selectmen's Meeting, two of them had read to the residents in attendance a new press release in which they claimed once again to be the latest incarnation of the Minute Men.

"We are assembling at Lexington Green much like the Minutemen but unarmed, bonded in our brotherhood of effecting revolutionary change in this country," the veterans asserted, before describing an even closer connection to the forefathers they claimed. "We now choose to assemble in the spirit of our Lexington forefathers, bearing witness to the illegal, immoral war in Indochina that has made all Americans prisoners of this war."[28]

When asked by one of the film crews to speak on the record about the occupation of the Green, VVAW's executive director, who had been instrumental in orchestrating Operation RAW the fall before and who had driven up from New York to be with the veterans on the Green, also spoke to the parallels.

"The same war, another battlefield."[29]

The veterans were claiming not only to be reenacting the gathering of the Minute Men on the Green but to be symbolically reborn as their forefathers in the process.

"The veterans had all agreed that if they were arrested," one resident later recalled, "they would give their birth date as April 19, 1775."[30]

"Some people may say they are Captain John Parker or Paul Revere," Bestor explained to one of the film crews of the protestors' plans, "They want to identify themselves as a Minute Man."[31]

The celebrated MIT linguist and internationally renowned antiwar activist Noam Chomsky, who had decided along with his wife to move to Lexington in the early 1950s because it "looked like paradise, a rural paradise," and who came to the Green with her to show the veterans support, was surprised that the people of Lexington, whose elite educations he blamed for making them "submissive and obedient people," were willing to be arrested. "It's not what ordinary middle-class people do," he later said. "It's very rare for a population to dissent." The demonstrations he had attended usually comprised college students and other young people, whereas the protestors on the Green, he later recalled, were "mostly people with children, people in their, I don't know, forties or something like that, which is not the usual demonstration." The majority of these people had never committed civil disobedience.[32]

It was the reenactment piece of the protest, the becoming Captain Parker and Paul Revere, that gave both the civilians and the veterans the courage of their convictions.

"It kind of gives you goose bumps, a strong sense of reality, when you realize that you have this cause and you believe in it, and that you are traveling in the same footsteps in the same direction [as the colonial militiamen] because you want to be heard," one veteran later explained. "You're a piece of history."[33]

As Joseph Baratta was learning, reenactment makes participants feel more alive because they are repeating "a piece of history" that has been deemed critically important in bringing the nation into existence.

The veterans' civilian supporters were so impressed by the connection the veterans forged between 1775 and 1971 that they still remembered it years later.

"It was easy to identity these Vietnam veterans' hard-wrought patriotism with the original Minutemen's," one resident recalled.[34]

Another woman recollected of the unfolding standoff on the Green, "You had the Tories on one side and the Patriots on another."[35]

"Instead of Captain John Parker," one resident put it, "there was Captain John Kerry."[36]

While Bestor Cram and his co-coordinator were the real captains of Operation POW, if that could even be said of anyone in a thoroughly democratic organization such as VVAW, the name of VVAW's national spokesman was more well known on account of his televised speech to the Senate Foreign Relations Committee the month before, during which he had asked in reference to the slow nature of Nixon's drawdown schedule, "How do you ask a man to be the last man to die in Vietnam?" Even as this Lexington resident failed to recognize that Kerry was in attendance solely as a member of VVAW, albeit an important one insofar as he helped draw media attention to the march, and not as one of its leaders, she enthusiastically embraced the idea that the nation's forefathers had been transubstantiated into the bodies of the living Vietnam veterans.[37]

"The Battle Green was alive again," one resident asserted, "not with people reading inscriptions about what other people did two hundred years ago, but with people making a stand now in the tradition of those who stood then." The Green, she continued, was transformed "from a museum to a working thing."[38]

When Bestor and the other veteran leaders returned to the Green at 11 p.m. after the religious community's hourlong, last-ditch attempt to avoid getting the police involved, they brought with them a very nervous chairman of the Board of Selectmen. He knew a mass arrest on the scale presenting itself would be financially costly for the town. It might also be politically costly for him personally. Worse, a mass arrest could be physically dangerous for the townspeople and local police. Unable to bring himself to simply ignore the protestors, the chairman wanted to make one last effort to clear the Green without police assistance. Seeing him, the crowd stirred in anticipation. But even as people pressed toward the rise on which the memorial obelisk stands and which the veterans were using as a kind of speakers' platform, the chairman was permitted to speak. Using the veterans' sound system, he offered the veterans the use of a new park on Lincoln Street that until recently had been a town dump.[39]

By then the protestors were convinced they had become Minute Men and were therefore emboldened to continue to take their stand on the Lexington

Battle Green. They had also come to realize that an overnight stay in a regular park would have none of the symbolic power of staying on the Green and would thus be far less likely to continue yielding the same terrific amount of media coverage they were receiving. Nor would it have the potential to generate the kind of energy propelling people to risk arrest for the first time in their lives.[40]

"No!" the energized crowd roared back in a spontaneous and unified response.[41]

And, with that, the protestors sat down to wait for the police while the chairman headed to the police station to confer with the chief and other officials about what to do next.

In the spring of 1775, the militia waited on the Green as temperatures dropped and the night grew uncomfortably cold. At 2 a.m., when the Regulars still had not appeared, Captain Parker dismissed his men. While some of them chose to return home, seventy-five or so were sufficiently concerned that they remained in and around nearby Buckman Tavern as Parker continued to send couriers down the road to watch for any arriving troops.

Almost two hundred years later, after waiting one, two, and then three hours to be arrested on what also became an increasingly cold night, several hundred people assumed the Selectmen must have decided not to enforce the curfew. They went home to their warm beds. Those who stayed to carry out their act of civil disobedience burrowed into heavy coats, blankets, and sleeping bags. While a few people went to sleep in the pews of the First Parish with the intention of returning to the Green if the police arrived, those who remained conversed, sang folk songs, dozed intermittently, and passed around bottles of wine and thermoses filled with hot coffee. Those who stayed later recalled being transformed by the fellowship.[42]

The twenty-nine-year-old assistant minister at Lexington's Follen Church where Emerson once served found himself next to the sixty-nine-year-old editor of the church newsletter. He had recently condensed an article she had written, to which she had responded emphatically, "I don't like ministers." But after sitting together on the Green in mutual protest of the Vietnam War, she softened, telling him that while she still did not like ministers, "you could be my friend," a gesture she followed up later with a poem thanking him for standing with her on that night.[43]

Betty Levin sat with a Lincoln woman whose son had enlisted and was serving in Vietnam while her teenaged daughter insisted on coming to

Lexington to protest the war with the veterans. After helping Betty and Don Carrico organize meals for the veterans in the week leading up to the protest ("We'll just take care of it the way we organize church meals"), she and her husband proceeded to commit civil disobedience on the Lexington Battle Green as a means of honoring both of their children.

"She was fabulous. I just adored her." Betty remembered thinking that "somebody should come and take a picture. These wonderful parents!"[44]

An MIT linguist who had been unable to forge a close relationship with his famous colleague later recalled finally being able to do so on the Green.

"You know that I am a colleague of Noam Chomsky's," he later recalled proudly when asked how he spent those long hours. "I don't get to talk to him very much, because he is extremely busy, because he has many students. So this was an opportunity for me to spend a lot of time talking to him about the things we do, about linguistics. And I heard a lot of things about politics and lots of things so it was a fine experience for me."[45]

At 2 a.m., when the plainclothes officers the chief of police had directed to mingle with the crowd on the Green reported that the number of people had decreased, the chief told the chairman of the Board of Selectmen that he could proceed with a mass arrest if that was what he still wanted. Most of the remaining protestors would fit in the large garage of the Public Works Department, already cleared of all trucks and large equipment. Of course, by this point, dawn was not far away, and the veterans and their supporters had already been on the Green for hours past the 10 p.m. curfew. As one resident had already pointed out at the Special Selectmen's Meeting earlier in the evening, the Selectmen could have gone home to bed and simply ignored the protestors. Instead, the chairman decided to proceed with arrests. His reason had nothing to do at that point with preempting the Green's occupation, which was already well under way. Nor at this point did it have anything to do anymore with the Selectmen's earlier voiced concerns about possible violence, which had proven unfounded. Rather, the chairman must have proceeded in order to purify a sacred space he regarded as having been defiled.[46]

Since the addition of monuments and markers at the Old North Bridge, along the Battle Road, and on Lexington Battle Green, as well as the subsequent enactment of laws from the local to the federal level that set aside these sites for memorial and sanctioned reenactment purposes, these former battlefields have served as portals through which Americans can return to 1775. Indeed, VVAW invented their performance-based and site-specific protests as a new form of nonviolent action precisely because, like traditional reenactors and their facilitators, they wanted to access the nation's foundational energy. From the chairman's perspective, however, the veterans were contaminating the Green by drawing a comparison between 1775 and 1971, thereby injecting the ongoing present time into a space where time is meant to have stopped. Declaring the protestors outside of the law and having the police clear the Green was the only way the chairman could reset the Green's internal clock to 1775 and stop it there for perpetuity. In other words, he seems to have regarded the arrests as a means of purifying the Green of chronological time and its many political burdens.[47]

Once the chairman gave the nod, the police chief assembled his men in the circular driveway in front of Cary Hall.

"We brought all our special police officers on board that night," the chief later recalled, "every one of our police officers."[48]

A local reporter counted, in addition to forty-five officers from Lexington, five from the town of Bedford and nine from Arlington.[49]

In 1775, Captain Parker finally received word from the scouts he had been sending down the road toward Charlestown that the Regulars were not more than fifteen minutes from the Green. An advance guard of six light-infantry companies, about 238 men in all, were approaching under the command of Major John Pitcairn, a Scotsman who joined the Marines at the age of twenty-three and who in 1774, at the age of fifty-one, had been put in charge of the six hundred Royal Marines sent to Boston in the wake of colonial unrest to support the British forces already there. Parker ordered his drummer to beat the call to arms and watched as about half of his remaining men quickly formed two short ranks on the Green. Hearing the drum after hours of listening to church bells and warning shots and recalling Revere's assertion upon being captured that the Regulars would face "near 200 of the rebels" or, as another officer later recalled, even "between two and three hundred," Pitcairn stopped his men at the last bend in the road from Charlestown. When a man appeared on horseback up ahead and warned them to turn back, Pitcairn ordered his men to load their weapons. His orders were to reach Concord, and to do so, his men would need to get safely past what he was now sure was an occupied Lexington Green.

The 1971 protestors also periodically sent someone down Massachusetts Avenue to check for activity. Finally, a car with its windows rolled down pulled up alongside the protestors.

"The police are coming!"[50]

Whether the informants meant to or not, they were echoing the words that Paul Revere is often said to have shouted.

"The British are coming!"

Revere, then still British himself, most likely said something such as, "The Regulars are coming out." But the myth has long trumped common sense, asserting as it does that the colonists were already a distinctly new people by virtue of hearing and heeding Revere's call. The Vietnam veterans and their supporters had entered into the nation's past precisely so that they had the same script and thus could enjoy the same outcome of rousing the people to action, which they proceeded to do down to the letter.[51]

Hearing the police were finally on the way, the protestors gathered their belongings and stood up to face them. Bestor quickly reviewed everything the veterans had done to avoid a violent clash with the police. He had informed the chief of police early Saturday morning of the veterans' intentions to occupy the Green peaceably. He and the other VVAW chapter leaders had been careful to keep a sharp lookout for provocateurs, recalling that six weeks earlier, during Operation Dewey Canyon III in DC, a man in olive drab trying to pass as a veteran had to be isolated after suggesting that the veterans "trash" the National Mall. VVAW leaders had also been very careful about how they publicized the march, fearful that people with more radical views than theirs, college students, or even imposters might attend and try to hijack the protest. Only once the march was well under way did WBCM, a Boston rock station, suggest that people should go to Lexington to support the veterans in their occupation of the Green. Finally, VVAW leaders had watched for those traumatized veterans who, still on high alert since experiencing combat, continued to carry firearms after being discharged from the military. (That morning at the Old North Bridge, one VVAW-NE leader had convinced a participating veteran to throw his gun in the Concord River.) Finally, the veterans had been scrupulous in modeling respect for others in the hopes that they would be treated well in return. When Bestor had announced over the loudspeaker that the chairman of the Board of Selectmen wanted to address the crowd and some of the residents started to boo, the veterans had immediately put a stop to that kind of antagonistic behavior. "If we expect respect from them," one veteran had called out, "we should give respect to them." Now, with the police en route and the standoff coming to a head, Bestor and other VVAW leaders walked among the protestors with final reminders of the veterans' commitment to nonviolence and the absolute necessity of complying peacefully with the police.[52]

"They're just doing their job like we did in Vietnam," was how they put it.[53]

The chief of police had also done what he could to ensure the mass arrest proceeded safely. When addressing his assembled men in front of Cary Hall, he had issued detailed instructions meant to ensure that calm prevailed.

"You don't tap them on the shoulder and say, 'You are under arrest.' You don't touch them," he told the officers. "If anyone becomes physical or resists, you back off. You back off. There will be no physical arrests made on the Green."[54]

Still, the chief had prepared for the worse.

"They said that if things got nasty," one local fireman recalled the police instructing his department, "we would wind up probably having to go down there and render first aid to people."[55]

"You never know what's going to happen at a protest," the chief admitted later, echoing the concern Bestor had voiced earlier. "Somebody decides that they want to become angry, start fighting with policemen, and the next thing you know you have got yourself a riot."[56]

The chief was sufficiently concerned that he had called for backup. In addition to the fifty-nine area officers, he had thirty-five officers on hand from the Massachusetts State Police.

"We kept them in reserve," the chief later explained, "not out in the open, but where we could reach them in case we needed them."[57]

"We knew the people that lived in the town better than they did," a former Lexington police cadet later explained of why the chief kept the state police nearby but out of sight, "and we would be better prepared to get voluntary compliance."[58]

Hearing the veterans voice their concern, some Lexington residents, who had thought to come to the Green dressed conservatively, rationalized that their respectability would protect them from police violence.[59]

"I remember looking for my longest dress," one Lexington woman later recalled of how she had dressed similarly for a student protest after the Kent State massacre. "We were wearing our skirts very short at that time, and I wanted to wear my most respectable looking outfit so that if I looked very middle class and very respectable and as old as I could, maybe the students wouldn't get shot. That's very magical thinking, but there was a notion that if the politicians could see that mainstream people like myself and my husband were in support of the students' right of expression that maybe they wouldn't be shot."[60]

Others were not so sure that Lexington's reputation as a bastion of middle-class propriety would be enough to protect the protestors.

A pregnant woman on the Green in support of her veteran husband later recalled having "a vision of maybe what I saw on television of other people at demonstrations getting arrested, that I might be thrown or I might be pushed or I might be shoved in some way that I could endanger my unborn child."

She kept telling her husband that she could not go through with getting arrested.

"Just hold my hand. We'll be okay," her husband had tried to reassure her.[61]

Another of the veterans' girlfriends later recalled how she also trembled with fear at the news of the police's imminent arrival.

"I had never been arrested and I was deathly worried," she later reported, adding that she had the dry heaves she was so scared. "It was circulating that the police were coming with dogs. Were they going to attack us? I was very, very worried about that."[62]

The head minister at Emerson's former church in East Lexington was convinced that the veterans' demonstration would probably turn into the same kind of riot he had witnessed in April 1969 when he had gone to Harvard Square to mail his income tax returns. Angry that Harvard University had an officers training corps and was thus supporting the Vietnam War, students had decided to occupy one of the college's oldest buildings. Even as the administration threatened to arrest the students, the number of protestors grew to five hundred. At 3 a.m. on the morning of April 10, four hundred city and state police moved in with billy clubs and mace, arresting more than one hundred students for trespassing. Students, faculty, and bystanders were enraged.

"They were trashing banks and they were throwing rocks," the minister recalled. "It's possible that in the name of doing good and bringing great masses of people together," he concluded, "that, whatever your cause, it's going to be destructive." He decided to leave the Green and go home before violence erupted.[63]

By the time Major Pitcairn's advance guard approached the Green at dawn on April 19, 1775, they had been awake for almost twenty-four hours. First, they had waited in a Cambridge swamp for all of the troops to be ferried across the water before setting off on foot for Lexington. Over the course of the ensuing thirteen miles, each of the eight hundred men had to carry sixty pounds on his back in the form of a ten-pound musket, a bayonet, a long sword, a short sword, thirty-six rounds, a full cartridge box, and two days' worth of provisions suspended from white belts crossed over their chests and around their waists or packed into a canvas haversack tied around their hips. For uniforms, they wore unwieldy headgear (tall bearskin caps for the grenadiers, tight leather helmets for the light infantry, and cocked hats for the rank and file), heavy and elaborately embellished woolen coats, tight winter gaiters, and square-toed brogans. Wet from the swamp and then from fording a stream when it was determined crossing a bridge would make too much noise, the troops' heavy uniforms were little protection against the chilly spring weather. They were a dangerous combination of cold, exhausted, and frightened.[64]

In 1971, the police were also tired and anxious. Some of them had worked the night before. Some were cadets with little to no experience. And some, including the chief himself, were upset that the veterans were breaking the law.[65]

"I have always felt that civil disobedience was not the way to go," he later admitted. "Anytime that I saw this happening obviously it was a displeasure to me." He was particularly upset that the veterans were breaking a law pertaining to the Battle Green.

"This is a place where we said, 'The shot was fired that was heard round the world,'" he later asserted, both misquoting and misappropriating the famous line penned by Emerson to honor the battle at Concord, not Lexington. "It was always considered to be a very, very special place. There were people buried on that Green and the Town of Lexington in its wisdom years ago created a special bylaw to protect the integrity of the Green, and to see to it that they didn't play ball on the Green. Part of our policing activity was to see to it that that Green was kept with a decorum that was meant to be."[66]

When two local school buses pulled up, the veterans and their civilian supporters were dismayed to see what the disembarking police were wearing. While they were in the same dress uniforms they wore every Patriots' Day and Fourth of July, as ordered by the chief, each officer also wore a hard helmet held on securely by a chin strap. The helmets might be a nonthreatening robin's egg blue, but they were unquestionably riot helmets nonetheless, meant to protect the police in the event that the protestors become violent.[67]

"It was kind of sad," one veteran later lamented, "to see the police come with all their riot control gear."[68]

"We were shocked," a local teenager later recalled.[69]

Some would later remember that the police were forbidden by the chief to use their nightsticks. Others, recalling how scared they had been, would imagine having seen billy clubs, even as there is no photographic evidence corroborating this impression.[70]

They "looked like they were about nine feet tall," one Lexington man would later recall of the police. "They were armed and they had the largest billy clubs I've ever seen in my life. I used to play baseball but to me they looked as long as a baseball bat. They were standing by those buses hitting their hands with their clubs. I had visions of Gestapo, I really did. I was frightened."[71]

As the police formed a phalanx on the side of the Green, the veterans, still intent on being nonviolent, invited the chief of police to use their sound system. Reporters and VVAW's own film team pressed close as he began to speak.

"If you persist at this point of staying on this Common then we are going to have to place you under arrest," the Lexington chief of police warned the protestors before inviting those who wanted to avoid arrest to move onto the sidewalk.[72]

The remaining crowd of over five hundred people broke into spontaneous applause, at which point the chief signaled to the officers to begin moving across the Green in formation toward the protestors. The applause stopped abruptly.

"It was really a terrible thing to behold," one protestor on the Green in 1971 later remembered. "They marched forward and they looked like Gestapo. They looked like storm troopers. They were dressed in battle gear essentially, in riot gear."[73]

Someone in the crowd, VVAW never learned who, hurled a bottle at the approaching police. This was exactly the kind of provoking behavior VVAW's leaders had feared.

"We didn't know all the members," Bestor later admitted, still uncertain if the offender was an angry veteran or someone who was there as a provocateur with the goal of making the veterans look bad.[74]

Contrary to the memorial on the Green that says otherwise, the Lexington captain never told his men to stand their ground when British soldiers arrived on the Green in 1775.[75]

"I immediately ordered our troops to disperse and not to fire," Captain Parker later testified.

As his men complied and were moving off the Green, someone fired a musket, although from which side, and whether an accidental discharge or an attempt to spark an incident, remains unclear.

Fearing they were in the same kind of kill-or-be-killed situation with which American soldiers in Vietnam would become intimately familiar almost two hundred years later, the exhausted and on-edge advance British guard began firing without any orders from Major Pitcairn. Revere, who was back on the Green after being released by his captors and attempting to carry a trunk full of John Hancock's important papers to safety, later described how the single shot was followed by a "continual roar of musketry." Some of the disbanding Lexington militiamen were shot in the back.[76]

They "rushed furiously, fired upon and killed eight of our party," Captain Parker testified a week later, "without receiving any provocation therefore from us."[77]

"We didn't want anything like that to happen," one veteran later recalled of the bottle hurled at the police in 1971. "The veterans in the crowd turned on that guy because that wasn't going to be tolerated. We didn't put up with that crap."[78]

Even as the bottle missed by a wide margin, the police chief immediately took additional precautions, asking the fire department to turn on their rescue truck's massive spotlights in hopes that arrests could proceed without further incident.

Once it became clear that the arrests were going to proceed in a well-lit area by respectful policemen, several of whom apologized to the people they were arresting, the veterans resumed the part of the protest that had already been so successful in mobilizing support and drawing attention to their message: historical reenactment. They sent an active-duty soldier, whom they wanted to keep out of sight anyway, up into the First Parish's steeple with the son of the First Parish's acting minister and two other of the many Lexington teenaged boys who were deeply impressed with the veterans' mobilization of masculine coolness for the antiwar cause. They started pulling the thick ropes that swing the massive bell.[79]

While Longfellow left the tolling of the bell on Lexington Green out of his account in order to heighten the significance of Revere's own signaling efforts, the people of Lexington have long celebrated the role of their town bell. The 1775 location of the stand-alone belfry on the Green was marked in 1910 by a stone erected there by the Daughters of the American Revolution, who also built a replica of the belfry, the original of which had been destroyed by fire the year before. Since being moved off the Green, the replica belfry has been located on a nearby hill where the town tolls it every Patriots' Day.

In 1971, the tolling of a bell had the same practical purpose it did in 1775, in this case awakening the protestors asleep in the First Parish's pews as well as those residents who had gone to their nearby homes to sleep or get warm. People within earshot leapt up and rushed to the Green to get arrested.[80]

The tolling was long remembered, however, for taking the protestors back to 1775 and thereby placing them in an already plotted and heroic narrative. Everyone became infused with the same conviction Joseph Baratta had voiced earlier: surely if they stood their ground, the Vietnam War would end.

"The just wonderful part of it," one veteran later recalled of that night, was that "there were an awful lot of bells and there was a stirring, very patriotic I guess in a way, and it just meant an awful lot, it really did."[81]

"I will just never forget it," one Lexington woman later asserted. "It was a very beautiful sound. It was a very dramatic moment. . . . It was probably the most exciting thing of the day. It was a very emotional moment for everybody who was involved because everybody felt that the battle was joined and the bells were on our side."[82]

Historical reenactment allowed participants to view their showdown with the Selectmen as another "battle," as the massacre on the Green is also often called, and not just any battle but a repetition of the 1775 battle that led to the birth of the nation.

The terrible anxiety one of the women there with her veteran boyfriend had been feeling as she anticipated what she feared would be a violent arrest was immediately assuaged by the recognition that what was happening was a repetition of the first day of the American Revolution.

"I swear I can still hear it in my head," she later recalled, her voice breaking with emotion. "They tolled that bell the entire time we were getting on those buses."[83]

"The excitement for me," a Lexington woman reported, "was to have the First Parish opening its doors to the veterans and having the bell ring."[84]

While making sure they were not separated from their civilian supporters, which could have created negotiating difficulties once they were imprisoned, the veterans proceeded to put their hands behind their heads and quietly submit to police. Despite the concerns Joseph Baratta had voiced Friday night, the press was there even at that late hour to help them spread the message that, as VVAW-NE had announced in the leaflet it distributed in Lexington, "We Are All Prisoners of This War." While a photograph of the

Figure 18. Bestor Cram gets arrested on the Lexington Battle Green. Photographed by Ted Polumbaum. Courtesy of the Newseum Collection.

well-known John Kerry and another photograph of a middle-aged and respectably dressed female protestor would appear Monday morning on the front page of the *Boston Globe* as evidence of the reasonableness of the antiwar cause, those photojournalists who had been following the march all day knew to seek out march organizer Bestor Cram, whose big smile revealed his satisfaction at having played an instrumental role in creating an opportunity to publicize the veterans' antiwar message while keeping protestors safe from the kind of telephoned threat he had received Thursday night, and Hart Perry, the head filmmaker in the tricorn hat who had decided to get arrested himself while continuing to film under the large lights called sun guns that the filmmakers had thought to bring with them (Figures 18 and 19).[85]

"The arrest," Bestor Cram later explained, "was a guarantee that the in cident was not going to go unnoticed."[86]

Many of those people who had already shown support by coordinating and providing meals or performing as the Vietnamese victims in VVAW-NE's mock search-and-destroy missions in Concord stayed on the Green in order to get arrested. Other people who had come to the Green to show their

Figure 19. Filmmaker Hart Perry continuing to film while getting arrested on the Green. Photographed by Ted Polumbaum. Courtesy of the Newseum Collection.

support for individual veterans also decided to get arrested, while some, such as Betty Levin, had already decided in consultation with the veterans not to get arrested because they were critically important in carrying out complicated logistics behind the scenes.[87]

"You know who showed up?" Pete Wilson exclaimed, recalling the arrests years later, "my flight instructor!" Perhaps recalling Pete's frustration during those years after high school when his height precluded him from enlisting and attending officer flight school, she decided to get arrested alongside her former pupil.[88]

Some stayed with a veteran on the Green even when they did not agree with his views about the war.

"I didn't think you had a big enough perspective to be able to see whether it was right or wrong," one man said to his younger brother about why he came down to the Green that night. But, he added, "I thought you needed support."[89]

While the VVAW-NE leadership could celebrate having found a way to be heard by the public and individual veterans could appreciate the support of even those family and friends who were not antiwar activists, the wounded,

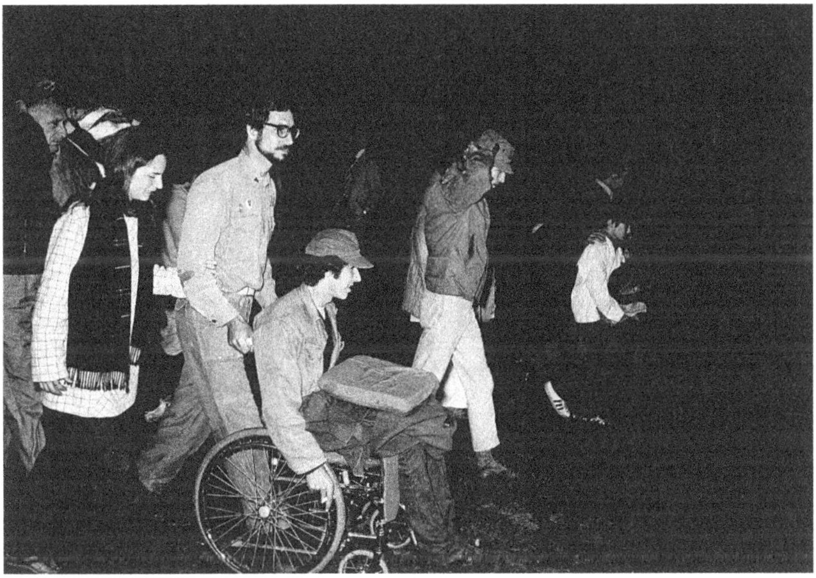

Figure 20. Joseph Baratta wheeling a wounded veteran to the buses. Photographed by Ted Polumbaum. Courtesy of the Newseum Collection.

whose presence had done so much to prove the lie of memorials that celebrate warrior immortality, were finding themselves excluded.[90]

"Stand aside," the chief later recalled telling one of the wheelchair-bound veterans. "When the time comes that we can put you on the bus, we will do it."[91]

In actuality, he had no intention of arresting anyone who was wounded.

"Obviously, we couldn't put him on the bus," he later conceded, referring to a wheelchair-bound veteran, although whether he was referring to the physical difficulty of such a feat or his sense that it would make the Lexington Selectmen and the local police look unreasonable is unclear.[92]

Joseph Baratta and his wife tried accompanying a wounded veteran to the bus in the hope the police would agree to arrest him, but their attempt failed, and they were forced to get on board without him (Figure 20).

However, twenty-two-year-old Phillip Lavoie of North Dighton, Massachusetts, a double amputee, would not take no for an answer.

"God damn it, I earned the right to be arrested," he exclaimed when the police turned him away. "I want to go on that bus!"[93]

Phil was determined that no one else would have to do what he had done in Vietnam.

"We did some things over there," he had explained to a reporter during VVAW's protest in DC, "that I can't even tell my mother."[94]

"After I was evacuated to Japan," he continued, "I had to see a psychiatrist, not so much because of my legs, but because of the nightmares about some things our unit had done to the Vietnamese."[95]

In order to demonstrate that he could get on the bus unassisted, Phil pulled himself out of his wheelchair and supported himself on his two prosthetic legs with the assistance of his hand braces.

"You gotta take him," the lawyer assisting the veterans said to one of the policemen he knew.

"We don't want to," the officer responded.

"You've gotta take him," the lawyer insisted.[96]

When the officer finally agreed, the crowd erupted in applause. Abandoning his wheelchair on the Green, Phil pulled himself onto the bus.[97]

While the chief continued to refuse to arrest other men confined to wheelchairs, he did allow children to get on the bus with their parents, prompting all of the photojournalists on the Green to photograph young kids taken in hand or on their parents' shoulders as they were escorted by helmeted police. The fact that the Lexington police would round up parents with young children in tow was an indication of how far they were willing to go to cleanse the sacred space after what the chairman of the Board of Selectmen regarded as its defilement, even as they stopped short of arresting the war wounded.[98]

"It was symbolic," Joseph Baratta later explained of the parents' willingness to keep their children with them on the Green. "They had to arrest the entire population!"

Because his own wife was with him and got arrested, Joseph was not aware that another segment of the population, in addition to the wounded, was also at least partially left out.

"A lot of women didn't get arrested because they had to go home to stay with their children," one Lexington woman later lamented.[99]

As Noam Chomsky said of his own marriage at that time, there was a "a kind of division of labor." Men went to work and women cared for the family. While he had already been arrested somewhere between four and six times by his estimation, his wife was only able to get arrested for her first time on the Green because one of their children was finally old enough to watch her siblings.[100]

In total, 104 Lexington men were arrested and 62 Lexington women. The ratios were similar for the residents of the nearby towns of Concord and Lincoln: five Concord and five Lincoln men got themselves arrested, whereas only three Concord and two Lincoln women did.[101]

"I didn't go back [to the Green] that night," one woman recalled, "because my husband took up our involvement after that."[102]

If the women in and around Lexington wanted to support the veterans, that was at least in part because they felt a kinship with them. One recalled being drawn to them because they too had not been able to control their own destinies.

"You're victims," one of the women who was not able to get arrested on account of having to watch her children later remembered telling one of the veterans.[103]

Another local woman who cooked for the veterans later described this kind of volunteer work as something that "helped us keep our sanity . . . when we had small children and weren't working full time."[104]

With only the two school buses running continuous loops between the Green and the makeshift jail at the town garage just over a mile away on Bedford Street, the mass arrest proceeded slowly. Finally, at 4 a.m., without any forewarning and with thirty or so veterans still on the Green, including two paraplegics and two other people in wheelchairs, as well as about seventy civilians, all eagerly awaiting arrest, the chief of police determined that the holding facility was full and gave the signal to his officers to stop. The protestors remaining were so bitterly disappointed to think they were not going to be arrested that they sought alternative ways of gaining access to the makeshift jail. One participant offered police his VW minibus so that they could arrest more people, but his offer was declined.[105]

"I believe if we drive down there we'll get in," one Lexington resident suggested.

"I think you probably could," a policeman standing nearby concurred.[106]

And so they did.

While the initial Boston-area newspaper headlines screamed in large type "500 Antiwar Vets Arrested on Lexington Green," in one case, and "458 Seized in Lexington," in another, the official number of people arrested and how many of them were veterans is impossible to determine exactly. Even if the court records had survived, they would not likely indicate which of those arrested were veterans. While newspapers could only estimate that approximately 100 to 150 of those arrested were part of VVAW, it seems certain that the total number of people arrested was around 400. According to Lexington police, 410 people in total were arrested, excluding juveniles, while the number of adults' names printed in the local newspaper the following week was 396. Either way, the Battle Green arrest was (and to date remains) the largest mass arrest in the Commonwealth's history.[107]

After waiting in long lines at the town garage, the protestors who did get arrested gave their adopted Revolutionary War names and their birthdates of April 18 or 19, 1775, to the court officials stationed there (the difference in dates a reminder that Longfellow's attempt to sacralize April 18 and not the day of the actual fighting was not entirely successful). Some chose to pay a fine so they could be released immediately. Most slept on the hard, grease-slicked floor for the few remaining hours of the night. When the judge of Middlesex District Court obtained permission to open on a Sunday, they waited in the town garage the long six hours it took to ferry everyone to court in alphabetical order and process their cases. During the wait, the veterans were finally able to perform guerrilla theater in Lexington, this time with the eyes of the public more securely on them. On its front page and above the fold, the *Boston Herald Traveler* ran a large photograph of the veterans in a clearing of the town garage putting on "an impromptu skit" of another deadly interrogation.[108]

Meanwhile, plenty of civilians outside of the garage found supportive ways to stay involved. The Bedford Peace Action Committee had already raised $273.25 from Bedford residents for the purchase of oranges, cereal, eggs, doughnuts, and coffee, which committee members had planned to serve Sunday morning on the Green or in Tower Park. Because Don Carrico was incarcerated, Betty Levin took charge. She coordinated thirty Bedford residents who showed up at the town garage to feed the protestors breakfast before she went back to the task of trying to get the Port-O-San company to come out to Lexington on a Sunday and empty the portable toilets the veterans had rented.[109]

"It was so awesome," Don, who just months earlier had felt completely isolated at college, later recalled. "Just to do all that food that they did for us was incredible, to get arrested with us, and donate money. It was mind boggling."

"I'm telling you, they were very welcoming," Joseph recalled of Lexington's residents. "People were really generous. Good food! We were never hungry."

Other area residents lined the walkway leading to the court's entrance back in Concord's Monument Square. Pleased to have the support and aware the media were also present, the veterans stayed in character, clasping their

Figure 21. Protestors enter Middlesex District Court in Concord's Monument Square. *Boston Herald Traveler* photo archives at the Boston Public Library.

hands behind their heads as they entered the courthouse (Figure 21). As serious as their message of being prisoners of the war was, Joseph Baratta and many other of the veterans could not help grinning as they passed through lines of applauding supporters.[110]

"Hell, that's the only welcome home I ever fucking got, to tell you the truth," one veteran later recalled of the cheers that meet him on the courthouse steps.[111]

No one was cheered more loudly than Phil Lavoie, who was confronted with the task of entering a building that was not handicapped accessible.[112]

"It almost broke your heart to watch the young man who could not use either of his legs trying to hobble to the second-floor courtroom in Concord," one woman later recalled. "He didn't ask for any help and the people backed away and let him do it on his own as they knew this meant so much to him."[113]

When the court proceedings began, the protestors learned that the injunction had never been invoked. They had been arrested for disorderly conduct after all, even as they had done nothing more than peacefully stay on the Lexington Battle Green. The young Lexington lawyer who had volunteered his assistance Saturday afternoon immediately conferred with the prosecution and worked out that the protestors would plead *nolo contendere* to the charge of violating a town bylaw if prosecutors would drop the disorderly charge. *Nolo contendere* is a way of accepting a conviction of guilt without admitting to being guilty. While Lexington law stipulated that the violation of a bylaw was fineable up to fifty dollars, the judge settled on five dollars, an amount he later explained setting as the equivalent of one night's lodging.[114]

One arrested Lexington resident was so disgusted with the Vietnam War and so inspired by the VVAW protest in Washington, DC, the month before, during which veterans had thrown away their war medals, that he tried to pay the five-dollar fine with his two World War II medals, the Distinguished Flying Cross and the Air Medal.

"Here," he said to the sergeant, "what are these worth?"

The sergeant's reply was reported the next day in the *Boston Globe*, which had learned from VVAW that participating in combat is not always the great honor the nation's war memorials insist it is.

"Sorry," he answered, "they aren't really worth much."[115]

While the World War II veteran was able to hand over five dollars, the majority of the arrested Vietnam veterans, many of whom like Bestor were protesting the war full-time while living off of the unemployment benefits to which they were entitled, could not.[116]

"I didn't have five dollars!" one veteran later exclaimed, noting how very young he was in 1971. "Where was I going to get five dollars?"[117]

In another gesture the veterans would later recall as healing their feelings of disillusionment about their country, the civilians waiting outside to cheer each bus's arrival started up a collection, amassing twelve hundred dollars with which to pay all of the veterans' fines.[118]

"It felt so cathartic to hear that some citizens paid our misdemeanor fine," the girlfriend who had been so afraid of getting arrested recalled later.[119]

Most important, the organization that the *Boston Globe* had relegated to the eighteenth page of the newspaper just two months before was featured Sunday morning on the front page above the fold with the photograph of the wounded veterans leading the march over the Old North Bridge seemingly accompanied by the Concord Minute Man Statue. The *Globe* also ran a lengthy magazine story about VVAW-NE's trip to Washington, DC, as well as a cartoon that captured how well the veterans had aligned their efforts to end the Vietnam War with the efforts of the American colonists to secure their independence. The cartoon depicts the veterans as the three Revolutionary War soldiers in Archibald Willard's well-known painting *The Spirit of '76* (Figures 22 and 23). (1775 is the date celebrated in Massachusetts as the nation's birth, but the rest of the nation recognizes the year the Declaration of Independence was signed.) On a ten-by-thirteen-foot canvas he painted in time for the nation's centennial celebration in 1876, Willard depicted two drummers, one wearing a tricorn hat, and a fife player whose head is wrapped in a bloodied bandage, marching across a smoke-covered Revolutionary War battlefield. A flag with thirteen stars flies behind them, and a wounded soldier lying on the ground salutes them. The cartoonist quoting Willard's painting put the Vietnam Veterans Against the War in the same colonial-era clothing, including a tricorn hat like the ones Jen Levin and Hart Perry had worn to the march. But rather than show the veterans resolutely facing a traditional war, he had them being shepherded at gunpoint by a man whose hat is labeled "Lexington Selectmen." If the veterans were unable to use their musical instruments to rally beleaguered but brave troops, that was because they had their hands clasped behind their heads in the same pose they had adopted on the Green and repeated upon entering court. They were prisoners, under arrest, the cartoon's caption explains, "for disorderly conduct." The cartoon ridicules the chairman of the Board of Selectmen's contempt for

Figure 22. Archibald Willard, *The Spirit of '76* (c. 1875). Courtesy of Marblehead, Massachusetts.

the Vietnam veterans by depicting him as tiny in stature and outfitting him like a greedy Monopoly banker. In contrast, it makes heroes of the veterans by putting them quite literally in the shoes of the nation's founders, which is precisely why so many civilians wanted to get arrested alongside of or otherwise help them.[120]

But it was the photograph of Phil Lavoie descending the steps with difficulty in front of the sign that designates the building as "District Court" that became the image Americans outside of New England saw of Operation POW (Figure 24). It ran with various captions in different newspapers around the country, each describing the protest in the exact way VVAW-NE presented it. The site of the mass arrest was where the "first battle of the Revolutionary

. . . for disorderly conduct

Figure 23. Vietnam veterans are *The Spirit of '76*. Cartoon by and courtesy of Paul Szep.

War" took place. "He surrendered at Lexington," another newspaper explained. That the veteran reenacting the Revolutionary War was gravely wounded only underscored his heroism in fighting for the Vietnam War's end as well as the state's immorality in not ending the war that had harmed him. In many newspapers, Phil's photo ran on the front page above the fold and next to articles reporting the death of America's most decorated World War II hero, Hollywood star Audie Murphy, in a plane crash. The end of World War II–era militarized masculinity seemed complete.[121]

Two hundred years earlier, in the days that had followed the 1775 massacre on the Green, Patriot leaders worked hard to keep the horrible incident

Figure 24. Phillip Lavoie descends Middlesex District Court House steps. Boston Public Library/United Press International.

before a shocked public's eyes, using it to make the case that the colonists needed a means to protect their families.

"The barbarous murders committed on our innocent brethren have made it absolutely necessary," Patriot leader Dr. Joseph Warren wrote to the Committees of Safety, "that we immediately raise an army to defend our wives and our children from the butchering hands of an inhuman soldiery."[122]

And, indeed, two months later, after colonial leaders learned the British forces occupying Boston were planning to send troops out of the city to occupy the surrounding hills and thereby take control of the harbor, the colonists established the Continental Army. On June 15, 1775, George Washington was unanimously elected commander-in-chief.

In 1971, the veterans were also keen to fuel the flames of indignity, in their case about their treatment in Lexington and, by extension, about the Vietnam War. When everyone had finally been processed at court, the veterans accepted rides from local residents back to the First Parish in Lexington, where they ate another dinner provided by area supporters and discussed how to proceed. If they wanted to continue to reverse Paul Revere's ride and garner news coverage of their efforts, their next stop would have to be Charlestown, from where Revere had set out on horseback and where two months later the Battle of Bunker Hill took place. The problem was that they should have arrived there hours ago and now it was starting to rain. Even after Lexington residents offered to drive the veterans there so they could get back on schedule, there was good reason to hesitate. The residents of Charlestown, a working-class Irish enclave since the 1860s, did not have the same ability to protect their children from the draft that the wealthy residents of Concord and Lexington did, whether by paying college tuition or exercising political clout with the local draft board. Approximately 80 percent of the men who served in Vietnam were from working-class or poor backgrounds, and thus young men from working-class Boston neighborhoods such as Charlestown were four times more likely to die in Vietnam than young men from Lexington and other affluent Route 128 suburbs. The veterans were worried residents might think along the same lines Pete Wilson's father once had and perceive the veterans to be dangerously undermining troop morale.[123]

"We did not necessarily have a feeling that this was a group of supportive people," Bestor later remembered worrying about Charlestown's residents.[124]

The veterans floated the idea of skipping Charlestown and meeting up on Memorial Day for the march's closing event on Boston Common. However, once again, the pull to reenact the events of the nation's birth proved strong.

"We've already begun the Battle of Lexington—the whole country knows it," a wounded veteran living at the Bedford VA hospital argued, invoking the same collapsed time that had structured the entire march. "So let's go on to Bunker Hill."[125]

CHAPTER 6

Memorial Day

After devoting Saturday and Sunday to protesting the Vietnam War on memorialized Revolutionary War battlefields, the veterans' plan for Monday was to appropriate for their antiwar cause the day set aside to honor soldiers killed in the nation's wars. The afternoon of the final day of their march would be devoted to hosting what, in the flier advertising it, VVAW-NE called a "Memorial Day Alternative." Instead of the traditional Memorial Day rituals performed in cities and towns across the country—hearing a roll call of the war dead, decorating the graves of dead soldiers, listening to Taps—participants could join antiwar veterans for what the flier promised would be theater, folk music, and a speech by Eugene McCarthy, who for a second time was planning to seek the Democratic presidential nomination on an antiwar platform.[1]

Bestor Cram and VVAW-NE's other chapter coordinator had spelled out the reason for offering the public a different way of observing Memorial Day in a letter to the editor of the *Boston Globe* published a week earlier. VVAW fervently hoped, they wrote, that the country would "cease to build memorials to death," of which Operation POW was essentially a tour, "and begin to glorify life." VVAW-NE's flier for its Memorial Day Alternative thus featured a photograph of a happy little boy as a means of posing a question: would honoring him on some future Memorial Day be worth the loss of his life on the battlefield? While they did not announce it in their flier, the veterans planned to have a Gold Star mother memorialize her own once little boy by denouncing both the war and the holiday that, while mourning his loss, also attempted to make glorious what for her was his senseless death in Vietnam. The Alternative would take place, the veterans' flier announced, on Boston Common, where they would finish their reverse march of Paul Revere's route a mere mile from the Patriot's family home, since 1905 a popular museum memorializing the silversmith's artisan and political careers as well as the departure point of his April 18, 1775, ride.[2]

The veterans had asked one of VVAW's most decorated and outspoken members to serve as the master of ceremonies or MC. Named after his father Ernest Sachs Jr., a professor of clinical neurosurgery at Dartmouth Medical School who had tended the wounded on the beaches of Normandy, the veterans' MC went by the nickname Rusty on account of his reddish blonde hair. Rusty's grandfather, Ernest Sachs, was the world's first professor of neurological surgery. Rusty's great-great-uncle discovered Tay-Sachs disease. Thus, when Rusty flunked out of Harvard in 1964, he decided that joining what was arguably the military's most demanding branch would be the only way to measure up to his family's achievements. It would also provide him with training in the activity that, like Pete Wilson, he loved most: flying. Rusty was proud to be assigned to the Ugly Angels, a Marine heavy helicopter squadron charged with transporting troops, and he quickly rose through the ranks to captain. His initial enthusiasm for the war, his ready smile, and good looks won him a starring role in one of the Marines' promotional films.

"Despite all the killing you find in a war, we save a lot of lives too," Rusty had enthused, sitting at the flight controls and grinning into the camera. "That's the main mission of this helicopter."[3]

When actor Robert Mitchum, famous for his roles in *The Story of G.I. Joe*, *Gung Ho!*, and numerous other war films, needed someone to pick him up at Chu Lai and take him around Vietnam to visit the troops, Rusty got that job too (Figure 25). With his closely cropped hair, a holstered pistol at his hip, and a gunner riding behind him, Rusty looked perfectly comfortable handing the six-foot-one Hollywood epitome of a tough American soldier an Ugly Angels patch. The message of the Ugly Angels' distinctly devilish face crowned with a yellow halo is clear: Rusty's unit was intent on saving their comrades' lives (being "angels"), but they were also willing to do whatever it took to accomplish their missions (because they were tough or "ugly").[4]

Rusty would be joined on the Boston Common stage by Patricia Simon, her title of Gold Star mother an honorific given by the U.S. military to a female citizen who has lost her child in an American war. The story Pat repeatedly told about her son David was of a young man who felt pressured to be one of the tough warriors he saw in the kinds of movies Robert Mitchum made and who are celebrated in larger-than-life statues at America's memorialized battle sites. David had enlisted in the Army shortly after she and her husband separated in 1965.

Figure 25. Rusty Sachs with Robert Mitchum in Vietnam (c. 1967).

"His father wanted him to go into the military to become a man," Pat would later explain.[5]

But for both David and Rusty, it had become increasingly difficult to ignore the immorality of the war.

"Whenever any prisoners were taken," Rusty explained in his testimony at VVAW's Winter Soldier Investigation, "the crewmen in the helicopters would blindfold the prisoners, holding the blindfold on with heavy wire, safety wire. They'd bind their hands, bind their feet and maybe bind them into a fetal position and upon landing, rather than releasing them so they could walk off the aircraft, they'd throw them out, get the grunts to mark how far they could throw them and have little contests. This was done with officers observing, at least all company grade officers," he continued. "There may have been a major present too."

Asked how many Vietnamese he had seen thrown this way, Rusty thought it was a "two-digit number, somewhere between 15 and 50 probably."

A lieutenant at the time, Rusty had tried to justify what was happening.

"Well, there's somebody senior to me here and I guess if this wasn't SOP he'd be doing something to stop it," Rusty recalled thinking, referencing standard operating procedure.

There were also, he testified, discussions about prisoners being thrown out midflight.

"We were given very specific oral orders from the colonel on down," Rusty explained in Detroit. "When you are carrying VCs—Viet Cong suspects—you don't count them when you get in the airplane, you counted them when you get out of the airplane because the numbers don't always jibe. And if one of them happens to get scared of heights and decides to get out, or something like that, or if he looks like maybe he's going to try and raise some shit in the belly of the aircraft and the crewman has to kick him out, that's none of your business; it didn't really happen because you counted the men when they got off."[6]

Rusty was given more dangerous work to do when he took the bold step of complaining to his superiors about what was happening on his helicopter and what he worried might be happening on others.

"They put him on night medevac only. Night medevac is a death sentence," another veteran recalled bitterly years later, using the military term for medical evacuations. "He was hit thirty or forty times. He was shot down two or three times. This does something to your nerves."[7]

But it was not being shot at that had the biggest impact on Rusty's nerves, according to him. It was the systemic racism. When calls would come in for a medevac, if the wounded person was Vietnamese, Rusty's major, the operations officer of the squadron, would not let him leave the base, even despite the fact that the United States was supposedly fighting the war to protect their South Vietnamese allies.

"Now hold it a minute. It's bad weather out there and you're going to get your asses killed and these are only ARVNs," Rusty remembered him saying, using the acronym for the Army of the Republic of Vietnam. "They aren't Americans. These are gook Marines. We don't need 'em. We're not going to risk ourselves for them."[8]

As the veterans had just illustrated in Concord's Monument Square, racial epithets, including "gook" and others, were sometimes used in the American military to express the conviction that a person does not deserve to live.

"When I got back from Nam, I woke up screaming every fucking night," Rusty told one of Hart Perry's film crews, not mincing words in describing how horrifying he continued to find the military's methods.[9]

Pat Simon's son David became convinced the war was immoral during basic training. Before shipping out for Vietnam, the nineteen-year-old told his mother that he dreamed of going AWOL. Being absent without leave was and remains punishable with dishonorable discharge, forfeiture of all military pay, imprisonment, and even the death penalty.

"I knew he wasn't kidding. I knew he hated it," Pat later recalled. She immediately got in touch with the American Friends Service Committee, a Quaker group working for peace.

"I wanted some male support for Davie to go AWOL."

When the Friends counselor had asked, Pat told him what her son wanted to do for a career.

"He'll never be able to be a teacher if he goes AWOL," the counselor replied.

Pat had been at her part-time job at a local women's college when a soldier arrived in formal military attire. At first, Pat pretended not to see him and kept on typing. She told herself she had to finish a letter for her boss.

"Just stop a minute," her boss told her, putting her hands over Pat's. "There's somebody here to see you."

"I just knew," Pat recalled sorrowfully.

After just three weeks in Vietnam, Pat's son had been killed.

"It was a search-and-destroy mission. It was an area that was supposed to be clear but it was not. Something was thrown in," Pat was later told by her son's friend Gordon, a fellow soldier serving in the same unit. "Something came in and everybody dropped to the ground, but then Davie stood up. Gordon said he tried to reach him to tell him to get down. You're supposed to get down. Everybody knows you're supposed to get down. I have the feeling he just wanted to end it. Because it was so unlike him to even think about killing somebody."

After returning from Vietnam, Rusty had decided to go back to school, was readmitted to Harvard, and began to speak out against the war, writing a letter to *Playboy* in defense of Lieutenant Calley, who had been charged with the murder of 109 residents at My Lai.[10]

"He may be some kind of homicidal pervert," Rusty repeated a few months later to the *Harvard Crimson*. "But if he is, the Army picked him to take all the blame. There are a whole lot of people who have done the same shit Calley did and thought it was the best thing for their country."[11]

VVAW national spokesman John Kerry tracked Rusty down in Harvard's married student housing and persuaded him to testify at the Winter Soldier Investigation in Detroit. Later, once VVAW formed a New England chapter,

Rusty teamed up with VVAW-NE den mother Betty Levin to fundraise for VVAW-NE's trip to Washington, DC. Betty would arrange for someone in Concord, Lincoln, Lexington, or another liberal suburban enclave to host Rusty and another veteran or two for a screening of the Winter Soldier film footage in which Rusty was featured prominently on account of being a senior officer.

"He'd testify in the movie," VVAW-NE's executive secretary later explained of Rusty's role. "It would be over and he'd get up and be right there in the living room. It was very effective."[12]

After Rusty's remarks at these fundraisers, the veterans would open the floor to questions. Someone would always want to know if they thought Lieutenant Calley was guilty.

"We're not interested in indicting individuals," the veterans would reply, "but in indicting the system which encourages this kind of thing, and the silent people who let it go on."[13]

Still, it was hard for the veterans not to feel responsible.

"I still carry within me the guilt of not having done anything to stop it," Rusty reported years later in reference to the treatment of the Vietnamese.[14]

After testifying in Detroit at VVAW's Winter Soldier Investigation, Rusty gave his medals to a Boston production of *Hair*, happy to be rid of awards handed out for participation in an immoral war. When it became clear there would be an opportunity during Operation Dewey Canyon III in DC for other veterans to disburden themselves but in a highly public way that would educate the people about the Vietnam War, he decided he would also discard his military ribbons.

"We discussed for a long time how we were going to return our medals," Rusty later explained, "whether we'd drop them into shitcans filled with blood . . . or carry them up to Congress in body bags. Finally we decided the best way to show our contempt was by throwing them over the fence they'd put up in front of the Capitol steps."[15]

When Rusty was two or three back in the line from those steps with his ribbons in hand, someone had handed him two medals. One was the Distinguished Flying Cross, awarded to members of the U.S. Air Force for "heroism or extraordinary achievement while participating in an aerial flight." The other was a Silver Star, the Air Force's third-highest decoration for valor in combat.

"I recalled two friends who had gotten killed recently, both in senseless accidents, not as a result of direct enemy action," Rusty later recounted. "One had gone down in the water with his helicopter, got out of the helicopter and was treading water and someone tried to hoist him out by hovering so low that he drowned in the downwash of the rotor blades. The other had been steered by radar vectors to a landing zone in terribly bad weather and something messed up and he flew into the side of the hill and got killed."[16]

Stepping to the microphone at the medal ceremony in DC, Rusty displayed his rejection of the American invasion of Vietnam while also memorializing at the same time two American men who died not for their country but because of it.

"For Captain Roger P. Harrell, United States Marine Corps, this is the Silver Star."[17]

When he turned to hurl it over the fence, a photographer captured Rusty in his aviation jacket with his captain wings and Ugly Angels patch clearly visible. The Silver Star he was in the act of rejecting is outlined against the sky. Here was one of America's heroic officers protesting the Vietnam War in no uncertain terms. Gone was the proud grin on display in the photograph taken with Robert Mitchum. In the photograph, Rusty's face is contorted in pain (Figure 26).

"And for Major Bob Cramer, U.S. Marine Corps, this is a Distinguished Flying Cross."[18]

Rusty turned and hurled it and his own ribbons as well.

"It was like two hours before I could stop crying," he later recalled. "It was very, very, very heavy."[19]

By then, Rusty, like Bestor and so many other Vietnam veterans, had stopped cutting his hair as a means of signifying his new relationship to his military affiliations and achievements. In a reference to his newly grown halo of curls, Betty Levin called him not an "Ugly" but a "Botticelli angel." The formerly gung-ho Marine had become a man who could appreciate softness as a moral basis from which to act politically.[20]

"Don't you think this [broadcast] is going to be turned off and that people will disregard a lot of what you say?" a reporter had asked him in Detroit in reference to his long hair before reminding the audience that he was interviewing a Harvard man. "You're an intelligent fellow."

Rusty's answer spoke to the deep transformation he had recently undergone.

"For six years, my hair never got longer than a quarter of an inch, and I always swore I'd keep it that short," Rusty explained. "I like it long now. It feels nice."[21]

Figure 26. Rusty Sachs throws away a medal on the steps of the U.S. Capitol Building. Photographed by Bernard Martell.

In the spring of 1971, Rusty Sachs, Pete Wilson, Bestor Cram, Don Carrico, Ross Fenton, and the other antiwar veterans were redefining masculinity, viewing a much softer version of it as a more potent means of securing peace while channeling their toughness into their antiwar work. The teenaged boys of Lexington had understood as much when they had followed the veterans to the Battle Green. Pat Simon was convinced their new conception of manhood was saving lives.

"If I had known about that kind of support, I'd have saved my child, you know?" she later lamented. "Because that's what he needed: some masculine support. He couldn't betray his buddies, he couldn't betray his father, he couldn't have his mother ship him off, take him to Canada."

Pat's daughters were also deeply impressed by the power of so many long-haired, fatigue-clad young men united in their embrace of softness and love. On the trip home from DC, Pat's youngest daughter declared that she felt like she had "one thousand brothers," using the same loving designation the veterans did to refer to one another.

"It seemed a wonderfully logical place for me to be," Pat later said of her time protesting the war in the nation's capital with her surviving children and the veterans, "a way of giving meaning to my son's death by taking a stand against the war he hated."

After the medal-tossing ceremony in DC, Rusty had wondered how the government could not fail to be impressed by the veterans' emotional rejection of what the military considered the highest honors a man could receive and by the love and fellowship the veterans demonstrated for each other.

"We wouldn't have been surprised if somebody had said, 'Hey, Nixon just announced that all the troops will be out of Nam and back home by suppertime.' We would have believed it at that instance. We really would have. We thought we'd finally done it and we'd reached everyone."[22]

And yet on Memorial Day, six weeks after Operation DCIII, the war dragged on. More Americans were being killed and wounded, and more Vietnamese were dying trying to liberate their country. Fearing another protest would do no good, Rusty had decided not to march with the veterans over Memorial Day weekend. When one of Hart Perry's film crews caught up with him on Boston Common and asked if he was hopeful that the veterans had in fact made a difference that weekend, he hesitated.

"What can you really do to end the war?" Rusty sighed. "Most of us are getting to a point of frustration, where we're thinking maybe you can't."[23]

In the end, he had agreed to be the MC for the Memorial Day Alternative only because he knew he was VVAW's most recognizable member after John Kerry, to whom the veterans were determined not to hand over their march for fear that his new celebrity status would overshadow their collective efforts and draw attention away from their mobilization of American history and myth.[24]

Pat Simon, in contrast, was not willing to give up yet. She had gone to the Lexington Battle Green Saturday night determined to get arrested with the veterans. And while a developing head cold prevented her from staying to get arrested, lest she be prevented from speaking the next day on Boston Common, she had stayed long enough to see a local woman succeed in getting enough women on the Green to fill a large white cardboard sign with their signatures.

"I Don't Want To Be A Gold Star Mother," it said.[25]

Waiting for the veterans to march onto Boston Common, Rusty still did not know how they had fared Sunday night in working-class Charlestown, a part of Boston that had lost so many more sons in Vietnam than had the wealthy towns of Concord and Lexington and whose residents were as proud as the people of Concord and Lexington to live where people had fought and died in the American Revolution.[26]

In the days and weeks following the events of April 19, 1775, the Patriots had been so successful in painting a horrific picture of what had transpired in Lexington and Concord that over ten thousand men from Massachusetts, Connecticut, Rhode Island, and New Hampshire were inspired to join the new Continental Army, headquartered just outside of occupied Boston in Cambridge. Finding themselves surrounded, the British army decided to take control of Dorchester Heights and the hills of Charlestown, the two highest points overlooking Boston. When Dr. Joseph Warren, who had just been appointed a major general of the Continental Army, became aware of this plan, he and other military leaders ordered 3,500 colonial troops to fortify Charlestown under the cover of darkness. When daylight broke on the morning of June 17, the colonists discovered that as a result of misunderstanding their orders or the confusion of working in the dark, they had not fortified Bunker Hill, Charlestown's highest point, but Breed's Hill, which is lower in elevation and closer to the harbor, then full of recently arrived British naval vessels. Daylight also exposed the Americans' entrenchment to the British. Soon the roar and hiss of cannonballs fired from the British ships filled the air. A thirty-five-year-old colonist from Billerica, Massachusetts, was instantly decapitated when a nine-pound cannonball hit him. Stopping only to bury him, the Americans continued to dig fortifications.[27]

By early afternoon, twenty-eight long boats carrying nearly fifty Regulars each had crossed the river from Boston to Charlestown. According to local legend, the entrenched Americans troops were told to wait until the advancing British were close enough to "see the whites of their eyes" before they started firing. In the meantime, American snipers were able to use the cover of Charlestown's many buildings to unleash their own deadly violence until the British decided to set fire to the town. John Quincy Adams would later remember being seven years old and watching with his mother from a hill near their home in Braintree as billows of black smoke rose into the sky. Dr. Warren had recently saved the young boy's finger after a bad accident. Now little John's father was far away in Philadelphia, a delegate to the Continental Congress, leaving his son terrified that the British army would invade the countryside and "butcher them in cold blood."[28]

The Americans were able to rebuff the British army's first two attempts to scale Breed's Hill. The third time the British advanced, however, they succeeded with four hundred reinforcements. Dr. Warren, who had insisted on fighting as a private, was killed with a gunshot to the head. The Adams's family physician was thirty-four years old. Low on ammunition after hours of fighting, the colonists resorted to throwing rocks and firing nails but were finally unable to keep the British from breaching their defenses. The British were so well trained with their bayonets that the colonists, who had few such weapons and were forced to use their muskets as clubs, could only retreat. When the smoke cleared, the British army had gained the ground for which it had fought, but half of its troops and more than half of their officers were dead or injured. Major Pitcairn, who had led the advance guard onto Lexington Green to such disastrous effect and who was in command of three hundred Marines in Charlestown, had been shot six times trying to advance up Breed's Hill. During the final advance, Pitcairn, like Dr. Warren, was shot in the head. He died several hours later. The victors, still in control of the city of Boston, buried their leader in the crypt at the Old North Church from which Dr. Warren had directed that the signal lanterns be flashed on the night of April 18, 1775. Dr. Warren's corpse, in contrast, was thrown into a shallow ditch on the battlefield after British troops, enraged and grief stricken over the loss of so many of their comrades, stripped the body of clothes and bayonetted it repeatedly.

But while the Americans lost the Battle of Bunker Hill, as it has traditionally been called, they put themselves in a better position to win what was now a full-scale war for American independence. There were not enough survivors from the British side left to pursue the colonists any further, and British troops remained confined to Boston. General Gage, who had orchestrated the march on Concord and Lexington, was soon removed of his command. And in subsequent fighting, the British were far more wary of the Americans than they would have been otherwise. Six years after the Americans prevailed at the Siege of Yorktown, they formerly declared themselves "we the people" in their Constitution.

On the evening before Memorial Day, the antiwar veterans had accepted the offer of a ride from their Concord and Lexington supporters. They asked to be dropped off in Sullivan Square so that they could proceed on foot to the massive obelisk that marks the site of the Battle of Bunker Hill and thereby ascertain the community's reaction (Map 6).[29]

Recalling the concerns voiced by so many of the VVAW marchers during Sunday's dinner in Lexington ("Was it gonna be food and acceptance or sticks and stones?"), Joseph Baratta was alarmed when he and another veteran walking along were stopped by two men identifying themselves as off-duty police officers.

"You think all cops are pigs, right?"

"You all smoke pot, right?"

"You think the war is wrong, right?"

Joseph was peppered with questions by the officers and the crowd that quickly formed around them. No, he replied, the Vietnam veterans did not think all cops were pigs and, yes, they did smoke pot once in a while. Then he used the march's framework and VVAW-NE's ability to continuously shift the American symbols it mobilized to make the veterans' case against the war.

"They're the Patriots," he argued of the Vietnamese, "and we're the Red Coats," he said of the Americans.

The comparison proved to be as effective in Charlestown as it had been in Concord and Lexington. According to the *Boston Herald Traveler*, the residents who had come out to greet the veterans began "cheering and applauding."[30]

"They were very moral, hard-working Americans. We met!" Joseph later exclaimed exultantly.

When one of Hart Perry's film crews caught up with John Kerry as he made his way uphill to the Bunker Hill Monument, VVAW's national spokesman also noted the warm embrace the veterans were enjoying.

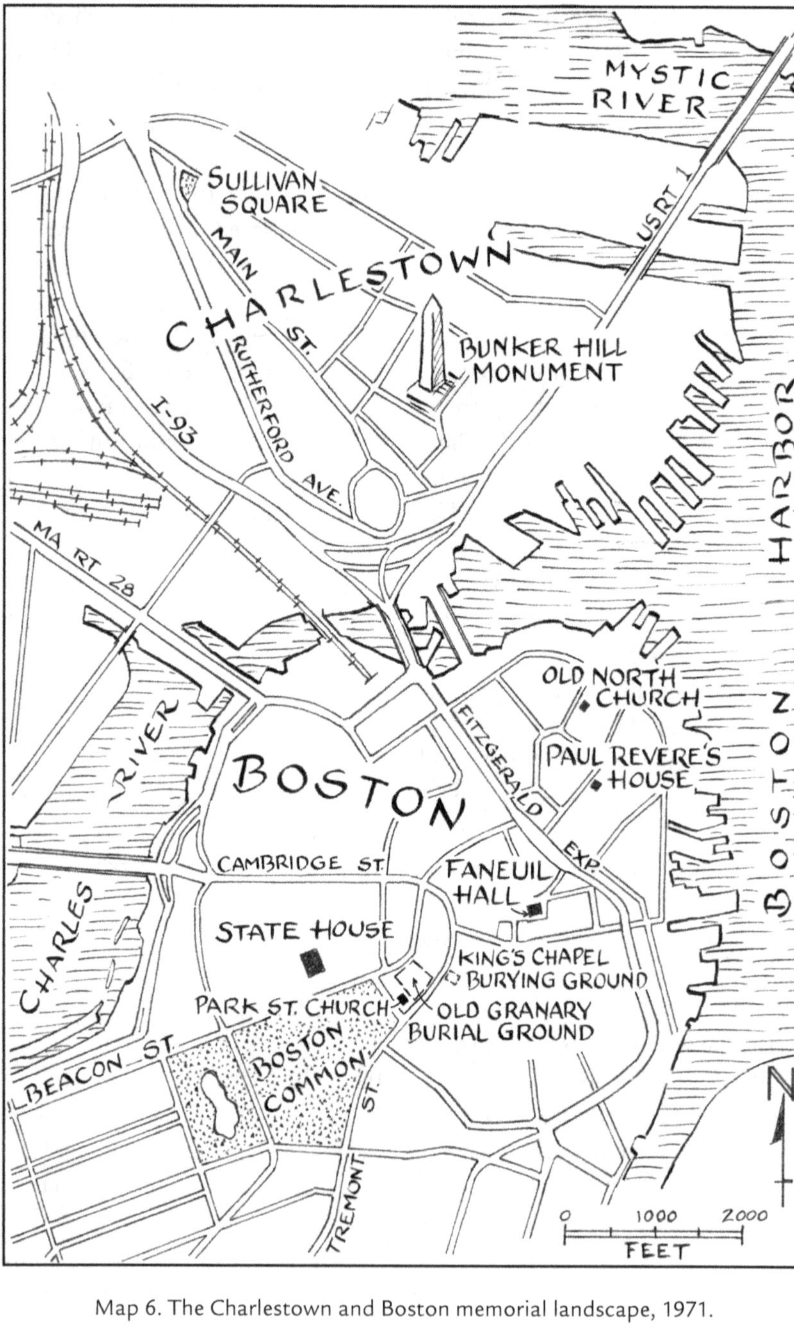

Map 6. The Charlestown and Boston memorial landscape, 1971.

"Everybody's been nice," he marveled. "They've been handing out soda and smiling and waving peace signs."[31]

Begun in the Civil War era as a day set aside to acknowledge the horrific cost of war, Memorial Day was supposed to unite communities through shared mourning. On account of Congress's decision in 1968 to move Memorial Day to the fourth Monday of May starting in 1971, it risked becoming an opportunity to enjoy a long weekend as spring turns into summer. On the first long Memorial Day weekend, VVAW reaffirmed the day's original meaning, uniting different classes around the shared sense that, given the terrible losses being incurred in Vietnam, ending the war was a goal worth fighting for.[32]

When the veterans emerged from the narrow streets lined with apartment buildings, they found themselves on a fifteen-acre expanse of grass that serves as a memorial site. In 1794, the King Solomon's Lodge of Free Masons had erected an eighteen-foot wooden column here topped with a gilt urn in honor of their slain Masonic brother, Dr. Joseph Warren. In 1822, when the owner of the memorial site announced plans to sell it, Daniel Webster and other prominent Boston residents formed the Bunker Hill Monument Association. Intent on honoring not an individual leader, as the Masons had done, but the role Massachusetts played in creating the world's greatest nation, they set out to build the biggest war memorial the country had ever seen. When the memorial cornerstone was laid in 1825, John Quincy Adams, whose broken finger Dr. Warren had saved from amputation, was president of the United States; however, he remained so traumatized by the death of his family's doctor that he could not bear to attend the elaborate ceremony. It took eighteen years to complete the 220-foot granite obelisk, of which the one at the Old North Bridge is its smaller sister by agreement between the Association and the town of Concord. It surpassed in height even a 160-foot monument to George Washington planned for Baltimore. (The obelisk erected in the District of Columbia in honor of George Washington was conceived of later.)[33]

"Its speech," Daniel Webster said at the dedication of the massive obelisk under which the Vietnam veterans assembled, "will be of patriotism and courage; of civil and religious liberty; of free government; of the moral improvement and elevation of mankind; and of the immortal memory of those who, with heroic devotion, have sacrificed their lives for their country."[34]

In a demonstration of that civil liberty, the veterans proceeded to repeat the actions they carried out upon their arrival in Lexington. Encircling the grassy portion of Charlestown's Memorial Square, they took turns dancing into the middle and ceremoniously discarding their weapons. In addition to once again singing "Give Peace a Chance" arm in arm, they sang an antiwar song Barbara Dane had first performed in 1970 at several different military bases in the United States.[35]

> I know I'm guilty, and I'm proud,
> I know I'm guilty, sing it louder.
> Don't try to tell me any lies,
> Cause you don't fool me with your jive![36]

The song gives the singer permission to attest without personal shame to involvement in American atrocities in Vietnam and further asserts that those involved should be proud of finally telling the truth about the war. The listener, in contrast, is initially imagined to be telling unspecified but easily imagined lies about the war, namely, that there are no atrocities being committed and that the war is a just one because it was being fought to save the South Vietnamese if not the entire world from communism. But after the singers' assertion that they cannot be fooled, the dishonest listener is discredited and everyone is free to reject further military orders and the nation's still ongoing attempts to erase the memory of American war violence. The chorus is a repetition of the word "insubordination" sung with each syllable emphasized equally. Having been insubordinate on the Lexington Green, the veterans gave the lyrics additional meaning. Yes, they had pled *nolo contendere* at Middlesex District Court, which was an assertion of "no contest" on the charge of breaking a Lexington bylaw and thus an admission of guilt. ("I know I'm guilty.") But they had pleaded as such in a declaration that they would no longer be lied to by the American government and by a culture that uses war memorialization to glorify death on the battlefield. ("You don't fool me with your jive!")

Prior to the march, the Metropolitan District Commission (MDC) had explained of Bunker Hill that "we don't let anyone camp there," citing a "standing rule" prohibiting it. However, at 9:30 p.m. on Sunday night, having seen the press coverage of the veterans' efforts, their subsequent arrest, and the hearty welcome extended to them in Charlestown, the MDC captain informed the veterans they could stay all night provided they turn off their sound system at 10 p.m. The veterans complied and remained vigilant about enforcing their code of peaceable behavior. When someone the newspaper described as a "local youngster" began "oinking" at one of the policemen keeping watch on the proceedings, a veteran retorted to the cheers of his fellow protestors, "You're the only pig here."[37]

The next morning, after carefully policing their camp site, the veterans mingled with the many Charlestown residents who appeared with breakfast.

"People, individuals, guys walking their dogs, came with ten cups of coffee," one veteran later recalled of that morning. "'Here is some coffee, boys. Here are some donuts. What do you want?' Really, it was extraordinary stuff."[38]

Taking note of the cross section of American classes coming together to end the war, a photojournalist took a picture of VVAW national spokesman John Kerry, sporting a pair of preppy moccasins that revealed his patrician background, next to an African American veteran whose bold plaid pants were the antithesis of Kerry's blue-blooded aesthetic (Figure 27). The two are united in the photograph by their shared commitment to the civil disobedience to which Ross Fenton and his slouch hat, also featured in the picture, speak. Like the American cowboys Hollywood celebrates for their commitment to a higher moral law than their own government's, the veterans had broken the law in order to right a moral wrong. The *Boston Herald* ran the photograph the next day, while the *Boston Phoenix* would call this diverse group of veterans' ability to draw residents out of the Charlestown multifamily buildings visible in the photograph's background VVAW's "greatest victory."[39]

Before setting out for their final march, the veterans met to review their plans at the foot of what is still the nation's tallest war memorial (Figure 28). Seeing the large crowd of exhausted but determined veterans, many of them visibly wounded and others wearing Purple Hearts, filmmaker Hart Perry was struck once again by how the veterans' presence immediately reframed a war memorial's meaning. Built to glorify the deadly battle waged here, the massive obelisk could not erase the horror of war John Quincy Adams remembered so well and to which the assembled veterans testified. Hart decided that in his documentary film about the march, he would use special effects to make the massive obelisk appear to crack, crumble, and fall (Figure 29). To make clear that it was imploding under pressure from the antiwar veterans' plea to stop building "memorials to death," he superimposed a still photograph of Pete Wilson, on the left, and two other veterans on the right.[40]

Don Carrico and one of the many wheelchair-bound veterans participating in the march took the lead as the veterans resumed their march in the same patrol formation they had used while traversing Minute Man National Historical Park. When the antiwar veterans crossed paths with a traditional

Figure 27. Ross Fenton and John Kerry at the foot of the Bunker Hill Monument. Courtesy of Associated Press.

Figure 28. Veterans hold final meeting at Bunker Hill Monument before marching to Boston. Courtesy of Associated Press.

Memorial Day parade comprising men in colonial-era dress and tricorn hats and led by a fife and drum, Hart Perry made sure to film the latter while continuing to compose in his head the film he was making about the antiwar veterans. Once in the editing studio back at Columbia University, he would make the traditional reenactors dissolve into the antiwar veterans as a means of expressing how patriotic he believed it was to express dissent about the Vietnam War.[41]

The route VVAW-NE chose from Charlestown to Boston Common, while not following Revere's footsteps, was very deliberately another walk through American history. The veterans stopped to perform a mock search-and-destroy mission in front of Faneuil Hall, where John Singleton Copley's portraits of John Hancock and Samuel Adams used to hang. Widely known as

Figure 29. The Bunker Hill Monument appears to crumble in Hart Perry's film of the march. Screenshot from *Veterans Against the War* (1971), directed by Hart Perry. Courtesy of Hart Perry.

the "Cradle of Liberty" in remembrance of the many speeches made there by Patriots in the years leading up to the American Revolution, it served as another powerful backdrop for the veterans in their aim to speak on behalf of the American people against the tyranny of their own government.[42]

After completing that performance and leafleting the large open space in front of Faneuil Hall, the veterans marched down a holiday-deserted Tremont Street, passing Kings Chapel Burying Ground on their left, where William Dawes is thought to be buried.[43]

"Patriot, Son of Liberty, and First Messenger," reads a plaque erected in 1899 by the Massachusetts Society of the Sons of the Revolution, "sent by Warren from Boston to Lexington on the night of April 18–19 1775 to warn Hancock and Adams of the coming of British troops."[44]

A few steps later, on their right, the veterans passed the Granary Burying Ground, where Dr. Warren's remains were reinterred after being dug up on Breed's Hill and identified by the artificial tooth Paul Revere had made him. (The doctor's remains were later moved again, first to a church in Boston and finally to his family's vault, each time conferring him anew with the status of a martyr.) Paul Revere and the two men he journeyed to Lexington to warn, John Hancock and Samuel Adams, are also buried here.

A few days earlier, this patriotic landscape might have reminded the Vietnam veterans now traversing it of the many promises their country had broken. But now, having been welcomed so warmly by so many, they were newly hopeful that their nation's most cherished myths might actually mean something. And thus, rather than marching to one of the many different military cadences VVAW had altered for their antiwar purposes ("Heighdy, heighdy, heighdy, ho! Richard Nixon's gotta go!"), they sang a Civil War–era song that is traditionally sung to express the nation's appreciation for its soldiers' efforts and its collective relief when a war is over.[45]

> When Johnny comes marching home again
> Hurrah! Hurrah!
> We'll give him a hearty welcome then
> Hurrah! Hurrah!
> The men will cheer and the boys will shout
> The ladies they will all turn out
> And we'll all feel gay
> When Johnny comes marching home.

"It was just us. There were hardly any members of the public there. It was totally unrehearsed," one veteran remembered. For the few moments they were out of the limelight, the veterans forgot the fatigue and the blisters they had accumulated over the many miles they had traversed on foot over the past three days and expressed their joy at being welcomed by so many who appreciated their attempts to realign the country with its most cherished values.[46]

"It always struck me, the symbolism of it," the veteran recalled of that moment. "What happens when Johnny comes marching home again? Well, here we were. We were marching home. And I remember it echoed off the walls of the bank buildings around us as we marched there. We sang that until we got back into the public again."[47]

Just the day before, Bestor had said in an interview with one of Hart Perry's film crews that Vietnam veterans could never feel at home again. But the love and acceptance the veterans received in Charlestown, perhaps more so even than the number of wealthy white suburbanites who occupied the

Lexington Green with them, had changed the veterans' minds. Maybe they could be at home in America after all. Yes, they had continued to run into opposition. (One man along their march route in Boston had called them "sons of bitches" and ordered them to "go fight the war where you're supposed to.") But the historic landscape they were traversing gave them the courage of their convictions at those moments when they worried support for their efforts might be flagging. They were as yet unaware how many people would attend their Memorial Day Alternative when they passed the last historic building en route to Boston Common. In 1831, one of the nation's traditional anthems, "My Country, 'Tis of Thee," debuted at Park Street Church with its famous exhortation, later taken up on the steps of the Lincoln Memorial by Dr. Martin Luther King Jr., to "let freedom ring." Moving forward resolutely from here, the veterans could see there were eight to ten thousand people awaiting their arrival on the Common.[48]

Purchased by the Massachusetts Bay Colony from a private citizen in 1634, Boston Common was originally a space for grazing cows, beating carpets, and practicing military drills. After the addition of promenades in the early nineteenth century, the banning of livestock in 1830, and the enclosure of the common by an ornamental iron fence in 1836, it became a city park. During the civil rights era and the Vietnam War, when Americans began to use centralized public spaces as protest sites, the Common became Boston's. In 1965, Dr. Martin Luther King Jr. led over twenty thousand people from Roxbury to a rally for civil rights on the Common. That same year, the Common was used to protest the Vietnam War for the first time. And while only one hundred protestors showed up, many times more people convened on Boston Common in 1969 for the Moratorium to End the War in Vietnam. Since then, however, the level of civilian antiwar activism in the United States had dramatically subsided. Only VVAW's performative brand of activism had succeeded in drawing attention back to the antiwar cause. While many had planned to gather on the Common after receiving the Memorial Day Alternative flier in the weeks leading up to the march, many times more people decided to come after reading the extensive press coverage of the veterans' standoff with the Lexington Selectmen. Those who had been arrested the night before on the Lexington Battle Green were awaiting the veterans' arrival wearing homemade POW pins that referenced both their status and the name of the veterans' operation. Others carried balloons inscribed with peace signs.[49]

Don Carrico led the veterans straight toward the densely packed throng.

Figure 30. Don Carrico leads the veterans onto Boston Common. Photo © Diana Mara Henry.

"They approached this mass of humanity," Joseph Baratta later recalled, still delighted years later at how many people had turned out to support the veterans, "and the humanity spread like the Red Sea of Moses. They just opened a lane" (Figure 30).[50]

Greeting the veterans like the patriotic heroes they had become that weekend, the crowd applauded and kept applauding for the amount of time it took all of the veterans to march onto the Common and into the clearing in front of a temporary stage they had arranged to have erected. There the veterans proceeded to repeat their weapons ceremony. This time, as they had planned that morning at the foot of the Bunker Hill Monument, they concluded by smashing their plastic M16s on the ground. This too was meant to be theater, but emotion took over. Many of the over two hundred veterans began to sob as they ground every last fragment of their plastic weapons under the heels of their well-worn combat boots, unloading the twinned burdens of grief and rage they had been carrying with them since serving in Vietnam.[51]

"I was crying," one veteran later recalled. "It was the first time I had ever really cried besides some drunken stupor. It was the first really awake tears that I had shed since coming back from Vietnam."[52]

With the shards of their weapons underfoot, the veterans grabbed each other and, arm in arm, began to jump en masse, yelling in unison.

"Peace now! Peace now! Peace now!"

The crowd watched silently, everyone sensing the importance of serving as the witnesses to the men's agony.[53]

"When I busted that M16, that was truly a cathartic moment in my life," one veteran later explained of how his anger and sadness were replaced with something new. "I had found my peers, my brothers. I found the place I was really accepted," he continued. "I knew I was solid."[54]

"It was absolutely therapeutic," a member of the film crew concluded of the gun-smashing ceremony. "They were not keeping everything inside and suppressing it. They were letting it out. And that's healing."[55]

Wearing an artificial flower tucked behind his ear in a demonstration of the faith he shared with the other antiwar veterans in the transformative potential of Flower Power, Rusty Sachs kicked off the speech and music portion of the celebration by asking the people assembled to reject the new version of Memorial Day that overlooks war's violence in order to celebrate the arrival of spring over a long weekend. What the veterans wanted, Rusty explained to the crowd's cheers, was to acknowledge war's horror by celebrating life instead of commemorating death on the battlefield.[56]

When it was her turn to speak, Gold Star mother Pat Simon simultaneously mourned the dead and honored the antiwar cause with a poem written in 1941 by Archibald MacLeish. "The young dead soldiers do not speak," she began. "Nevertheless, they are heard in the still houses: / who has not heard them?" Pat read slowly at first. She began to speak louder and more emphatically when, several lines later, the poem urges listeners to take action on behalf of the dead. "Whether our lives and our deaths were for / peace and a new hope or for nothing we cannot say, / it is you who must say this."[57]

After more speeches and a concert, Operation POW ended on schedule, even despite the delays caused when Lexington officials undertook the largest mass arrest in Massachusetts history. Pete Wilson walked through the fading light back to where he had parked his family's Land Rover on the edge of Boston Common. Some veterans had already hopped into the roofless vehicle in the hopes of securing a lift home. An animated young boy with a wide smile was standing close enough to the veteran's largest performance prop to be able to touch it, although whether he did so out of the desire to play with war equipment or admiration for the veterans' antiwar theater was not immediately clear. One of the photojournalists who had walked with

Figure 31. Veterans prepare to depart Boston Common in the Wilson family Land Rover. Photographed by Ted Polumbaum. Courtesy of the Newseum Collection.

the veterans from Concord to Lexington was also heading home. Seeing the veterans strike up a conversation with the boy, he took a picture (Figure 31). Operation POW might be over, but Vietnam Veterans Against the War would continue to educate the public about the Vietnam War, embracing their role as truth tellers uniquely qualified to enlighten America and America's future soldiers about the realities of war. The photographer was careful to frame the conversation so that the four letters Pete had spelled out in masking tape on the side of the Rover three long but glorious days earlier would serve as a caption for this last photograph taken of the march. Over the course of the past six weeks, "VVAW" had become a nationally recognized acronym for the country's most powerful antiwar group.[58]

In the weeks and months that followed, as some of VVAW-NE's leaders moved on to graduate school and other endeavors, new leaders came to the fore, and the chapter stayed active. In the fall of 1971, Joseph Baratta and other chapter members organized three days of testimony at Faneuil Hall they called Winter Soldier II. The 1,300-page typed transcript of the testimonies of

Figure 32. Record sleeve for the Winter Soldier II recording.
Private collection of Joseph Baratta.

seventy-three people made the case that, while the American public was being told that the war was "winding down," it was actually "being ruthlessly escalated" in the form of a brutal air war. Both a partial transcript and an audio recording of the testimonies of ten veterans, two of whom had been arrested on the Lexington Battle Green, were sent to every member of the Senate, House of Representatives, and Supreme Court. The recording, produced on 45 RPM seven-inch records, was sent out in paper sleeves imprinted on the front with a version of the cartoon of the Vietnam veterans that had been published in the *Boston Globe* after the mass arrest on the Lexington Battle Green (Figure 32).[59]

The three veterans marching abreast on the record sleeve are playing a fife and drum under the original American flag with its thirteen stars. This time, however, they did not need to be depicted wearing colonial-era clothing and tricorn hats; VVAW had already established itself as the newest incarnation of the Minute Men. Instead, the artist put a tremendous amount of energy into accurately rendering jungle fatigues to which are affixed patches that show the veterans' division (U.S. Army) and under what command they served (MACV). One of the veterans wears a helmet with a cover inked, as so many were in Vietnam, with little hash marks counting down to the last day of his tour. Another wears a boonie hat, while the third, being injured, has an eye patch held on by a bandage wrapped around his head. That they are marching as "an army for peace," in the words Bestor Cram intoned at the Old North Bridge, is evident by the peace signs drawn on the middle soldier's helmet cover and the medallion hung on a chain around his neck, as well as by the fact that all three of them have long hair, sideburns, and mustaches. By making one of the veterans African American, the artist insists that veterans from different backgrounds were united in their desire to see the war end even as the membership of VVAW-NE was, in reality, predominantly white. The letters on the middle drum name this organization of tough antiwar fighters using their by then famous acronym.

In December, Don Carrico and other members of VVAW-NE continued to bring attention to the ongoing air war with Operation Peace on Earth. This time, the antiwar veterans occupied the Statue of Liberty for forty-two hours. A photograph taken from a helicopter of the veterans sending the universal military signal of distress in the form of a massive upside-down American flag hung from Lady Liberty's crown ran in newspapers around the world. As with the Memorial Day weekend march, Don and the other antiwar Vietnam veterans continued to stage their concerns at the nation's most hallowed sites, reworking its sacred symbols and iconography.[60]

Finally, in 1973, President Richard Nixon signed the Paris Peace Accords. After agreeing to a ceasefire, North Vietnam sent home all 591 of its American prisoners of war. Two years later, the Vietnamese cemented their victory, reunifying their independent country under communist rule. For a time, it appeared that the deaths of over 58,000 American soldiers, 1,500,000 Vietnamese soldiers, and as many as two million civilians in a war that divided the American citizenry had taught the United States a valuable lesson. Yet fifty years after New England's antiwar veterans marched Paul Revere's route in reverse, the United States has troops around the globe, fighting in what has become a state of perpetual warfare. And thus VVAW continues its protests, noting on its website that "the struggle continues, perhaps these days more than ever."[61]

EPILOGUE

Memorializing the Vietnam War

A decade after VVAW members Rusty Sachs and Bestor Cram occupied the National Mall in Washington, DC, and then carried out Operation POW back in Massachusetts, they returned to DC together, and, as with the reverse Revere march, they documented their journey on film. The Vietnam Veterans Memorial had just been completed, although not yet dedicated. The veterans were not to be honored with a soaring memorial obelisk or with a larger-than-life statue that captured their physical and military prowess. In a radical departure from this tradition, the Vietnam Veterans Memorial is formed of stacked black granite blocks embedded into the side of an almost 500-foot-long V-shaped trench and etched with the names of the 57,939 American soldiers who died in Vietnam between 1955, when the United States first had military advisers in the country, and 1975, when communist forces captured the capital of what had been South Vietnam. (More names have since been added as records are revised.) One line of the V stretches toward the Washington Monument, the colossal obelisk dedicated in 1885 that dwarfs even the Bunker Hill Monument. The other stretches toward the temple-shaped Lincoln Memorial, inside of which sits the nineteen-foot-tall white marble statue of the Civil War–era president carved by the same artist who sculpted Concord's Minute Man Statue. In contrast to both of these, the Vietnam Veterans Memorial, or The Wall as its shape has made it popularly known, functions less as a source of pride about the nation's democracy and more as an expression of the nation's sorrow over the loss of so many in a war most Americans regret precisely because it did not reflect the ideals associated with the president who oversaw the nation's birth and the one who orchestrated its rebirth as a free country for all.[1]

The resulting film, *How Far Home: Veterans After Vietnam*, follows Rusty with his distinctive head of tousled curls as he descends into the Vietnam

Veterans Memorial. It is the Veterans Day before the memorial's dedication, and the camera has to push through a crowd of other veterans, many dressed in fatigues. Rusty has on the same flight jacket with its Ugly Angels patch that he was wearing when he stepped onto VVAW's makeshift stage in front of the Capitol Building and threw away two medals he dedicated to men who died in flight accidents in Vietnam.

As Bestor's camera rolls, Rusty begins to scan The Wall. Names are not listed alphabetically but in chronological order, according to the date on which the service person was killed. At its deepest point, where the names are stacked ten feet deep, The Wall represents how the Vietnamese stepped up their efforts to be free, unleashing their largest military campaign against the Americans, and how, in response, the United States sent more and more of its young people into combat in a futile attempt to control the tiny but undaunted country on the other side of the world. At this nadir, which represents the American losses in May 1968, The Wall turns and its height tapers off painfully slowly, reflecting what Pete Wilson knew too well: as Nixon gradually drew down the troops, he left those in Vietnam during that period in mortal danger.

The fatigue-clad veteran accompanying Rusty says they should consult one of the directories on site for the locations of their friends' names.

"What difference does it make if you find one name?" Rusty asks, gesturing hopelessly at the expanse of granite now towering over them. "Look at all of the names!" He begins to sob inconsolably. "Names just keep coming into my head. It seems absurd to try to pick one out!"[2]

Several times throughout the film, the camera pulls back to reveal the new memorial site already covered in flowers, flags, photographs, and other personal mementoes. We see veterans, some wearing their medals, touch the names of their lost comrades. We see a woman hold up a rose so it can be photographed next to her loved one's name. Another veteran recognizes Rusty, and the two share a tight embrace. After a segment in which Rusty and several other veterans linger over coffee in a nearby restaurant sharing stories about the harrowing long-term effects of the war on their lives and on those dear to them, the film ends with veterans parading through Washington, DC, not in protest of the war, as they had during Operation Dewey Canyon III, but in somber acceptance of the nation's very belated acknowledgment of their service.

While Vietnam Veterans Against the War did not achieve the organization's goal in the spring of 1971 of ending the Vietnam War immediately,

How Far Home reminds us that VVAW can be credited with changing the political and cultural landscape in other important ways. In addition to successfully fighting for the medical profession's recognition of what is now called posttraumatic stress disorder and for a more responsive Veterans Health Administration, both important achievements that are beyond the scope of this book, the organization convinced at least a part of the country, for a brief historic moment, that the traditional American way of memorializing war is an idealization and thus the utterly wrong approach to the Vietnam War. The men who joined VVAW used the power of performance to bring home the horrors of the atrocities they believed the United States was committing daily in Southeast Asia. By staging their performances at memorialized Revolutionary War battlefields and other nationally sacred sites, they showed that while American war memorialization is meant to remind the citizenry to honor those killed on the battlefield, it also elides war's violence and reifies American exceptionalism. If the Vietnam Veterans Memorial as originally conceived was a different kind of memorial, that was in large part because VVAW changed the narrative of what the Vietnam War was and how it should be remembered while raising fundamental questions about the role of traditional war memorialization.[3]

And yet despite VVAW's efforts on this front, a more traditional statue was erected next to the Vietnam Veterans Memorial two years after Bestor and Rusty returned home to New England. Under political pressure from members of Congress, the White House, and others who threatened to block construction of The Wall unless an American flag and a statue of "heroic fighting men" were also added to the site, the Federal Commission of Fine Arts erected *The Three Infantrymen* or *The Three Soldiers*, as the statue is variously called (Figure 33). Three eight-foot-tall soldiers wear the same distinctive Vietnam War–era gear that the antiwar veterans wore when they performed their mock search-and-destroy missions in order to establish that they had served in Southeast Asia and were thus authorities on the matter of American military tactics. Here is the distinctive M1 helmet with camouflage cover, the boonie cap, the fatigues, and the jungle boots. But while the grouping of three forward-facing soldiers is reminiscent of the appropriation of *The Spirit of '76* by VVAW supporters, these three soldiers are hypermilitarized, in sharp contrast to the two drummers and the fifer of the celebrated painting. The three bronze Vietnam-era soldiers may hold their weapons down by their sides, perhaps in a gesture toward the Cincinnatus tradition embodied by the Minute Men statues, but the sheer number, size,

Figure 33. *The Three Soldiers*, Washington, DC. Photographed by and courtesy of Lissandra Melo.

and power of their weapons is a celebration of American military might. In addition to an M16, the soldiers have a .45 caliber pistol, an M16A1 rifle, and a M60 machine gun with its massive accompanying bandolier. If The Wall seems to sink into the ground under the weight of the nation's sorrow for the losses incurred in an unjust war, *The Three Soldiers* suggests that the strength of the American firepower deployed in Vietnam should be appreciated regardless of the death and destruction it caused.[4]

The Three Soldiers has not proved to be an aberration. Rather, it marks not merely the resurgence of traditional memorial practices but an intensification of them. In recent years, the National Mall has been radically altered by the addition of two more war monuments. In 1995, the Korean War Veterans Memorial was unveiled on the other side of the Lincoln Memorial Reflecting Pool from the Vietnam Veterans Memorial. This time, the inclusion of both a polished black granite wall and representational statuary was part of the original design. The wall, which does not include a list of the American war dead but rather photographic images from the war, is much smaller in scale than that of the Vietnam Veterans Memorial, while the representational statuary is far more massive than *The Three Soldiers*. A platoon of nineteen larger-than-life, stainless steel American soldiers wearing full combat gear is depicted patrolling with M-1 rifles and other weaponry in hand. While the memorial is ostensibly in remembrance of American servicemen and not a celebration of another string of wars the United States waged in Asia across the twentieth century, American firepower is again a central feature.[5]

In 2004, a massive World War II memorial was installed directly between the Lincoln Memorial and the Washington Monument. Whereas the two-acre Vietnam Veterans Memorial is unsettling in its design, black in color, and with a reflective surface that embeds visitors in a dialogue about war and its costs, the over seven-acre World War II Memorial is neoclassical, all white marble and bronze, and triumphal in tone. While The Wall lists the names of all of the American dead and thereby makes explicit war's human toll, the World War II Memorial includes quotations from great men that erase war's trauma in favor of celebrating masculine leadership and winning at whatever cost. President Franklin D. Roosevelt, for example, is quoted asserting that "the American people, in their righteous might, will win through to absolute victory." And, of course, the break in the National Mall's east-west axis has reframed the meaning of the Washington and Lincoln memorials, which are now separated by this glorification of World War II. While the Washington and Lincoln memorials were originally intended as celebrations of the nation's first president, who refused to be king and thereby helped to birth a democracy, and of the nation's sixteenth president, who ended slavery and thereby theoretically expanded the scope of that democracy to all, they are now at risk of being understood as war memorials themselves, one to the American Revolution and the other to the Civil War. Finally, the location and size of the World War II Memorial, which was dedicated at the height of the Iraq War and thus seemed to justify it, takes away from the ability of the public to gather on the Mall in expressions of dissent. There is now significantly less space for people to gather at the foot of the Lincoln Memorial, as they did during the March on Washington for Jobs and Freedom when Dr. King gave his "I Have a Dream" speech, or to camp, as the antiwar Vietnam Veterans did in 1971. Fifty years after Vietnam Veterans Against the War marched on Washington and its New England chapter reversed Paul Revere's ride in a bid to wake the nation, our memorialization practices as well as our overseas military incursions indicate that we have forgotten the lessons VVAW imparted.[6]

ABBREVIATIONS OF SOURCES AND ORGANIZATIONS

Archival and Oral History Collections

COHP	Concord Oral History Program Collection, Concord Free Public Library, Concord, MA
LOHP	Lexington Oral History Project, Cary Memorial Library, Lexington, MA
MMNHP-AHP	Minute Man National Historical Park Administrative History Project
SCPC	Swarthmore College Peace Collection
VVAW-AP	Vietnam Veterans Against the War Archive Project, Wisconsin Historical Society
WSI-T	Winter Soldier Investigation Transcript

Newspapers

BG	*Boston Globe*
BHT	*Boston Herald Traveler*
BP	*Boston Phoenix*
LMM	*Lexington Minute-man*

Organizations, Entities, and Protests

DCIII	Operation Dewey Canyon III
MACV	U.S. Military Assistance Command, Vietnam
Mass PAX	Massachusetts Political Action for Peace
NPS	National Park Service
VVAW	Vietnam Veterans Against the War
VVAW-NE	New England Chapter of Vietnam Veterans Against the War
WSI	Winter Soldier Investigation

NOTES

Introduction

1. Quoted in Hersh. On the breaking of the My Lai story, see Oliver, 40–44.

2. On the American misnaming of the location of the massacre, see Oliver, 192, 211–212, who notes that "Americans had the power to call the massacre what they wanted" (211). On the hearings, called the Winter Soldier Investigation, see Nicosia, 73–93, and Hunt, 55–76.

3. Opening statement, WSI-T. In addition to the transcript, see the 1972 documentary film *Winter Soldier.*

4. On the Vietnam War as a Vietnamese war for independence, see Young, Chomsky, and Hunt and Levine. On the military's naming of search-and-destroy missions, see Young, 162–166. On the causal link between the kinds of missions ordered of American soldiers on the ground and the killing of Vietnamese citizens, see Young, Shay, Lifton, and Turse, the latter of whom argues that "murder, torture, rape, abuse, forced displacement, home burnings, specious arrests, imprisonment without due process . . . were virtually a daily fact of life throughout the years of the American presence in Vietnam" (6). Kulik argues, in contrast, that "Vietnam was the first war in which men lied about committing war crimes" (19), noting of the Detroit hearings that "years later, a thoughtful former Winter Soldier recalled that some of the Marines . . . seemed determined to trump each other, as if they were in competition to tell the most shocking story" (149). While Kulik raises valid concerns that some of the men testifying "succumbed to the power of rumor, second- and third-hand evidence, 'boot camp propaganda,' and imputed motive" (154), he concludes that "some, perhaps many, veterans spoke the truth at the WSI about what they personally witnessed in Vietnam" (151). What is important for our purposes is that the veterans testifying were offering a particular reason to end the war, the success of which in galvanizing the public has to be measured against other arguments that were made against the Vietnam War, such as its financial cost.

5. John Kerry, Vietnam Veterans Against the War's national spokesman, told a *Boston Globe* reporter that "one liberal businessman told me that war crime stories are 'glutting the market,' to use his words" (Thomas Oliphant, "Vets' New War Needs Funding," BG, April 15, 1971).

6. On the various performative means of staging a protest, see Sharp.

7. King (1963). There has recently been a robust academic conversation about the role of place in protest. See, for example, Endres and Senda-Cook. For case studies of the ways in which physical space and symbolic meaning have been used for more recent protests, see Hatuka.

8. In the book-length histories of the Vietnam veterans' antiwar movement, the May 1971 march to Massachusetts' Revolutionary War battlefields is only mentioned briefly and without any agreement as to its significance. Moser calls it "the most striking Memorial Day observance in American history" (117–118), while Hunt describes it as "little more than [a] repetition . . . of earlier VVAW events" (123). Nicosia, despite writing the most extensive history of organizers Vietnam Veterans Against the War, does not even mention it. The three in-depth examinations of this march to date, each of which focuses on the importance of dissent in American democracy, are the hourlong 2001 documentary film *Unfinished Symphony*, directed by Bestor Cram and Mike Majoros, which comprises march film footage provided by Hart Perry and framed by a discussion with historian Howard Zinn; a short article by Lexington march participant Eugenia Kaledin; and a personal recollection by ecologist Bill McKibben, whose father participated in the protest. The march is described most insightfully, although only very briefly, by Edward Linenthal (1991), where he notes that the antiwar veterans "believed the real defilement had been perpetrated by a new class of American Tories who had severed the link between revolutionary war principles (especially the principle of dissent) and contemporary American life." The antiwar veterans believed, Linenthal continues, that their protest "would spark the recovery of the American revolutionary tradition, which was viewed as crucial to the resuscitation of authentic American values that had fallen into disrepair because of public apathy" (12). I agree with this assessment and attempt in these pages to expand this argument in order to explain the veterans' use of performance as well as place, while chronicling how and why six Vietnam veterans with different backgrounds and wartime experiences attempted to re-release the same energy that spurred the colonists in 1775.

9. On the steps involved in sanctifying a space, see Foote. On how the preservation of certain places is a means of "channel[ing] the ongoing currents of American civic life" and fostering "patriotic nationalism," see Bluestone (15, 20). In addition to being frontpage news for several days in New England's newspapers, the veterans' protest was covered in the *New York Times* ("Memorial Day Observed Traditionally and by Protests on War," June 1, 1971), the *Washington Post* ("Vets March from Concord Draws Fire," May 29, 1971, and "Vets March in Boston as War Protest," June 1, 1971), the *Philadelphia Inquirer* ("550 War Protestors Seized at Camp-In," May 31, 1971), and the *Chicago Sun-Times* ("Arrest of 400 in War Protest on Historic Lexington Green," May 31, 1971), while many other smaller papers ran United Press International or Associated Press articles about the march. The march was also covered by the NBC Sunday Night News on May 30, 1971, and on ABC News on May 31, 1971. Both broadcasts are preserved at the Vanderbilt News Archives.

Chapter 1

1. On the height and weight restrictions imposed during the Vietnam War, see Abney, 58.

2. All of Peter Wilson's recollections and comments are taken from his interview with the author.

3. The stashed toy M16 is visible in one of several photographs Cary Wolinsky took of Peter Wilson over Memorial Day weekend, 1971.

4. On VVAW's founding and early efforts, see Nicosia, 15–36, and Hunt, 5–33. On the air war the United States waged in Southeast Asia, see Gibson, 319–420, among others.

5. The Moratorium to End the War in Vietnam was the brainchild of Massachusetts businessman Jerome Grossman, who, as head of Mass PAX, would help VVAW open its New England office in the winter of 1970–1971. See Grossman, 36–38, 48–57, 59–61, and Jerome Grossman LOHP interview, 12. See also Arthur Johnson LOHP interview, 8.

6. On Operation RAW, see Nicosia, 56–67; Hunt, 45–54; and Moser, 108–110.

7. On the essay that introduced the term and the concept of guerrilla theater, see Davis. On the origins of guerrilla theater in the 1960s, see Doyle. On the NYU protest against the Kent State massacre, see Schechner.

8. For a history of the First Indochina War, see Prados and Young, among others.

9. Quoted in Gibson, 25.

10. One of the New England members of VVAW who participated in the Memorial Day weekend march left the naval academy after being debriefed about the Gulf of Tonkin incident. "I learned more than the public had yet," Richard Colton explained. "I was appalled that the government had taken advantage of this situation to then just walk in." See his interview with the author. The Pentagon Papers, which revealed so much about why the United States entered into a war with Vietnam and how the federal government was conducting the war illegally while misleading the American people, were not made public until the month after VVAW-NE's Memorial Day weekend march.

11. In 1971, Valley Forge was a Pennsylvania state park. It is now a National Historical Park.

12. Paine.

13. On the jeremiad in American history, see Miller and Bercovitch. On the veterans' actions along the march route and at Valley Forge, see the documentary film *Different Sons*.

14. On the VVAW *Playboy* ad, see Hunt, 67–68, and Nicosia, 91–92, who notes under a reproduction of the ad that it brought "more than 10,000 new members into the organization." VVAW-NE's executive secretary was Marvin Gross. See his interview with the author.

15. On Operation Dewey Canyon III, see Nicosia, 98–157; Hunt, 94–119; and Moser, 112–116.

16. On the rise of liberalism in the suburbs west of Boston, see Geismer. On the New England chapter's role in Operation DCIII, see Bestor Cram interview with the author. On Mass PAX and its role in supporting the New England chapter of VVAW, see Grossman and Jerome Grossman LOHP interview. On the role of Citizens for Participation in Political Action in helping the veterans organize their Memorial Day weekend march, see Betty Levin, Marvin Gross, and Lenny Rotman interviews with the author. For an example of the kind of fundraisers VVAW had in people's homes, see Jean Gogolin, "Vets: Anti-War Stand Explained," untitled newspaper, box 26, folder 2, VVAW-AP. On VVAW-NE's journey to DC, see Joe Pilati, "The Vietnam Veterans' March on Washington," BG, May 30, 1971. On the veterans' transportation to DC, see Chris Gregory LOHP interview and his interview with the author.

17. On the number of veterans who attended Operation Dewey Canyon III, see Hunt, 96.

18. On the history of protests in Washington, DC, see Barber. On John Kerry's role in VVAW, see Kranish et al., 116–140, and Brinkley, 342–389. See John Kerry's speech at http://

www2.iath.virginia.edu/sixties/HTML_docs/Resources/Primary/Manifestos/VVAW_Kerry_Senate.html (accessed December 18, 2019).

19. On deciding to reenact Paul Revere's ride during the bus ride home, see Arthur Johnson LOHP interview, 12. Johnson does not mention it, but he was the editor of Holy Cross's student newspaper when it reported that a student was reenacting the 1775 British march from Boston Common to Concord in order to "'awaken the general public to an awareness' of the American Revolution." The student reported having originally wanted to reenact Revere's ride but decided it would be impractical to ride a horse through Boston ("Holy Cross Jun. Plans to Repeat British March from Boston in '75," *Crusader* 44, no. 10, April 6, 1967). Johnson knew from this march and a spring 1970 march from Concord's Walden Pond to Boston in protest of the Vietnam War that the distance was walkable and the way laden with important American symbols (box 19, folder "Thoreau Walk 1970," SCPC).

VVAW's Memorial Day weekend march was not the first time political activists had staged alternative celebrations of the nation's birth as a means of advancing their cause. On how the abolitionists held alternative commemorations of the Fourth of July as a means of calling attention to the fact that not all Americans were free, see Branham and Bellah. See Foner on how, in later years, labor groups, farmers, and others used the Fourth of July to advance their causes. It was not until 1976, however, that a group other than the veterans used the Old North Bridge to stage a protest on Patriots' Day. On the People's Bicentennial Commission and their interruption of the orthodox bicentennial celebration at the Old North Bridge, see Hall (2016) and Linenthal (1991), 41–43.

20. "Vietnam Vets Plan Reverse Revere March," *Fence Viewer* (Sudbury, MA) (and elsewhere), May 20, 1971.

21. Quoted in Franklin, 51, and Nicosia, 156. Nicosia notes that "even as the VVAW were moving from Winter Soldier to Dewey Canyon, Nixon was honing his new strategy like a knife blade that would hamstring the peace movement" (156). On the Nixon administration's POW/MIA campaign, see Franklin.

22. "We Are All Prisoners of This War: Operation P.O.W.," flier in the personal collection of Eugenia Kaledin.

23. Peter Wilson had wanted to participate in Operation DCIII, but his family's Land Rover broke down en route and he had to turn back. See his interview with the author. He did participate in the mock search-and-destroy mission VVAW-NE staged in Boston's Government Center the week before Operation DCIII. A photograph of him sitting in the converted Land Rover was featured in an article about that action: "Veterans Against the War," BP, April 20, 1971.

24. DeWitt, 59.

25. John Singleton Copley's portrait of Paul Revere is now proudly displayed at the Boston Museum of Fine Arts as one of its greatest treasures. On the painting's history, see www.mfa.org/collections/object/paul-revere-32401 (accessed October 15, 2018).

26. For a broad overview of the American Revolution in the nation's historical memory, see Kammen (1978). For a history of the reception of "Paul Revere's Ride," see Gartner. On the poem's use in American schools, see Sorby.

27. All of the passages quoted from the poem are from Longfellow.

28. On Dr. Warren's role in the messengering system, see Fischer, 95.

29. On the full extent of the alarm system, see Fischer, 138–142. In his otherwise definitive account of Paul Revere's ride and the delays experienced by the king's troops, Fischer declines to point out that the signaling described in Longfellow's poem proved irrelevant, so powerful is the myth.

30. For an explanation of how the poem forges a citizenry, see Sorby, 14–24.

31. See Betty Levin interview with the author and Jennifer Levin interview with the author.

32. On draft card burning in Boston, see Foley, 19–23, 96–109.

33. All of Jennifer Levin's recollections and remarks are from her interview with the author. The person she recalls being shot in the head was handcuffed National Liberation Front officer Nguyan Van Lem. South Vietnamese general Nguyen Ngoc Loan shot him point blank in the street on February 1, 1968. Eddie Adams's photograph of the execution, in which the bullet can be seen exiting the NLF officer's head, is one of the most well-known images of the Vietnam War. Film footage of the execution also ran on television, as Levin readily recalled.

34. In 1961, Paul Revere's sixth-generation descendant, eleven-year-old George Haskett, "re-enacted the lighting of the lanterns" ("Africans Witness Ceremony Marking Paul Revere's Ride," *New York Times*, April 20, 1961). On the use of flares, see Christopher Gregory interview with the author. On the number of flares sent up, see "VVAW History," n.d., personal papers of Joseph Baratta. On the air war the United States waged against Laos and Cambodia, see Kiernan and Owen. On the signal lanterns used in 1775, of which the Concord Museum claims to have one, see Cooke, 123.

35. The typed directions survive in the personal papers of VVAW-NE member Jerry Lund. See Jerry Lund interview with the author. In her interview with the author, Jennifer Levin recalls that the reproduction signal lantern she carried most likely belonged to her family.

36. On the history of memorialization at the Concord Old North Bridge area, see Dietrich-Smith and Olmstead Center for Landscape Preservation; Linenthal (1991), 11–51; Zenzen and National Park Service U.S. Department of the Interior; and Gross (1999, 2003). On the sacred nature accorded to American battlefields, see Linenthal (1991). On the sacred as the place where there was once a hierophany, see Eliade, who argues that a sacred place "constitutes a break in the homogeneity of space" brought about by "an opening by which passage from one cosmic region to another is made possible" (37). While Americans experience Revolutionary War battlefields as places where, in Eliade's terms, a door opened between heaven and earth, I follow Chidester and Linenthal ("Introduction") in viewing sacred spaces as designated as such by humans.

37. On the nation's modern managerial practices as an extension of religious custodianship, see Chidester and Linenthal, 27. On the steps taken to achieve sanctification, including "a change of ownership, often a transfer from private to public stewardship," see Foote, 9 and passim. On NPS's ruling on the antiwar veterans' request, see "VVAW Protestors Spend Quiet Night, Costly Day," *Concord Free Press*, June 3, 1971, and John O'Keefe, "Concord Board Escaped Sticky VVAW Ruling," *Lowell* (MA) *Sun*, June 6, 1971.

38. See VVAW-NE's request letter to the Lexington Selectmen, May 20, 1971, from the personal collection of Eugenia Kaledin. The letter's contents are also included in the minutes from the May 24 Selectmen's meeting, available online at http://www.lexingtonbattlegreen1971.com/files/SelectmenMinutes1.pdf (accessed June 5, 2019). On VVAW-NE organizers' initial

preference for Tower Park on account of it being closer to Charlestown, see Arthur Johnson LOHP interview, 14.

39. Cited in Robert Cataldo LOHP interview, 17–18. The bylaw dates back to 1923 or earlier, according to the footnote in the Cataldo interview.

40. Minutes of Regular Selectman's Meeting, May 24, 1971, http://www.lexingtonbattlegreen1971.com/files/SelectmenMinutes1.pdf (accessed December 19, 2019). On the veterans' views on the political importance of always cleaning up after themselves, see Bob Barbanti's LOHP interview, 38. On the veterans' response to the number of toilet units, see "Selectmen Deny Permit for Bivouac, Guerilla Theater Demonstration," LMM, May 27, 1971. On the arrangements made to pick up a Port-o-San trailer for Operation RAW, see VVAW's paperwork on the four support vehicles they engaged, one for carrying food, one for water, one for toilets, and one for medical support in box 13, folder 7, VVAW-AP. In VVAW's first edition of its newsletter, the *First Casualty*, VVAW published "Guidelines for VVAW Marches and Guerrilla Theaters," in which it was noted that "it goes without question that prior planning is of the utmost importance from porto-sans [*sic*], location of encampments, routes of march, to alternatives in case of emergencies for successful operations" (*First Casualty* 1, no. 1, August 1971, 6).

41. Robert Cataldo LOHP interview, 9.

42. Ibid., 22.

43. Allan Kenney LOHP interview, 20.

44. Minutes of Special Selectmen's Meeting, May 27, 1971, http://www.lexingtonbattlegreen1971.com/files/SelectmenMinutes2.pdf (accessed January 19, 2020); Allan Kenny LOHP interview, 5; Robert Cataldo LOHP interview, 8; Kenney, ibid., 5.

45. On the contested nature of public memory, see Bodnar (1994) and Linenthal (2001), the latter of whom rightly argues that preserved battlefields are "contested terrain where Americans come to compete for the ownership of powerful national stories and to argue about the nature of heroism, the meaning of war, the efficacy of martial sacrifice, and the significance of preserving the patriotic landscape of the nation" (303). On what Revere may have shouted, see Fischer, 109–110. Revere was still British himself so would not have called out that "the British are coming!" as so many assume.

46. One of the co-coordinators of VVAW-NE was quoted as saying of the Battle Green and Bunker Hill that "we're going to have a meeting Friday night, and if we decide we want to camp at these two symbolic places, we will—without official permission." Robert B. Hanron, "Viet Vets Protest War," BG, 18, March 31, 1971. On VVAW-NE's Mobile Information Center, see Lenny Rotman interview with the author and Marvin Gross interview with the author. For Operation RAW, VVAW purchased food in bulk at a cost of $938.58 and cooked it themselves en route using sterno cans ("Food," box 13, folder 7, VVAW-AP). For Operation POW, the veterans worked with local supporters. In a short announcement about the planned march in the *Fence Viewer* (Sudbury, MA) on May 20, 1971, "Vietnam Vets Plan Reverse Revere March," the final two paragraphs address food: "Citizen and church groups from Lincoln and Concord will provide Friday dinner and Saturday breakfast for the vets in Concord. Anyone wishing to donate food or help is asked to contact Mrs. Philip Villers of Concord." A similar announcement in the *Concord Journal*, "Vietnam Veterans to March Concord to Bunker Hill," also published on May 20, 1971, notes that "contributions of food and help are urgently needed." The names of two additional

women were added as contacts, along with all three women's telephone numbers. On Friday evening, the volunteers served the veterans a "chicken dinner" in what the newspaper described as "the old Sohier field next to the North Bridge entrance" ("VVAW Protestors Spend Quiet Night, Costly Day," *Concord Free Press*, June 3, 1971). Betty Levin's father had just passed away, and she brought his Trinidadian nurse with her to the Old North Bridge on Friday where the press interviewed her only to discover that, not being American, she was unable to interpret the symbols VVAW-NE was mobilizing (Betty Levin interview with the author).

47. Reports of the number of veterans in Concord on Friday night vary widely. The *Boston Globe* reported on May 29, 1971, in an article by William J. Cardoso, that "about 250 anti-Vietnam War veterans bivouacked last night at the Old North Bridge." Another article, "VVAW Protestors Spend Quiet Night, Costly Day," asserts that there were "some 100 veterans and their friends gathered . . . for a chicken dinner provided by local supporters" and that the following morning, the number "had grown to about 150" (*Concord Free Press*, June 3, 1971). The *Sun* (Lowell, MA) reported that the number of veterans over the weekend "ranged from 50 to more than 200 at times" ("Concord Board Escaped Sticky VVAW Ruling," June 6, 1971). When LOHP asked Bestor Cram if there were 150 veterans on Friday night in Concord, he replied, "I don't even think we had that many. . . . I think a number of people joined us on Saturday" (19). Chris Gregory, another principal VVAW-NE organizer, remembered there were "only a few guys, forty, fifty, sixty guys camping out at the bridge" (LOHP interview, 28). The *Globe* appears to have mistakenly assumed that the number of veterans arrested in Lexington was the same number that started the march. I suspect that both the *Concord Free Press* and the Lowell *Sun* are the more accurate reports of how many veterans camped Friday night, especially as their numbers are in keeping with what participants Bestor Cram and Chris Gregory remember. On the filming of Jack Ofield's *Different Sons* (1971), see Saunders, 29–46. Hart Perry applied for a grant from the PBS show *The Great American Dream Machine* to make a film of the march, and based on the strength of a previous short docudrama he had shot about the American prison system, the show agreed to fund him. Hart Perry assembled enough people to man four film crews. They borrowed four Éclair NPR 16-mm cameras and four Nagra III portable audio recorders. Hart Perry also borrowed a camper from his cousin, a Vietnam veteran, and used that to store equipment. Ultimately, however, PBS declined to broadcast the film, arguing that it was too one-sided. See Hart Perry's interview with the author. On the other young filmmakers following the veterans that weekend under the direction of Hart Perry, see Deborah Crockett-Rice, Guy Pommares, Ted Timreck, and David Helperin, interviews with the author. On the care taken by VVAW-NE's executive director not to appear as a veteran, see Marv Gross interview with the author. On stolen valor, see Burkett and Whitley. Hart Perry wearing his tricorn hat is shown in Figures 16 and 19.

48. Jerry Lund read the veterans' warning. See Jerry Lund interview with the author as well as a picture of him receiving it from Jennifer Levin that appeared in the *Minute-man Supplement* on June 3, 2017. "Portraying Paul Revere, Miss Jennifer Levin of Old Winter rd., Lincoln hands the VVAW List of Grievances to Jerry Lund of Brookline at the Old North Bridge, Friday night." VVAW's "Open Letter to Congress of the United States" is from the personal files of Eugenia Kaladin and was also published in "Over 400 Arrested, Fined in Lexington, Sunday, as Antiwar March Stalled," *Minute-man Supplement*, June 3, 1971.

49. Transcribed by the author from *Unfinished Symphony*.

Chapter 2

1. Three months after Operation POW, in August 1971, VVAW would publish its first newsletter, the *First Casualty.* In it, the organization set forth "Guidelines for VVAW Marches and Guerrilla Theaters," which included instructions on transporting all of the necessary gear: "Trucks and other vehicles should be restricted in number. Have as many as are required for the transportation of food and gear and the required emergency medical vehicle. . . . There should be one roving vehicle for general coordination" (*First Casualty* 1, no. 1, August 1971, 6). On Daniel Chester French's work on the Minute Man Statue, see Robbins.

2. An article reporting on the Lexington Selectmen's decision appeared in the *Boston Globe* on Thursday, May 27, 1971 ("Lexington Forbids Antiwar Vets Bivouac"). On Friday, May 28, 1971, the *Globe* published an editorial in support of the veterans ("The People Will Be Heard"). And on Saturday morning, May 29, 1971, the *Globe* reported on the Friday night encampment at the Old North Bridge ("Antiwar Vets Camp at Concord Bridge"), noting that the veterans were going to ignore the Selectmen's restrictions. Harvard senior David King reported in the *New Republic* that by Saturday morning, there were 178 veterans, "including about 20 ex-officers and three disabled veterans, joined by a couple of active duty GIs" ("Paul Revere Had a Horse: The Veterans' March to Boston," *New Republic*, June 12, 1971, 11). King's report is in keeping with the *Concord Free Press*, which reported that the number of veterans "had grown to about 150" on Saturday morning ("VVAW Protestors Spend Quiet Night, Costly Day," June 3, 1971).

Bullhorns and walkie talkies appear in several of the photographs taken of Operation POW. While a budget has not survived, the budget for Operation RAW shows that VVAW rented ten walkie talkies for $400, a PA system for $1,200, and four bullhorns for $80.

3. Bestor Cram's remarks at the Old North Bridge were transcribed by the author from *Veterans Against the War*, the documentary film of the march made by Hart Perry in cooperation with VVAW-NE.

4. The press release was later reprinted in an article entitled "VVAW Gives Reasons for Green Bivouac," which begins by noting that "the following is the statement approved by the Vietnam Veterans Against the War after the group had voted Friday night in Concord to bivouac on the Battle Green" (LMM, June 2, 1971).

5. On Bestor Cram and his family, see his interview in *J'ai vecu*, 26–49; his LOHP interview; his interview with the author; and his mother's memoir (Cram). On memories of World War II as "the good war," see Bodnar (2010).

6. On the traumatization of war Bestor Cram witnessed in the men assigned him, see Fussell, Shay, and Lifton.

7. Bestor Cram, interview with the author. Shay names this type of behavior among traumatized soldiers the berserk state, 77–99.

8. Bestor Cram's reply to "Urgent" memo sent from Al Hubbard, VVAW executive secretary, on October 13, 1970 (box 13, folder 8, VVAW-AP).

9. Bestor Cram's co-coordinator was Arthur Johnson, pictured addressing march participants in Figures 10 and 28 and occupying the Green in Figure 14. On his tremendous efforts for VVAW-NE and his crucially important role in organizing and carrying out Operation POW, see his LOHP interview, his interview with the author, and the 2010 panel discussion, "Peace, Protest, Patriotism," in which both he and Bestor participated.

10. On how breaking a minor law unrelated to the issue of concern can be a highly effective form of civil disobedience, see Zinn, 18–19, and Sharp, 420–421.

11. Quoted in Nicosia, 126. See the photo taken by Steven Clevenger of Edward Kennedy meeting with the veterans on the National Mall in which Bestor Cram is visible sitting near him: https://www.gettyimages.fi/detail/news-photo/ted-kennedy-speaks-with-members-of-vietnam-veterans-against-news-photo/526094724 (accessed December 22, 2019).

12. On the veterans' decision to make their democratic deliberations publicly as part of their theater, see Bestor Cram LOHP interview, 24–25; Bestor Cram interview with the author; and Howie Baker interview with the author.

13. Gary Rafferty LOHP interview, 25.

14. Transcribed by the author from *Unfinished Symphony.*

15. Ibid.

16. Joseph Baratta's remarks were transcribed by the author from *Unfinished Symphony* and were reiterated by him in his interview with the author.

17. While civil disobedience can be understood as principled nonviolent disobedience of the law, theorists generally understand it to be aimed at persuading others that a law or government policy is morally wrong and must be changed. See Lyons.

18. Transcribed by the author from *Unfinished Symphony.*

19. The four votes opposed to proceeding onto the Lexington Battle Green were reported in "Over 400 Arrested, Fined in Lexington, Sunday, as Antiwar March Stalled," *Lexington Minute-man Supplement*, June 3, 1971. See also Joseph Baratta interview with the author.

20. George W. Ashworth, "The Mission Was Impossible, but Veterans Made Their Point," *Christian Science Monitor*, April 26, 1971. For Operation RAW, participants were instructed to "wear fatigues (preferably jungle fatigues)" ("The Objective of Operation RAW," box 13, folder 7, VVAW-AP). For DCIII, participants were instructed to "wear your fatigues and combat ribbons. Jungle boots and gas masks optional but recommended" ("Vietnam Vets March on D.C.," Vietnam Veterans Against the War collection, 1967-, SCPC). The pairing of fatigues with beards began with Fidel Castro, who visited New York City so adorned in 1959, and Ernesto "Chi" Guevara, of whom the 1960 photograph by Alberto Díaz Gutíerrez became after Guevara's death in 1967 one of the most disseminated images in the world. See Casey. In other words, by the time VVAW adopted the look, it had already been thoroughly masculinized and associated with revolution.

21. *J'ai vecu*, as translated for the author by Sylvia Bitton, 4.

22. *The New Soldier*, 152.

23. Weems quoted in Albanese (1976), 178. Based on a single account of a Pepperell farmer who "left his plow in the furrow," Fischer concludes that "the folk image of the minuteman leaving his plough was literally the case in many towns that first heard the alarm after the sun was up" (Fischer, 157, quoting from Hurd, 231). But to assert that some farmers literally left their fields distracts us from the construction of the myth and the myth's purpose. On the use of French's Minute Man Statue to sell Victory bonds, Victory stamps, and advertisements for war loans, see Linenthal (1991), 26. The image of the virtuous warrior as one with restrained strength goes back to the ancient Greeks. See Mosse, 102.

24. For accounts of the skirmish at the Old North Bridge, see Gross (2001), 109–132; Bradford, 39–54; Tourtellot, 149–168; Fischer, 202–219; Galvin, 147–155; and, most recently, Atkinson. On whether or not "White Cockade" was played during the approach to the bridge, see Ryan.

25. Emerson. On how places are made sacred through "ritual dedication," see Foote, 8.

26. According to local legend, Bedford's Nathaniel Page carried a flag at the Old North Bridge made for a cavalry troop of the Massachusetts Bay militia during the French and Indian War and now in the possession of the town of Bedford. See Martucci, 22. On the history of flags in colonial New England and later the United States, see Teachout, especially 25–27. On how violence is often erased at sacred American sites, see Foote.

27. The patch is clearly visible in the photographs of the Memorial Day weekend march taken by Richard Robbat and Cary Wolinsky.

28. One of the first people to identify the Vietnam War as an imperialist endeavor was Noam Chomsky, who wrote the following about the United States in 1967: "Our reasons for wanting to control Vietnam are not those of the British in India in 1829, but in Vietnam, as in the Philippines and Latin America, our efforts are directed to organizing (or restructuring) the society so as to ensure the domination of those elements that will enter into partnership with us. That we should do so is not surprising, surely not to anyone who is familiar with the history of imperialism" (Chomsky, 252). In John Kerry's speech to the Senate Foreign Relations Committee during VVAW's Operation Dewey Canyon III, he echoed Chomsky's view, noting that Vietnam posed no threat to the United States and describing the Vietnamese as fighting a "civil war" against "colonial influence." For the most recent argument that the Vietnam War was part of "an arc of empire" established by the United States in Asia, see Hunt and Levine.

29. For a history of disabled veterans, see Gerber. On VVAW's display of wounded veterans and the organization's argument that American GIs were victims, see Huebner, 219–237. Christopher Gregory explains the decision to have the wounded go first: "It was Bestor's idea. 'These guys should go first'" (Christopher Gregory LOHP interview, 28–29). Each of the wounded veterans who arrived Saturday morning from area VA hospitals had most likely signed the same kind of release form VVAW required for Operation RAW, one acknowledging that march organizers were "interested in my participation primarily because of the physical condition resulting from wounds suffered in Vietnam." By signing, they agreed not to receive any compensation for their participation or for any materials, including photographs, that the organizers created using their images. This latter point was important in case anyone accused them of selfish motives. No such form survives from Operation POW, but the form created for Operation RAW the fall before survives in VVAW's national archives (box 13, folder 7, VVAW-AP). On the effort required of the veteran with his legs in braces to push the other wounded veteran in a wheelchair, see Sally Hale LOHP interview, 5. On the role of memorialization in masking death, see Mosse, especially 88.

30. "Vietnam Vets March on D.C.," Vietnam Veterans Against the War collection, 1967-, SCPC. On William Wyman, see Vietnam Veterans Against the War, "An Interview with a Veteran." Photographs of and articles about Wyman ran in the *Christian Science Monitor* (April 24, 1971), the *Washington Post* (April 23, 1971), *Newsday* [New York] (April 19, 1971), the *Chicago Tribune* (April 20, 1971), the *Chicago Sun-Times* (April 19, 1971), the *Chicago Daily News*

(April 19, 1971), BG (April 20, 1971), the BHT (April 11, 1971, and April 23, 1971), the *Blade* [Toledo, OH] (April 22, 1971), *St. Petersburg* [Florida] *Times* (April 30, 1971), and the [Bergen County, NJ] *Record* (April 19, 1971). John Kerry's statement, WSI-T.

31. Bestor Cram interview with the author. Bestor Cram also describes receiving death threats in his LOHP interview, 21.

Chapter 3

1. On the ways in which Americans create a living sense of the past that reflects present concerns, see Kammen (1991). On the historic preservation movement in New England, see Lindgren. On the population and politics of Concord in 1960, see Geismer.

2. On the creation and dedication of Concord's Civil War Monument, see Frese, chap. 10.

3. My recreation of what happened in Monument Square is based on photographs and film footage as well as on news reports of other VVAW mock search-and-destroy missions, including Karen Rhodes's report of her participation in a mock search-and-destroy mission VVAW-NE had performed at Government Center a month earlier ("V.C. Numba Ten, Me No V.C.!" BP, April 20, 1971). Rhodes was arrested on Lexington Green with the veterans and thus likely performed in Concord.

4. Karen Rhodes, "V.C. Numba Ten, Me No V.C.!" BP, April 20, 1971. I have used the script Rhodes recalls from that day to illustrate the kinds of things the veterans would have said in Monument Square and what their civilian coperformers, several of whom photographs indicate were women, would have experienced.

5. Three months later, in the first edition of its newsletter, VVAW stipulated that guerrilla theater "should be done where the largest amount of people can see it. There is no use in doing it for ourselves" ("Guidelines for VVAW Marches and Guerrilla Theaters," *First Casualty* 1, no. 1, August 1971, 6). For children's reactions, see *Veterans Against the War* and *Unfinished Symphony.*

6. All of Donald Carrico's comments, unless otherwise noted, are from his interview with the author.

7. Donald Carrico fought with the 1st Battalion, 27th Marines. For his account of the battle that took place on April 13, 1968, see Jarvis, 36–37, 222.

8. On Concord's World War I memorial, see https://www.waymarking.com/waymarks/WMWAJK_Concord_World_War_Memorial_Concord_MA (accessed May 3, 2020).

9. William Calley (Court-Martial Testimony), in Hammer, 263, as quoted in O'Brien (1994), 141.

10. On the role of Vietnamese women in the war, see Taylor.

11. See Shay on the berserk state in Vietnam and Kehoe on its earlier manifestations in Concord and Lexington.

12. Quoted in Kehoe, 113.

13. Ibid., 128.

14. The flier announcing Operation POW that VVAW-NE distributed to veterans was attached to a timeline for the weekend that includes a list of "suggested equipment." In addition to "Bedroll or Sleeping Bag, DD form 214 or retirement papers, Canteen, Poncho, Nam

Fatigues, and dry socks," veterans were asked to bring "plastic weapons—m16, 45, Thompson's" (personal collection of Eugenia Kaledin). It is also possible the national VVAW office supplied all or some of the toy weapons for the Memorial Day weekend march, as they did for Operation RAW ("Budget for Operation RAW," box 13, folder 7, VVAW-AP). Unfortunately, most correspondence for the New England chapter of VVAW has not survived. Several veterans reported that they had thrown or immediately given away their military uniforms upon being discharged. See, for example, Richard Colton interview with the author. Then again, some, such as Dale Reese, wore their fatigue jackets for months and even years afterward. See his interview with the author. My description of the clothing and gear featured in Ted Polumbaum's photograph of guerrilla theater in Monument Square (Figure 7) was provided to me by David Brubaker, who serves on the Board of Directors of the Kansas Museum of Military History. In terms of choosing their weapons, veterans used the toy version of what they carried in Vietnam. For most of them, that was the M16. Others, such as Richard Colton, chose the Thompson because that is what they had used in the Navy. See Richard Colton's interview with the author.

15. Mort Schultz, "VC Firepower: Can We Match It?" *Popular Mechanics* 127, no. 6 (June 1967), https://archive.org/stream/PopularMechanics1967/Popular%20mechanics-06-1967_djvu.txt (accessed February 18, 2020).

16. For Mattel ads from the period, which spell the sound made by the M16 as I have here, see, for example, *Hawkman*, issue 21, 1967. The ad is also reprinted at fromthebarrelofagun.blogspot.com/2010/12/mattel-m16-marauder.html (accessed February 18, 2020).

17. "Budget for Operation RAW," box 13, folder 7, VVAW-AP. The budget for Operation POW has not survived.

18. Engelhardt, 176. On the history of G.I. Joe, see Engelhardt, 175–178.

19. One of the best explorations of the link between American war toys and enlistment in the Vietnam War is Ron Kovic's memoir *Born on the Fourth of July.*

20. Jim Walsh resignation letter, box 5, folder 12, VVAW-AP.

21. Gary Rafferty interview with LOHP, 29. Bestor Cram later recalled worrying that guys "standing in the dress of their war, carrying toy guns that look very much like the real thing" might flashback (Bestor Cram LOHP interview, 27).

22. On the history of the term "gook," see Roediger. On the use of the term "gook" in basic training, including in written materials and films, see Eisenhart, 28. In *Born on the Fourth of July,* Ron Kovic recalls hearing the enemy described by officers as "COMMIES JAPS AND DINKS" during basic training as he prepared for combat in Vietnam (106).

23. Former Marine Scott Camil at the Winter Soldier Investigation, WSI-T.

24. Quoted in Young, 11.

25. Quoted in Giguere, 75. Fischer notes of the Lexington battle that "eight pairs of fathers and sons had mustered on the Common. Five of those eight were shattered by death. Most families in that small community suffered the loss of a kinsman—if not a father or son, then an uncle or cousin" (200).

26. On the Bunker Hill Monument, see Purcell, Boston National Historical Park, and Foote, 114–122.

27. Quoted in Boston National Historical Park, 25.

28. On Concord's connection to the Bunker Hill Association, see Gross (1999), 262. Concord son George Washington Dugan, the son of two formerly enslaved parents, was not included in the list of names on Concord's Civil War Monument despite having been killed fighting with the 54th Regiment Massachusetts Voluntary Infantry during the famous storming of Fort Wagner in South Carolina on July 18, 1863. Nearly half of the company, which never retreated, was killed or, like Dugan, "never accounted for." See Frese, 61–63, and Rick Frese, "Let's Acknowledge Concord's 49th Fallen Soldier," *Concord Journal*, June 16, 2016, http://concord.wickedlocal.com/news/20160616/guest-commentary-lets-acknowledge-concords-49th-fallen-soldier (accessed February 19, 2020).

29. On PBS's decision not to broadcast Hart Perry's documentary, see his interview with the author.

30. Letter from VVAW-NE to the Board of Selectmen, May 20, 1971 (personal collection of Eugenia Kaledin).

31. Quoted in Davis, 130. VVAW-NE had also spent a good part of a day performing mock search-and-destroy missions in Boston prior to heading to Washington. Those efforts were covered in the Boston-area press with both articles and photo essays that the Selectmen would have seen. See, for example, "Mock War Held by Viet Vets," *Record American* (Boston), April 15, 1971; "Viet Vets Hold Hub Anti-War Rallies," BG, April 14, 1971; "Vets' Boston Mission Warm-up for Washington," BG, April 15, 1971; "Bringing the Atrocities Home," BP, April 20, 1971; and "Mock War Too Realistic," BH, April 15, 1971. In other words, the Selectmen knew what guerrilla theater was when the veterans approached them.

32. The minutes from both of these public meetings are posted at www.lexingtonbattlegreen1971.com (accessed January 20, 2020).

33. Robert Cataldo LOHP interview, 19.

34. Ibid., 19; Allan Kenney LOHP interview, 13.

35. See *Veterans Against the War.*

36. This is what Al Hubbard, VVAW's national executive secretary, said after each performance of guerrilla theater during Operation RAW to the crowd that would have inevitably gathered to watch the brutal interrogations the veterans performed along the way to Valley Forge (see Nicosia, 65–66). I have assumed similar words were used to explain the situation to the Concord crowd at Monument Square.

37. "A U.S. Infantry Company Just Came Through Here," undated pamphlet in the private collection of Eugenia Kaledin. "Guidelines for VVAW Marches and Guerrilla Theaters," published three months later in the first edition of VVAW's newsletter, suggested that organizers "designate at least five people to stay back and talk and leaflet the townspeople" (*First Casualty* 1, no. 1, August 1971, 6).

38. On the arrangements VVAW-NE made with the Concord police chief, see "VVAW Protestors Spend Quiet Night, Costly Day," *Concord Free Press*, June 3, 1971. Ted Polumbaum's photographs of the veterans' departure from Monument Square show civilians trailing them. One Concord resident who later recalled following them along with his draft-age son was Amedio (Al) Armenti. See his LOHP interview, 2, and his COHP interview. Al Armenti also wrote his biography and posted it online. In part V, he also recounts walking behind the veterans. https://alarmenti.com/non-fiction/part-5/ (accessed May 29,

2019). Veteran Joseph P. Baratta would later recall a large number of civilians following along. See his interview with the author.

39. One of the people Don called was Norma McGavern-Norland. Norma was the head of the Lexington division of Citizens for Participation in Political Action, founded by Betty Levin's husband. Don asked Norma to organize residents in providing a spaghetti dinner on Saturday night in Lexington. See Norma McGavern-Norland LOHP interview, 5–6. On the acquisition of plastic utensils from a local plastics factory, see Lenny Rotman interview with the author.

40. Quoted in "Veterans Against the War: Bringing the Atrocities Home," BP, April 20, 1971.

Chapter 4

1. For a history of the Lexington Green, see Brockway.

2. Clarke.

3. "The first photograph of the Common, an image dated 1865, shows the haying operation" (Brockway, 15). On the practice of reinterring the dead as a figurative resurrection that confers additional honor, see Kammen (2010).

4. On the memorialization of the Lexington Battle Green, see Linenthal (1991), 11–51.

5. On the deliberations about whether or not to include the Lexington Battle Green in what would become Minute Man National Historical Park, see Boston National Historic Sites Commission, especially 105–112.

6. Unless otherwise specified, Ross Fenton's comments are taken from his interview with the author.

7. "Rhode Island Chapter of Vietnam Veterans Against the War," box 5, folder 12, VVAW-AP.

8. On war as a contest of mutual injuring and the metaphors used to disguise that fact, see Scarry.

9. Boston National Historic Sites Commission, 9. On the human role in making space sacred, see Chidester and Linenthal.

10. The road on which the running battle took place is not called "the Battle Road" in the history books written before 1959, which leads me to believe the capitalized name was developed by NPS. See, for example, Shattuck.

11. On the history of high-tech development along Route 128 as a result of the relationship between the Massachusetts Institute of Technology, other universities, and the federal government, see Tsipis and Kruh, Leslie, Schiffrin, Saxenian, Rosegrant and Lampe, and O'Mara. On the invention of industrial parks and what they looked like and why, see Rand.

12. NPS has studied the traffic issue on several occasions. See, for example, Rothweiller et al., Steinitz, Bryan et al., Swikes et al., and *The Battle Road Scenic Byway*. One of the Ted Polumbaum photographs of the veterans' march in the Newseum collection shows the veterans handing out leaflets to people outside of Swanson's Pontiac dealership. Rental trucks and private sag wagons are visible in many of the photographs and in the film footage of the march. While no budget survives for the reverse Revere march, the budget for Operation RAW shows that VVAW spent $440 on four rental trucks ("Budget for Operation RAW," box 13, folder 7, VVAW-AP). In advance of Operation RAW, VVAW issued typed instructions, including on

how to walk: "Line of March: The march will be tactical in nature with 5 meter intervals between men and 25 meters between platoons" ("The Objective of Operation RAW," box 13, folder 7, VVAW-AP).

13. Tom Curran LOHP interview, 8.

14. Bruce Gordon LOHP interview, 8.

15. Chris Burns LOHP interview, 8.

16. John Hopkins LOHP interview, 44.

17. Fenton.

18. Bestor Cram interview with the author.

19. See Don Carrico interview with the author and Jarvis.

20. Boston National Historic Sites Commission, 2. Cary Wolinsky's photographs of the lunch stop at Fiske Hill show men treating their blisters.

21. Amedio Armenti LOHP interview, 4.

22. Quoted in Rand, 17–18.

23. Eugenia Kaledin LOHP interview, 2.

24. George McKibben LOHP interview.

25. Massachusetts Advisory Committee to the U.S. Commission on Civil Rights and the Massachusetts Commission Against Discrimination.

26. In her study of the park's founding and early history, Alicia M. Flynn notes, "The Park was not founded entirely on altruistic impulses. It is clear that many local residents hoped to decrease the pace of development and wished to preserve the semi-rural status of their communities" (23).

27. Betty Levin MMNHP-AHP interview, 9. On the Levin family's experience with polio, see Black, 29, 33–34, 35, 108, 195. On the Levin family's loss of their home to NPS and elite support for MMNHP, see Betty Levin MMNHP-AHP interview.

28. Betty Levin MMNHP-AHP interview, 13.

29. Betty Levin interview with the author.

30. "The People Will Be Heard," BG, May 28, 1971.

31. A photograph of the marker can be accessed at https://www.hmdb.org/m.asp?m=18249 (accessed January 20, 2020).

32. On NPS's efforts at Fiske Hill, see "Fiske Hill" and "Fiske Hill: Development Concept," box 2, folder 20, MMNHP-AHP.

33. Ginsberg, 10, and Raskin, 96–97.

34. Bruce McCabe and Gerald F. Mahoney, "500 Antiwar Vets Arrested on Lexington Green," BG, May 30, 1971. Photo caption: "Arms for Peace—Flower-bedecked and stacked 'weapons' are in reality toys" (11).

35. Ted Polumbaum's photographs of the march feature several veterans who decorated themselves with lilacs.

36. Sally Hale LOHP interview, 19–20.

37. Transcribed by the author from *Unfinished Symphony*.

38. Richard Robbat photographed the veterans flashing the peace sign at the Lexington police station. Three months later, in the first edition of its newsletter, the *First Casualty*, VVAW set forth "Guidelines for VVAW Marches and Guerrilla Theaters," in which the organization

noted the importance of having a march route "through the most populated area available": "If the period of marching includes a Sunday morning the route should pass as many churches as possible. . . . If schools are in session the route should pass as many schools as possible. . . . In all instances the route should pass shopping centers" ("Guidelines," *First Casualty* 1, no. 1, August 1971, 6).

39. Christopher Gregory interview with the author.

40. In his COHP interview, Armedio Armenti reported thinking there were three hundred civilians following the veterans in an expression of support. The *Boston Globe* reported that by the time the veterans arrived on the Lexington Green, there were "a hundred or so Lexington residents [who] cheered and applauded" (Bruce McCabe, "500 Antiwar Vets Arrested on Lexington Green," May 30, 1971).

41. Joseph Baratta interview with the author.

42. On the prowl cars deployed, see "A Bell Tolls for Lexington. . . ." BG, Op-Ed, June 2, 1971. Spencer Sullivan was one of the Lexington teenaged boys in awe of the antiwar veterans who came to Lexington. See his interview with the author. The teenaged boys are visible in photographs of the march taken by Richard Robbat. On the role of war violence as a gendering activity, see Leed and Mosse, 72.

43. "We Are All Prisoners of This War," leaflet in the private collection of Eugenia Kaledin. Concord and Lexington spell the names of their statues differently. Concord's is the Minute Man Statue and Lexington's is the Minuteman Statue.

44. In addition to Hart Perry's footage, one of Richard Robbat's photographs shows a Lexington policeman hammering in the "No Parking" signs midday Saturday. See Richard Robbat's photograph of the First Parish youth group's welcome sign and Richard Robbat's photograph of the veterans using the First Parish parking lot for their trucks and vans. On the First Parish's contributions to the march, see Richard Harding LOHP interview. He reported at the Special Selectmen's Meeting on Saturday night at Cary Hall that "the Executive Committee of the Church had voted to allow the VVAW members to use the church's parking and other lands owned by the church" ("410 Arrested in Defiance of Court Injunction," LMM, June 3, 1971, 15).

45. Arthur Johnson, VVAW-NE's other co-coordinator, along with Bestor Cram, is pictured between Bestor and Ross Fenton.

46. On the use of phone chains, see Norma McGavern-Norland LOHP interview, 10, and Bruce Gordon LOHP interview, 7. On the sign, see Eva Gordon LOHP interview, 5. On the antiweapons dance the veterans performed, see Christopher Gregory LOHP interview, 35; Lenny Rotman interview with the author; *Veterans Against the War*, in which it is included; and Ted Polumbaum's photographs of the march.

47. Christopher Gregory LOHP interview, 35.

48. Joseph Baratta interview with the author.

49. Christopher Gregory interview with the author.

Chapter 5

1. Quoted in Fischer, 76. For an account of Revere's time in Lexington prior to continuing toward Concord, see Fischer, 109–112.

2. On the Massachusetts officers who were combat veterans of the French and Indian War, see Fischer, 154.

3. Julian Soshnick agreed to assist the Vietnam veterans at the request of Nancy Earsey. See his LOHP interview, 2, and Nancy Earsy's LOHP interview, 3. The judge was John Forte. See his LOHP interview.

4. Julian Soshnick LOHP interview, 4. The chairman of the Board of Selectmen repeatedly expressed concern that violence would erupt if the veterans were allowed on the Green. Asked later what the Selectmen's initial reaction to the veterans' request had been, he recalled that "we wanted somebody to be able to answer to us, in case somebody was going to get hurt. Because we knew from the other marches there were a lot of drugs and liquor involved" (Robert Cataldo LOHP interview, 8). He worried about what would happen "if somebody got killed" (ibid., 24). On the Saturday evening of Memorial Day weekend, at the Special Selectmen's Meeting at Cary Hall, he told the hundreds of Lexington residents who attended while the veterans occupied the Green that he was concerned the Lexington residents opposed to the veterans' use of the Green would go down there and physically remove them themselves (transcribed by the author from *Veterans Against the War* and *Unfinished Symphony*). The Selectmen thus appear to have preselected a charge of disorderly conduct because, as a recent Massachusetts case, *Alegata v. Commonwealth* (1967), had made clear, it was the legal means used to prevent someone from provoking violence in others: "A person is guilty of disorderly conduct if, with purpose to cause public inconvenience, annoyance or alarm, or recklessly creating a risk thereof, he: (a) engages in fighting or threatening, or in violent or tumultuous behavior; or (b) makes unreasonable noise or offensively coarse utterance, gesture, or display, or addresses abusive language to any person present; or (c) creates a hazardous or physically offensive condition by any act which serves no legitimate purpose of the actor" (https://cite.case.law/mass/353/287/, accessed January 20, 2020). The punishment for disorderly conduct was no more than six months in jail, a fine of not more than two hundred dollars, or both.

5. Julian Soshnick LOHP interview, 6.

6. The caption of one of the photographs published later in the local Lexington newspaper reads as follows: "Attorney Julian Soshnick, 4 Douglas rd., tells New England Coordinator of the VVAW Bestor Cram, right, and attorney Bob Flanagan that the town had received an injunction barring the VVAW from camping Saturday night on the Battle Green. The announcement came minutes before the 7 p.m. meeting last Saturday of the Board of Selectmen." The injunction is quoted in "410 Arrested in Defiance of Court Injunction," LMM, June 3, 1971, 1.

7. Betty Levin interview with the author. On the Chicago riots, see Farber.

8. Bestor Cram LOHP interview, 31.

9. Gary Rafferty LOHP interview, 25.

10. Julian Soshnick, the young Lexington lawyer who was helping VVAW, suggested that local woman Nancy Earsy, who had just applied to law school, not get arrested because it might hurt her chances for admission. Nancy Earsy LOHP interview, 12. One active-duty soldier who attended the Memorial Day weekend march was John "Jack" Tracey. He describes how VVAW-NE leaders made sure he stayed out of sight of the authorities. See Tracey and John "Jack" Tracey interview with the author.

11. Quoted in Tourtellot, 123.

12. Joseph Baratta's interview on the Green is included in *Unfinished Symphony* and was transcribed by the author.

13. Unless taken from his interview on the Lexington Battle Green during the protest, Joseph Baratta's comments were made during his interview with the author.

14. Women who marched with their Vietnam veteran boyfriends or husbands include Norma Jacqueline Rich (see Don Carrico interview with the author); Gay Baratta (Joseph Baratta interview with the author); Melanie Fletcher-Howell, then Melanie Fletcher (Gordan and Melanie Fletcher-Howell interviews with the author); and Sheila Hopkins (John and Sheila Hopkins LOHP interviews). On the experiences of those Vietnam veterans in VVAW who were gay, see Bill Homans interview with the author.

15. On America's wars in Asia, see Hunt and Levine.

16. On historical reenactment, see Handler and Saxton, Turner, Hall (1994), Agnew, and Allred. "The play identity transforms the reenactor into someone else," Turner writes of historical reenactment, "and at the same time someone more fully himself: a creative individual freely engaging in a personally meaningful activity" (126). Note that Agnew, Hall (1994), and Turner focus on reenactment of the Civil War. As of yet, there is no scholarly study of Revolutionary War reenactment, and historians have thus not yet claimed a connection between the Cold War and the rise of historical reenactment of the American Revolution. Instead, they link the rise of historical reenactment to the anniversary of the Civil War and the impending bicentennial. "As the 1960 centennial approached," Rory Turner writes of the Civil War, "planners thought that battle demonstration would be a dramatic and effective means of commemoration" (123). What Turner does not explain, however, is why there was a perceived need for commemoration.

17. Lawrence and Lee, 67. Thoreau, "On the Duty of Civil Disobedience," http://www.gutenberg.org/files/71/71-h/71-h.htm (accessed January 2, 2020).

18. Eugenia Kaledin LOHP interview, 2.

19. Mim Donovan LOHP interview, 7.

20. In his sweeping survey of tradition in American history, *Mystic Chords of Memory*, Kammen proves that, in times of upheaval, "a usable past has been needed to give shape and substance to national identity" (6). For a history of the pageants on Lexington Green that preceded battle reenactments, see Glassberg, 27, 30, 32, 204, 250. On the early observances of April 19, 1775, in Lexington, see Pullen and Cobb. An article in the *Boston Globe* makes clear that observances prior to the 1960s did not include reenactments: "Flag raising ceremonies on the Battle Green followed a sunrise parade in which the Lexington Drum Corps and the Girl and Boy Scouts participated. The Lexington Minute Men, who gathered at historic Buckman Tavern, placed a wreath on the Minute Man Memorial" ("25,000 Hear Gen Merrill at Lexington," BG, April 19, 1951). In "Sacred Ground: Martial Landscape in American Culture," Linenthal notes that there are three means by which American battlefields are made sacred: (1) commemorative rhetoric, (2) monument building, and (3) physical preservation. He includes "battle reenactment" as "another form of veneration" (303). On the history of the modern Concord Minute Men, see Linenthal, *Sacred Ground* (1991), 17. For an account of historical reenactment in Concord in the 1960s, see Vincent Kehoe MMNHP-AHP interview.

21. Chairman of the Board of Selectmen Robert Cataldo later asserted, "I personally was against the war—I even wrote President Johnson, as an individual" (Robert Cataldo LOHP interview, 16). Selectman Allan Kenney said similarly, "It's difficult for me to speak for all the Selectmen, but I think generally speaking, at least the [World War II and Korean] veterans, we were not hot for the war" (Allan Kenney LOHP interview, 2). On the women antiwar protestors on the Lexington Green, see Geismer, 130–131.

22. The *Lexington Minute-man* reported that "following the VVAW marchers' arrival on the Battle Green at about 4 p.m. Saturday afternoon, an estimated 125 persons, mostly Lexington residents, marched to the Town Hall to demand a meeting with the Selectmen in an attempt to have the board reverse its decision denying the camping permit" (Tom Curran, "Veterans, Supporters Defy Bivouac Injunction," LMM, June 3, 1971). On the residents' parade to the Selectmen's temporary office trailer, see also Bruce Gordon LOHP interview, 9, and Allan Kenney LOHP interview, 14. Lexington resident Sally Hale later recalled "an angry kind of crowd milling around . . . demanding that they meet, demanding that they make a decision, demanding that they decide that they would be allowed to stay on the Green" (LOHP interview, 6–7). Photographs taken by Richard Robbat and film footage shot by Hart Perry confirm these reports. The *Boston Herald Traveler* reported that "about 700 townspeople, the majority apparently in sympathy with the veterans, met with the Board of Selectmen in a lengthy special session at the town hall" ("Antiwar Veterans Ousted," BHT, n.d., box 26, folder 12, VVAW-AP). The *Boston Globe* reported that "nearly 1000 Lexington residents . . . attended the special meeting" (Bruce McCabe, "500 Antiwar Vets Arrested on Lexington Green," May 30, 1971). The *Lexington Minute-man* reported that "on Saturday night, over 500 persons turned out for a mass meeting in Cary Hall" ("Over 400 Arrested, Fined in Lexington, Sunday, as Antiwar March Stalled," June 3, 1971). On residents' reaction to the number of police officers on hand at the Special Selectmen's Meeting, see Jackie Davison LOHP interview, 15–16, and Mary Shunney LOHP interview, 6. The extent of the support for the Selectmen's view that the bylaw governing use of the Green must be upheld is evident in the letters to the local newspaper following the events of Memorial Day weekend. According to a tally made by LOHP, of the 139 letters submitted, 45 letters were in support of the Selectmen's position while 94 were in support of the protestors ("Lexington Minute-Man Headlines and Letters," n.d., personal files of Eugenia Kaledin). On the cluster of issues around which liberalism cohered in the greater Boston area during the Cold War era, see Geismer. Regarding the way in which Lexington was split between turn-of-the-century immigrant families and recently arrived liberals, see Nathan Cobb, "Lexington: A Town Divided," BG, June 27, 1971. Cobb notes that there was one group composed of "ethnic groups whose families had tilled the town's soil during the years Lexington was primarily a farming community. One such example is Robert Cataldo, the current chairman of the Board of Selectmen. Another is Alfred S. Busa, elected to the board in March." Then there were the "new arrivals" who were "articulate academic-professionals able to come in and immediately make their presence felt." This group "was made up of first-generation suburbanites who had saved their money to escape the city after half a lifetime of hard work." Those locals who were asked when interviewed by LOHP agreed with this assessment of the town's political landscape. See, in particular, Pat Swanson LOHP interview, 5–7; Jackie Davison LOHP interview, 2–5, 18–19; Mim

Donovan LOHP interview, 1–3; Emily Frankovich LOHP interview, 17–31; and Bonnie Jones LOHP interview, 1–2, 5.

23. On the line at the Cary Hall pay phone after the Special Selectmen's Meeting, see the Carol Chomsky LOHP interview. When asked to estimate how many demonstrators were on the Green, police estimated that there were "more than 1,000" but added, according to one newspaper account, that "a constant flow of spectators hindered a factual count" ("Vets, Townspeople Held in Lexington Protest," BHT, May 31, 1971). The *Lexington Minute-man* also reported an "estimated 1,000 persons" on the Green ("Veterans, Supporters Defy Bivouac Injunction," June 3, 1971). If there were over two hundred veterans, as eyewitness accounts attest, then 800 or so of the people on the Green were civilian supporters of the veterans. In noting that the veterans had not yet been welcomed home, I am not suggesting that the veterans were spat upon. On the myth that Vietnam veterans were spat upon, see Lembcke.

24. Christopher Gregory LOHP interview, 12.

25. Dale Reese interview with the author.

26. Christopher Gregory LOHP interview, 38.

27. Gary Rafferty LOHP interview, 39.

28. The local paper reported that the veterans read "a statement approved Friday night by the veterans" ("Special Meeting Held to Avert 'Bust,'" LMM, June 3, 1971). See "VVAW Gives Reasons for Green Bivouac," in which VVAW's statement is reprinted (LMM, June 3, 1971).

29. Transcribed by the author from *Veterans Against the War.*

30. Kaledin, 148. The *Boston Herald Traveler* also reported that protestors were instructed by the veterans to, "if arrested . . . 'give our names, serial numbers and date of birth—April 18, 1775—an important day in American liberty'" ("Held in Lexington Protest," BHT, May 31, 1971). The difference in dates represents the difference between the date Longfellow celebrated (April 18) and the date celebrated by the state holiday (April 19).

31. Bestor Cram interview with the film crew in *Unfinished Symphony* as transcribed by the author.

32. Noam Chomsky LOHP interview, 28, 15, 16.

33. Chris Burns LOHP interview, 27.

34. Kaledin, 149.

35. Jackie Davison LOHP interview, 6, 11.

36. Florence Bernier, "Bells," Letter to the Editor, LMM, June 10, 1971, 18.

37. VVAW statement by John Kerry, WSI-T. At the 2010 panel discussion held in Lexington about the march, "Peace, Protest, Patriotism," Bestor Cram had to clarify to the man who was chairman of the Board of Selectmen in 1971 that it was he and co-coordinator Arthur Johnson, not John Kerry, who organized and led the march.

38. Carlene A. Raper, Letter to the Editor, LMM, June 3, 1971.

39. On Robert Cataldo's nervousness about stepping onto the Battle Green during its occupation, see his LOHP interview, 33. Selectman Allan Kenney warned Chairman Cataldo that "there's a possibility here that if arrests are made that's the thing that people might remember and not all the good work you have done" (Allan Kenney LOHP interview, 19–20). He strongly recommended that the chairman read a statement condemning the occupation while declining to arrest for safety reasons. The Selectmen had considered the park on Lincoln Street, until

recently a town dump, as an alternative Thursday night, only to reject the idea because it had just been seeded with grass.

40. On the perceived importance of staying on the Green for the media coverage it would garner, see Tom Curran LOHP interview, 10–11.

41. Allan Kenney LOHP interview, 18.

42. Jackie Davison was one of the residents who went home because she did not think the Selectmen were going to enforce the injunction (Jackie Davison LOHP interview, 14). On people's use of the pews as beds, see Sheila Hopkins LOHP interview, 14, and a photo of people sleeping in the pews in the supplement the *Minute-man* devoted to the arrests on June 3, 1971. Several veterans mention that they drank Boone's Farm wine in those days at their get-togethers, and one bottle is clearly visible in one of Richard Robbat's photographs of the protestors on the Lexington Green. In his report on the march for the *New Republic*, David King notes, "One resident went through the crowd handing out bottles of apple wine from a case" (11). He admitted to finding it "puzzling" that the veterans had such a rapport with the suburban communities through which they passed given that "liquor and drugs were in evidence throughout the weekend" and concluded that "they succeeded in seducing the emotions of almost everyone they encountered," which I attribute to their use of historical reenactment (12–13). Film crew members Deborah Crocket-Rice and Ted Timreck both describe leaving the Lexington Battle Green, although not with each other, for romantic trysts during the protest. See their interviews with the author.

43. Hall (2002), 7. Frank Hall remembers his interaction happening in the Public Works Department's garage after the mass arrest. I have taken the liberty of shifting it forward chronologically.

44. Betty Levin interview with the author about Lincoln parents Margaret and Warren Flint Sr.

45. Kenneth Hale LOHP interview, 5.

46. On assigning policemen in plainclothes to the Green during its occupation, see James Corr LOHP interview, 15 and 18. Corr also kept the FBI apprised of what was happening on the Green. His and the Concord police chief's reports to the FBI over Memorial Day weekend, 1971, are included in the Vietnam Veterans Against the War FBI Files. On the way in which sacred spaces become "more intensely sacred" when "in danger of being defiled," see Chidester and Linenthal, 5, and Linenthal (2001), 302. The suggestion that the Selectmen go home to bed was filmed and transcribed by the author from *Unfinished Symphony*. It was also reported in the local paper ("410 Arrested in Defiance of Court Injunction," LMM, June 3, 1971, 15).

47. Chidester and Linenthal note that "defilement can be easily addressed through rites of purification or rites of exclusion, such as excommunication, banishment, or execution, which effectively eliminate a polluting influence from the pure space of the sacred" (2).

48. James Corr LOHP interview, 14.

49. "Veterans, Supporters Defy Bivouac Injunctions," LMM, June 3, 1971, 1. Lexington resident Charles E. Forrester also reports seeing policemen from Arlington and Bedford in "Botching," Letter to the Editor from Charles E. Forrester, LMM, June 3, 1971.

50. John Grossman, "Eyewitness Account: Veterans' Demonstration," *Musket*, June 10, 1971.

51. On what Revere most likely shouted, see Fischer, 109–110.

52. Joe Pilati, "The Vietnam Veterans' March on Washington," BG, March 30, 1971. On how the veterans took care not to invite "radicals and college students" on the reverse Revere march, see King (1971), 11. VVAW was always exceedingly careful to ensure that its members and the participants in its events were indeed Vietnam veterans. Participants in marches and demonstrations were always asked to bring discharge papers, for example. Prior to the Winter Soldier Investigation, testimonies were crosschecked to ensure that there were always corroborating witnesses (a point Kulik overlooks in his critique of the testimonies made at the Winter Soldier Investigation). There was, however, one man participating in Operation POW who was indeed a veteran but who greatly exaggerated his service record. Paul Withers, since deceased, told VVAW-NE leaders and others that he had been a sergeant in the Green Berets and that he had served as a Special Forces agent in Laos. At the medal ceremony during Operation Dewey Canyon III in DC, he told those gathered that he had been awarded nine Purple Hearts, the Distinguished Service Cross, and Silver and Bronze Stars. By the mid-1980s, Withers was exaggerating even more, describing his service to his local newspaper in terms that almost exactly replicate the outlandish script of the Vietnam War film *Rambo* (Steve Rosenbush, "Vietnam Hero to Be Honored Endured Capture, Torture, and Shootings," *Day* [New London, CT], November 10, 1986). Paul Withers's service records indicate that his highest rank was actually Specialist Fourth and that he had one Purple Heart, not nine, as well as a Vietnam Service Medal with two Bronze Service Stars, and other medals, but not the Distinguished Service Cross, which is the second highest medal the Army awards. In his interview with the author, Chris Gregory explains that VVAW-NE leaders were initially very eager to use Withers's stories about illegal American operations in Laos (included in *The Opium Trail*, 50), but they were unable to corroborate them and declined to put him forward, although he was allowed to testify at the VVAW-NE–organized Winter Soldier II, held in Boston on October 9, 1971. On the veteran with the firearm, see Chris Gregory LOHP interview, 29, and his interview with the author. The veteran calling for respect is quoted in Joan Mahoney, "Citizens and Veterans Share Cold Night Vigil," BG, May 31, 1971. David King also reported in an article for the *New Republic* that during Cataldo's remarks, someone tried to interrupt only to be shouted down by the veterans (12).

53. Chris Burns LOHP interview, 30.

54. Allan Kenney's recollection of Chief Corr's briefing to his officers, Kenney LOHP interview, 22.

55. John Quinlan LOHP interview.

56. James Corr LOHP interview, 13.

57. Ibid., 14.

58. Joe O'Leary at 2010 panel, "Peace, Protest, Patriotism."

59. Hart Perry directed one of his film crews to film an older man in a suit and the woman on his arm in a dress and heels strolling among the veterans congenially.

60. Nancy Earsy LOHP interview, 4.

61. Sheila Hopkins LOHP interview, 23.

62. Melanie Fletcher-Howells interview with the author.

63. Herb Adams LOHP interview.

64. On the Regulars' clothing and gear, see Fischer, 118-123. On the story of the Regulars' fatigue and its role in their subsequent berserk state that resulted in the massacre of eight colonists, see Fischer, 184-195, and, most especially, O'Brien (1993).

65. Chief Corr's son was a cadet (James Corr LOHP interview, 21), as was Joe O'Leary (2010 Lexington Panel).

66. James Corr LOHP interview, 9–10, 7.

67. On the chief ordering his men to wear the same dress uniforms they wore on Patriots' Day, see Joe O'Leary, 2010 Lexington panel, "Peace, Protest, Patriotism."

68. Chris Burns LOHP interview, 29.

69. Jo Hanna Katz at 2010 Lexington panel, "Peace, Protest, Patriotism."

70. Selectman Allan Kenney would later insist of the chief of police that "he told them that there [would be] no nightsticks" (LOHP interview, 22).

71. Edgar Smith recalled seeing massive nightsticks in his LOHP interview, 10. It is possible Smith was recalling seeing the state police so armed, although there are no corroborating reports.

72. Transcribed by the author from *Unfinished Symphony.*

73. Amedio Armenti LOPH interview, 7.

74. Bestor Cram LOHP interview, 30.

75. Tourtellot calls Parker saying "stand your ground" a "myth," noting that the quotation was born in an 1825 deposition given fifty years after the events of that day and printed in Phinney, 289.

76. Quoted in Fischer, 195.

77. Quoted in Tourtellot, 123.

78. Gary Rafferty LOHP interview, 41.

79. On officers apologizing, see Gary Rafferty LOHP interview, 40–41. On who rang the bell, see Tracey, Jack Tracey interview with the author, and Richard Harding LOHP interview. One of the film crews followed them into the church and filmed the ropes being pulled in close up.

80. "As the wait for the police continued, the number of persons appeared to dwindle to less than 400 but when the arrests started, the number of persons in the Green area increased" ("Veterans, Supporters Defy Bivouac Injunction," LMM, June 3, 1971). "I woke up to hear the bells, the church bells in First Parish. They were ringing just two blocks from my house," one woman later recalled. "I got up and went down to the Green to get arrested" (Nancy Earsy LOHP interview, 8–9).

81. Chris Burns LOHP interview, 28–29.

82. Norma McGovern-Norland LOHP interview, 9.

83. Melanie Fletcher-Howell interview with the author.

84. Lucille Longview LOHP interview, 12.

85. The photo caption reads "Left photo, John Kerry, a leader of Vietnam Veterans Against the War, walks with hands behind his head. Right, man and wife in custody. Son, in blanket, accompanied them on bus," BG, May 31, 1971.

86. Bestor Cram LOHP interview, 29–30.

87. For example, Karen Rhodes, who had written a first-person account of her participation in an earlier VVAW-NE mock search-and-destroy mission, got arrested on the Lexington

Battle Green. See the arrest list printed in the *Lexington Minute-Man* on June 3, 1971. Karen Rhodes, "V.C. Numba Ten, Me No V.C.!" BP, April 20, 1971.

88. Pete Wilson's flight instructor was Landon T. Stores of Cambridge. See the arrest list printed in the *Lexington Minute-man* on June 3, 1971.

89. Quoted by Gordon Fletcher-Howell in his interview with the author.

90. Allan Kenney recalled there being fifteen to twenty veterans in wheelchairs (Allan Kenney LOHP interview, 23). And while no one else cites such a large number, photographic evidence indicates that there were more than a few.

91. James Corr LOHP interview, 18.

92. Ibid., 18–19.

93. Quoted in Julian Soshnick LOHP interview, 10.

94. Quoted in Brooks Jackson, "Protesting Veterans to Turn in Medals," *Ledger-Star* (Norfolk, VA), April 23, 1971.

95. Quoted in Jim Tice, "Vets Keep Their Cool," *Times* (Washington, DC), May 5, 1971.

96. Exchange recalled by Julian Soshnick in his LOHP interview, 10.

97. King (1971), 12. Peter Wilson has similar memories of wounded veterans seeking ways to get arrested. He later recalled that one wounded veteran asked his comrades to hide his wheelchair behind a tree so that, seeing him sitting on the grass, the police would put him under arrest. Peter Wilson interview with the author.

98. A photograph of a husband and wife with their young son getting arrested together was featured on the front page of the *Boston Globe* on May 31, 1971. The *Lexington Minute-man* also ran a photo of children being arrested with the following caption: "Young and old await buses to bring them to DPW garage following their arrest on the Battle Green last Sunday morning" (June 3, 1971). For accounts of parents who stayed on the Green with their minor children, see John Maguire LOHP interview, 17, 19; Marion Coletta LOHP interview, 6; and Eugenia Kaledin LOHP interview, 1. Several people remembered years later the presence of children during the arrests, among them Chief James Corr (LOHP interview, 16) and Lexington resident Bruce Gordon (LOHP interview, 16–17).

99. Eugenia Kaledin LOHP interview, 20. George McKibben's wife and two young children, one of whom would grow up to be an important environmentalist and who would write an article about how the arrests were his introduction to activism, came to the Green, but when it grew late, his wife went home with the children. "Someone had to stay home with the kids" (George McKibben LOHP interview). For his son Bill's article, see McKibben. John Maguire's wife also stayed home with their children during the protest, even though, as John put it, his wife "was, at the time, as sympathetic as I to the aims of war protestors" (John Maguire LOHP interview). Norma McGavern-Norland was only able to stay on the Green because her parents were visiting and volunteered to babysit her young children (Norma McGavern-Norland LOHP interview, 8).

100. Noam Chomsky LOHP interview, 12. On the gendered division of labor in the Chomsky family, see too Carol Chomsky LOHP interview and Barksy, 124–126.

101. See the arrest list printed in the *Lexington Minute-man* on June 3, 1971.

102. Sally Hale LOHP interview, 7.

103. Ibid., 4.

104. Norma McGavern-Norland LOHP interview, 4.

105. John Wood, "Antiwar Veterans March on Bunker Hill," BG, May 31, 1971. On the number of protestors remaining, see Ted Polumbaum LOHP interview, 15.

106. Lucile Longview LOHP interview, 10.

107. The Lexington police tally of 410 excluding juveniles was reported in the local newspaper ("401 Arrested in Defiance of Court Injunction," LMM, June 3, 1971). See also Kaledin, 148. The *Boston Globe* headline announcing "500 Antiwar Vets Arrested on Lexington Green" ran on Sunday, May 30, 1971. The following day, the *Boston Herald Traveler* was more specific, running a headline announcing "458 Seized in Lexington" and noting in the article that "about 100" of those arrested were members of VVAW. The *Boston Globe* concurred on Monday, also noting that "about 100 of those arrested were veterans" ("Antiwar Veterans March on Bunker Hill," BG, May 31, 1971). The *Boston Phoenix* reported the following week that 150 of the people arrested were veterans ("Memorial Day: Antiwar Vets on the March," BP, June 8, 1971). Lexington had the largest number of residents arrested at 168 people, followed by Cambridge (36) and Boston (20). People from ten other states were arrested, with the most from Connecticut (20) and Rhode Island (13) on account of both states having VVAW chapters who came up to Massachusetts to participate.

108. On the length of the lines at the town garage, see John Maguire LOHP interview, 4. The *Boston Herald Traveler* reported in "Special Events—Dedications, Anniversaries—Vietnam Veterans—5/31/1971" that people were saying they were born on April 18, 1776 (quoted in Linenthal [1991], 50, fn78). Bestor Cram, conversely, told the filmmakers while incarcerated in Lexington's town garage that people were giving their birthdates as April 19, 1775 (transcribed by the author from *Unfinished Symphony*). For a detailed account of how court workers were called in to the town garage, see James Corr LOHP interview, 17. Bonnie Jones and her husband were two of the people who paid their fine and went home (Bonnie Jones LOHP interview, 11). John Maguire did not wait to be booked and simply left with his children (LOHP interview, 4). On how Judge John Forte got permission to open court and then ran the session, see his LOHP interview. The photograph of the skit, taken by Frank Kelly, ran on the front page of the *Boston Herald Traveler* on May 31, 1997.

109. "Feeding VVAW," letter to the editor from Anita J. Sethares, Bedford Peace Action Committee, *Concord Journal*, June 17, 1971; Don Carrico interview with the author; Betty Levin interview with the author.

110. Diana Mara Henry took many photographs outside of the courthouse that reveal the veterans smiling broadly as they were greeted by applause. In one of her photographs, Joseph Baratta is beaming as he leaves the courthouse.

111. Gary Rafferty LOHP interview, 43.

112. "There had been times on other occasions," Judge Forte explained, "where I've had to arraign people outside on the ground because there is no access for a wheelchair" (Judge John Forte LOHP interview, 10).

113. Ruth McCarthy, editorial, *Springfield Union*, June 15, 1971.

114. Judge John Forte LOHP interview, 13–14.

115. "500 Antiwar Vets Arrested on Lexington's Battle Green," BG, May 31, 1971.

116. Bestor Cram interview with the author.

117. Dale Reese interview with the author.

118. John Wood, "Antiwar Veterans March on Bunker Hill," BG, May 31, 1971.

119. Melanie Howell-Fletcher interview with the author.

120. Joe Pilati, "The Vietnam Veterans' March on Washington," BG, May 30, 1971.

121. The photo ran in the *Chicago Sun-Times* and the *San Rafael Daily Independent* (CA), as well as on the front pages of the *Progress Bulletin* (Pomona, CA), the *Kingsport News* (TN), and the *Ogden Standard-Examiner* (UT), among other newspapers. "He surrendered at Lexington," *Chicago Sun-Times*, May 31, 1971. In all captions, Phillip Lavoie is mistakenly identified as "Philip LaBois." The march was also covered in "409 Fined in Protest on Lexington Green," *Los Angeles Times*, May, 31 1971; "400 Fined $5 Each in Antiwar March: Arrested for Camping at Lexington, Mass. Site," *New York Times*, May, 31 1971; "Vets March from Concord Draws Fire," *Washington Post*, May 29, 1971; "400 Fined in Massachusetts War Protest," *Washington Post*, May 31, 1971.

122. Quoted in Tourtellot, 215–216.

123. On the economic divide between the suburbs along Route 128 and the urban Boston area, see Massachusetts Advisory Committee to the U.S. Commission on Civil Rights and the Massachusetts Commission Against Discrimination. On the working-class demographics of the draft in the Vietnam War era, see Appy and Baskir and Strauss.

124. Bestor Cram LOHP interview, 33. In his LOHP interview, Bob Barbanti recalled hearing that the "townies" of Charlestown were going "to kick the shit out of us" (33).

125. John Wood, "Antiwar Veterans March on Bunker Hill," BG, May 31, 1971.

Chapter 6

1. On the history and rituals that comprise Memorial Day, see Mosse, Warner, and Albanese (1974, 1976). "Bring our brothers home alive," flier for "Memorial Day Alternative," personal collection of Eugene Kaledin.

2. ". . . to Glorify Life," Letter to the Editor, BG, from Bestor Cram and Arthur Johnson, May 23, 1971. The Gold Star mother who spoke on the Boston Common on behalf of the veterans and who was not announced on the flier was Pat Simon. See her interview with the author. On the formation of the Paul Revere Memorial Association, see Lindgren, 37–41.

3. Transcribed by the author from *People's Century*. "Young Blood (1968).

4. This photograph is online at https://visions.popasmoke.com/Vietnam/HMM-362/i-4vPJHgk/A (accessed January 7, 2020).

5. All of Pat Simon's remarks are from her interview with the author.

6. WSI-T. For an in-depth critique of Rusty Sachs's testimony, see Kulik, 131–132. Kulik argues that Sachs was asked a "leading question" at the start of the Winter Soldier Investigation and "communicated a desire to be accommodating." Kulik points out that Sachs could not have seen a prisoner thrown out while he was piloting. What Sachs was recounting, Kulik argues, was a joke repeated in Vietnam. He points out that Sachs's testimony was subsequently manipulated by the press so that it appeared he routinely witnessed prisoners being thrown from his helicopter while it was in flight. I have tried to make clear that Rusty Sachs testified to prisoners being thrown from *grounded* aircraft. As Kulik rightly points out, Rusty Sachs never claimed to have seen prisoners thrown from an airborne helicopter.

7. Christopher Gregory interview with the author. Rusty Sachs describes several particularly vivid memories of conducting medevac missions under fire in a 2008 interview as one of the "Timeless Voices of Aviation!" available online at https://www.eaa.org/videos/1590219863 (accessed January 2, 2020).

8. WSI-T.

9. Transcribed by the author from *Veterans Against the War.*

10. Rusty Sachs interview with the author.

11. Lubow.

12. Marvin Gross, interview with the author.

13. Arthur Johnson, quoted in Jean Gogolin, "Vets: Anti-War Stand Explained," newspaper name not indicated, April 18, 1971, box 26, folder 2, VVAW-AP.

14. Rusty Sachs National Public Radio (NPR) interview, August 10, 2005, https://www.npr.org/templates/story/story.php?storyId=4793878 (accessed January 9, 2020).

15. *The New Soldier,* 138.

16. Rusty Sachs NPR interview, August 10, 2005, https://www.npr.org/templates/story/story.php?storyId=4793878 (accessed January 9, 2020).

17. Ibid.

18. Ibid.

19. *The New Soldier,* 142.

20. Betty Levin interview with the author.

21. Transcribed by the author from the film *Winter Soldier.*

22. *The New Soldier,* 138.

23. Transcribed by the author from *Veterans Against the War.*

24. The VVAW-NE veterans respected the fact that Rusty was such a high-ranking officer, that he had flown night medevac missions under fire, that he had testified in Detroit, and that he had thrown away his ribbons during Operation DCIII. His credibility in their minds was unshakeable, whereas there were members of VVAW who were concerned that John Kerry was more interested in starting a political career than he was in their cause. VVAW-NE gave Rusty a central role in the Memorial Day weekend march while they made sure that John Kerry did not speak publicly and thereby draw attention away from their efforts to situate the Vietnam War in American history. On the veterans' respect for Rusty Sachs, see Christopher Gregory interview with the author.

25. A photo caption reads, "Mrs. Mariel Kinsey 19 Cedar st, Lexington, Left, signs a plaque reading 'I Don't Want to Be a Gold Star Mother' held by Virginia Nolan, 4 Grimes rd," LMM, June 3, 1971.

26. On which Americans served in Vietnam, see Appy.

27. For accounts of the Battle of Bunker Hill, see Ketchum and Philbrick.

28. John Quincy Adams, quoted in Philbrick, xiii.

29. "Antiwar Vets End 3-Day Protest, Leave Common," *Record American* (Boston, MA), June 1, 1971. Reports on the number of veterans at Bunker Hill vary wildly. The *Sun* (Baltimore, MD) reported "about 300" in one article ("300 Anti-War Vets Camp on Bunker Hill in Trek," May 31, 1971) and "more than 400 veterans" in another ("War Foes March from Bunker Hill," June 1, 1971). The UPI reported, in contrast, that about 75 veterans camped on Bunker Hill (see

"Vets Camp Out on Bunker Hill," *Desert News* [Salt Lake City, UT], May 31, 1971). Other reports include "250 Vietnam Vets Camp on Bunker Hill," *Record American* (Boston, MA), May 31, 1971, and "Veterans Gain Front Ranks in Antiwar Fight," *Christian Science Monitor*, June 2, 1971.

30. Residents' reactions to the veterans are described in "Marchers Bivouac at Bunker Hill," BHT, May 31, 1971. See also John Wood, "Antiwar Veterans March on Bunker Hill," BG, May 31, 1971.

31. Transcribed by the author from *Unfinished Symphony.*

32. On the nineteenth-century origins of Memorial Day, see Blight. On Memorial Day as a "cult of the dead" that creates national unity, see Warner.

33. On the history of the Bunker Hill Monument, see Giguere, 91–115. On John Quincy Adams's reaction to Dr. Warren's death, see Philbrick, xiii, 293–294.

34. Webster, 6.

35. "458 Seized in Lexington," BHT, May 31, 1971.

36. The lyrics can be found at https://www.antiwarsongs.org/canzone.php?id=27503&lang=en (accessed January 2, 2020).

37. "Marchers Bivouac at Bunker Hill," BHT, May 31, 2020.

38. Arthur Johnson interview with the author.

39. Stu Werbin, "Memorial Day: Antiwar Vets on the March," BP, June 8, 1971. This photograph ran in newspapers around the country. See, for example, in addition to the *Boston Herald*, the *Times Union* (Albany, NY), June 1, 1971. The photograph of Ross Fenton and John Kerry would reappear during Kerry's career (see, for example, the September 16, 1974, edition of *People* magazine, shortly after Kerry was named executive director of Mass Action, a Massachusetts advocacy association) and most explosively during his 2004 presidential campaign, when Swift Boat Veterans for Truth argued that Kerry was "unfit to serve" as president, having made what the organization considered "phony" charges of American war crimes in Vietnam. While the group's insistence that Kerry did not deserve his combat medals was ultimately proven to be a smear campaign, it contributed to Kerry's defeat. For the case against Kerry, see O'Neill. Kerry's counterargument is represented by his biographer, Brinkley.

40. See *Veterans Against the War.*

41. Ibid.

42. On the stop at Faneuil Hall, see "Observances Over, Protest Points Made," BG, June 1, 1971.

43. William Dawes is now thought to be buried in his wife's plot in Forest Hills Cemetery in Jamaica Plain. See Ron Fletcher, "Who's Buried in Dawes's Tomb," BG, February 25, 2005.

44. The plaque honoring Dr. Joseph Warren is transcribed at https://www.waymarking.com/waymarks/WMDZJ5_William_Dawes_Jr_One_of_the_Riders_with_Paul_Revere_Boston_MA (accessed April 22, 2020).

45. Quoted in Nicosia, 110.

46. Richard Colton interview with the author.

47. Ibid.

48. The detractor's comments were transcribed by the author from *Veterans Against the War*. On the size of the crowd, see "Observances Over, Protest Points Made," BG, June 1, 1971.

49. For a history of Boston Common, see Rawson, 22–74.

50. Also visible in the photograph of Don Carrico leading the veterans onto the Common is Al Hubbard, VVAW's executive secretary (second from right), and Dale Reese (pushing the wheelchair), who had driven all the way from New Jersey to participate in the march. See his interview with the author and Jane Brayton's interview with the author.

51. See Shay on Vietnam veterans' grief and rage, a concept he borrows from anthropologist Renato Rosaldo.

52. Bill Homans interview with the author.

53. Shay argues that Vietnam veterans experienced what we now call PTSD in part because they were denied communal mourning for their deeds and the war dead.

54. Bill Homans interview with the author.

55. Deborah Crockett-Rice interview with the author.

56. Robert J. Sales, "Antiwar Vets End Protest on Common," BG, June 1, 1971.

57. MacLeish, 172.

58. One of the musicians was a young Bonnie Raitt, and another was Vietnam veteran Bill Homans. See his interview with the author. See *Veterans Against the War* for film footage of children playing with the veterans' discarded weapons along the march route of Operation POW. The photojournalist was Ted Polumbaum. See his LOHP interview.

59. The 45 RPM record is entitled *Air War/1984, MIA Testimony by 10 Vietnam Veterans, Faneuil Hall, Boston, October 7–9, 1971*. Private collection of Joseph Baratta.

60. For his account of occupying the Statue of Liberty, see Don Bristow-Carrico, "Seizing the Statue of Liberty 1971: Three Days with a Lady," *Veteran* 29, no. 1 (Spring/Summer 1999), www.vvaw.org/veteran/article/?id=195 (accessed January 4, 2020). For scholarly considerations of Operation Peace on Earth, see Nicosia, 217; Hunt, 140–142; Moser, 119–120; and especially Teachout, 1–4.

61. www.vvaw.org (accessed January 4, 2020). Nixon's POW/MIA campaign did not end in 1973. The U.S. government continued to list over one thousand American men as POW/MIA until VVAW's former national spokesman, Massachusetts senator John Kerry, led a U.S. Senate committee in the early 1990s that ultimately concluded there was no evidence indicating there were still Americans held captive in Southeast Asia. Still, the U.S. Capitol and towns and cities across the United States continue to fly the POW/MIA flag, which declares to American prisoners of war that "you are not forgotten." This message is aimed at POWs held anywhere but specifically refers to those held in Southeast Asia, insofar as they were the ones for whom the Nixon administration created the POW/MIA campaign. On the way in which the flag rewrites history by asserting that the United States was the victim and not the aggressor in the Vietnam War, see Franklin. Today, the only reminder of the Vietnam War era on the Lexington Battle Green is the POW/MIA flag that flies on the same pole as the American flag. Its meaning directly contradicts the message brought to the Lexington Battle Green in 1971 by VVAW during its Operation POW.

Epilogue

1. On how the Vietnam Veterans Memorial came into being, see Hagopian (2009). There are numerous excellent interpretations of the Vietnam Veterans Memorial. See Wagner-Pacifici and Schwartz for a particularly good study that considers the memorial within the context of prior war memorials.

2. Transcribed by the author from *How Far Home: Veterans After Vietnam.*

3. On VVAW's many achievements, see Shay, Nicosia, and Horwitz.

4. Representative Henry Hyde, quoted in Hagopian (2009), 127. On the controversy surrounding the design of the Vietnam Veterans Memorial and the decision to add a statue, see Hagopian (2009).

5. For a description of the design process and an interpretation of the resulting Korean War Veterans Memorial, see Hagopian (2012).

6. For an in-depth reading of the World War II Memorial, see Doss, 186–216.

BIBLIOGRAPHY

Interviews Conducted by the Author

Key:

- * Vietnam War veteran
- # Vietnam War–era veteran
- @ Veteran of other wars or eras
- + Member of the film crew organized by Hart Perry
- % Civilian supporter of VVAW

Howard Baker, December 16, 2011*

Joseph P. Baratta, October 25, 2011@

Jane (Williams) Brayton, June 24, 2010%

Don Carrico, November 1, 2011*

Richard Colton, June 10, 2011*

Christopher Coyle, February 12, 2014*

Bestor Cram, June 25, 2010*

Deborah Crocket-Rice, August 19, 2010+

Ross Fenton, December 14, 2011*

Gordon Fletcher-Howell, June 9, 2012*

Melanie Fletcher-Howell, June 9, 2012%

Christopher Gregory, December 15, 2011*

Marvin Gross, October 4, 2011%

Peter Haggerty, April 17, 2012#

David Helperin, September 7, 2011+

Bill Homans, November 4, 2011*

Arthur Johnson, March 8, 2012*

Harry Knaster, June 1, 2012*

Betty Levin, November 13, 2010%

Jennifer Levin, March 5, 2011%

Jerry Lund, July 26, 2011#

Rand E. Martin, June 6, 2012*

Richard Nichols, September 10, 2012%

Hart Perry, May 27, 2010+

Richard Hayes Phillips, July 29, 2016%

Guy Pommares, May 16, 2012+
Sally Raisbeck, November 30, 2010%
Dale Reese, January 26, 2011*
Richard Robbat, November 25, 2011#
Lenny Rotman, November 9, 2011*
Rusty Sachs, September 19, 2010*
Robert Shapiro, May 20, 2012%
Patricia Simon, December 30, 2011%
Spencer Sullivan, May 31, 2017%
Ted Timreck, September 10, 2010+
Jack Tracey, October 23, 2011*
Peter Wilson, January 6, 2011*
Tim Wright, February 13, 2012@

Interviews Conducted by the Lexington Oral History Project

Key:

- * Vietnam veteran
- \# Interview that LOHP transcribed, paginated, and supplied on their website, www.lexingtonbattlegreen1971.com, accessed February 15, 2020 (other LOHP interviews exist solely on videotape and are thus cited without page numbers)

Herb Adams, October 29, 1994
Amedio Armenti, August 1, 1991#
Bob Barbanti, April 7, 1994*#
Lois Brown, January 29, 1994
John Buehrens, May 25, 1994#
Chris Burns, December 31, 1994*#
Helena Butters, April 17, 1993
Keith Butters, April 26, 1993
Robert Cataldo, August 24, 1993#
Carol Chomsky, February 29, 1992
Noam Chomsky, March 7, 1992#
Blythe Clinchy, April 20, 1994
Lincoln Cole, July 21, 1993
Dario Coletta, February 2, 1994
Marion Coletta, November 1, 1993#
James Corr Jr., September 16, 1994#
Bestor Cram, June 19, 1992*#
John Crowley, February 8, 1993
Tom Curran, January 26, 1994#
Fred Davis, October 26, 1992
Jackie Davison, October 6, 1992#

Mim Donovan, June 25, 1991#
Nancy Earsy, July 1, 1991#
Dan Fenn, March, 20, 1993
John Forte, April 27, 1994#
Emily Frankovich, February 28, 1992#
Richard Gillespie, April 29, 1995
Bruce Gordon, August 24, 1992#
Eva Gordon, September 8, 1992#
Christopher Gregory, March 14, 1995*#
Jerome Grossman, December 3, 1996#
Kenneth Hale, January 15, 1991#
Sally Hale, September 10, 1991#
Richard Harding, October 29, 1991
John Hopkins, June 24, 1995*#
Sheila Hopkins, June 24, 1995#
Virginia Hutchinson, May 25, 1994
William Hutchinson, May 25, 1994
Arthur Johnson, March 20, 1995*#
Bonnie Jones, December 3, 1991#
Jim Jones, August 27, 1991
Arthur Kaledin, January 9, 1993
Eugenia Kaledin, September 3, 1991#
Allan Kenney, June 11, 1994#
Lucille Longview, November 18, 1992#
John Maquire, November 30, 1992#
David McGavern, June 30, 1992
Norma McGavern-Norland, August 22, 1991#
Gordon McKibben, October 3, 1991
Frank Michelman, December 13, 1993
Paul Plasse, April 24, 1995#
Nyna Polumbaum, April 2, 1995
Ted Polumbaum, April 2, 1995#
John Quinlan, February 4, 1993*
Gary Rafferty, March 23, 1994*#
David Reiner, September 29, 1992
Anne Scigliano, July 15, 1992#
Mary Shunney, November 10, 1992#
Ardyth Smith, April 11, 1994
Edgar Smith, May 24, 1993#
Julian Soshni[c]k, August 15, 1991#
Pat Swanson, September 28, 1995#
Philip Taylor, March 28, 1995

Jackie Ward, March 29, 1994
Weiant Wathen-Dunn, June 25, 1992

Interviews Conducted by the Minute Man National Historical Park Administrative History Project

Vincent Kehoe, May 14, 1994
Betty Levin, April 26, 2005

Texts

Abney, Wesley. *Random Destiny: How the Vietnam War Draft Lottery Shaped a Generation.* Wilmington, DE: Vernon Press, 2018.

Agnew, Vanessa. "Introduction: What Is Reenactment?" *Criticism* 46, no. 3 (2004): 327–339.

Albanese, Catherine. "Requiem for Memorial Day: Dissent in the Redeemer Nation." *American Quarterly* 26, no. 4 (October 1974): 386–398.

———. *Sons of the Fathers: The Civil Religion of the American Revolution.* Philadelphia: Temple University Press, 1976.

Allred, Randal. "Catharsis, Revision, and Re-enactment: Negotiating the Meaning of the American Civil War." *Journal of American Culture* 19, no. 4 (Winter 1996): 1–13.

Appy, Christian G. *Working-Class War: American Combat Soldiers and Vietnam.* Chapel Hill: University of North Carolina Press, 1993.

Atkinson, Rick. *The British Are Coming: The War for America, Lexington to Princeton, 1775–1777.* New York: Henry Holt, 2019.

Barber, Lucy G. *Marching on Washington: The Forging of an American Political Tradition.* Berkeley: University of California Press, 2002.

Barsky, Robert F. *Noam Chomsky: A Life of Dissent.* Cambridge: MIT Press, 1998.

Baskir, Lawrence M., and William Strauss. *Chance and Circumstance: The Draft, the War, and the Vietnam Generation.* New York: Vintage, 1978.

The Battle Road Scenic Byway: Road to Revolution Corridor Management Plan, May 2011. http://www.mapc.org/wp-content/uploads/2017/09/BRSB_CMP_FINAL_webversion.pdf (accessed June 20, 2019).

Bellah, R. *The Broken Covenant.* New York: Seabury, 1975.

Bercovitch, Sacvan. *The American Jeremiad.* Madison: University of Wisconsin Press, 1978.

Black, Kathryn. *In the Shadow of Polio: A Personal and Social History.* Reading, MA: Addison-Wesley, 1997.

Blight, David. *Race and Reunion: The Civil War in American Memory.* Cambridge, MA: Harvard University Press, 2002.

Bluestone, Daniel. *Buildings, Landscapes, and Memory.* New York: W. W. Norton, 2011.

Bodnar, John. *The "Good War" in American Memory.* Baltimore: Johns Hopkins University Press, 2010.

———. *Remaking America: Public Memory, Commemoration, and Patriotism in the Twentieth Century.* Princeton, NJ: Princeton University Press, 1994.

Boston National Historic Sites Commission. *The Lexington-Concord Battle Road: Interim Report of the Boston National Historic Sites Commission*. [Boston, MA]: [The Commission], 1958.

Boston National Historical Park. *Bunker Hill: Battle, Monument, Memory*. Fort Washington, PA: Eastern National, 2007.

Bradford, Charles H. *The Battle Road*. Boston: Rotary Club of Boston, 1975.

Branham, Robert. "ISSA Proceedings 1998: Abolitionist Reconstructions of July Fourth." *Rozenberg Quarterly*. http://rozenbergquarterly.com/issa-proceedings-1998-abolitionist-reconstructions-of-july-fourth/ (accessed July 1, 2019).

Brinkley, Douglas. *Tour of Duty: John Kerry and the Vietnam War*. New York: William Morrow, 2004.

Brockway, Lucinda. *Lexington Battle Green Area Draft Master Plan*, 2011. https://www.lexingtonma.gov/sites/lexingtonma/files/uploads/battlegreenapprovedfinalreport3-14-11.pdf (accessed June 1, 2019).

Bryan, Jeff, et al. *Minute Man National Historical Park: Rte 2A Traffic Analysis and Its Impact on the Park's Visitor Experience*. Cambridge, MA: Volpe, The National Transportation Systems Center, 2002.

Burkett, B. G., and Glenna Whitley. *Stolen Valor: How the Vietnam Generation Was Robbed of Its Heroes and Its History*. Dallas, TX: Verity, 1998.

Casey, Michael. *Che's Afterlife: The Legacy of an Image*. New York: Vintage, 2009.

Chidester, David, and Edward T. Linenthal. "Introduction." In *American Sacred Space*, edited by David Chidester and Edward T. Linenthal, 1–42. Bloomington: Indiana University Press, 1995.

Chomsky, Noam. *American Power and the New Mandarins*. New York: New Press, 2002.

Clarke, Jonas. "The Fate of Blood-Thirsty Oppressors, and GOD's Care of His Distressed People" (1776). https://quod.lib.umich.edu/e/evans/N32919.0001.001/1:3?rgn=div1;view=fulltext (accessed February 19, 2020).

Cooke, Lawrence S. *Lighting in America: From Colonial Rushlights to Victorian Chandeliers*. Pittstown, NJ: Main Street/Universe Books, 1976.

Cram, Mary Frances Bestor. *Chautauqua Salute: A Memoir of the Bestor Years*. Chautauqua, NY: Chautauqua Institution, 1990.

Davis, R. G. "Guerrilla Theatre." *Tulane Drama Review* 10, no. 4 (1966): 130–136.

DeWitt, William A. *History's 100 Greatest Events: Selected by Famous Educators and Journalists*. New York: Grosset & Dunlap, 1954.

Dietrich-Smith, Deborah, and Olmsted Center for Landscape Preservation. *Cultural Landscape Report: North Bridge Unit Minute Man National Historical Park*. Brookline, MA: Olmsted Center for Landscape Preservation, 2004.

Different Sons. Directed by Jack Ofield. Bowling Green Films, 1971. https://www.youtube.com/watch?v=jWAZCDmy0C8 (accessed January 16, 2020).

Doss, Erika. *Memorial Mania: Public Feeling in America*. Chicago: University of Chicago Press, 2010.

Doyle, Michael William. "Staging the Revolution: Guerrilla Theater as a Countercultural Practice, 1965–1968." In *Imagine Nation: The American Counterculture of the 1960s and '70s*, edited by Peter Braunstein and Michael William Doyle, 71–98. New York: Routledge, 2002.

Eisenhart, R. Wayne. "'You Can't Hack It Little Girl': A Discussion of the Covert Psychological Agenda of Modern Combat Training." *Journal of Social Issues* 31, no. 4 (Fall 1975): 13–23.

Eliade, Mircea. *The Sacred and the Profane: The Nature of Religion*, translated by Willard R. Trask. San Diego: Harcourt, 1987.

Emerson, Ralph Waldo. "Concord Hymn." In *Ralph Waldo Emerson: The Major Poetry*, edited by Albert J. von Frank, 130. Cambridge, MA: Harvard University Press, 2015.

Endres, Danielle, and Samantha Senda-Cook. "Location Matters: The Rhetoric of Place in Protest." *Quarterly Journal of Speech* 97, no. 3 (August 2011): 257–282.

Engelhardt, Tom. *The End of Victory Culture: Cold War America and the Disillusioning of a Generation*. Amherst: University of Massachusetts Press, 2007.

Farber, David R. *Chicago '68*. Chicago: University of Chicago Press, 1988.

Fenton, Ross. "On Memorial Day, a Veteran Questions the Futility of War," May 30, 2011, http://archive.boston.com/bostonglobe/editorial_opinion/blogs/the_angle/2011/05/on_memorial_day.html (accessed June 5, 2019).

Fischer, David Hackett. *Paul Revere's Ride*. New York: Oxford University Press, 1995.

Flynn, Alicia M. *Embattled Heritage: The Troubled History of Minute Man National Park*. Senior thesis, Brandeis University, 1995.

Foley, Michael S. *Confronting the War Machine: Draft Resistance During the Vietnam War*. Chapel Hill: University of North Carolina Press, 2003.

Foner, P. S. *We the Other People: Alternative Declarations of Independence by Labor Groups, Farmers, Woman's Rights Advocates, Socialists, and Blacks, 1829–1975*. Urbana: University of Illinois Press, 1976.

Foote, Kenneth E. *Shadowed Ground: America's Landscapes of Violence and Tragedy*. Austin: University of Texas Press, 1997.

Franklin, H. Bruce. *M.I.A., or, Mythmaking in America*. New Brunswick, NJ: Rutgers University Press, 1992.

Frese, Rick. *Concord and the Civil War: From Walden Pond to the Gettysburg Front*. Charleston, SC: History Press, 2014.

Fussell, Paul. *The Great War and Modern Memory*. Oxford: Oxford University Press, 1975.

Galvin, John R. *The Minute Men; The First Fight: Myths and Realities of the American Revolution*. Dulles, VA: Potomac Books, 1989.

Gartner, Matthew. "The Cultural Career of Longfellow's 'Paul Revere's Ride.'" In *Reconsidering Longfellow*, edited by Christoph Irmscher and Robert Arbour, 121–138. Madison, NJ: Fairleigh Dickinson University Press, 2014.

Geismer, Lily. *Don't Blame Us: Suburban Liberals and the Transformation of the Democratic Party*. Princeton, NJ: Princeton University Press, 2015.

Gerber, David A. "Post-Modern American Heroism: Anti-War Heroes, Survivor Heroes, and the Eclipse of Traditional Warrior Values." In *Disabled Veterans in History, Enlarged and Revised Edition*, edited by David A. Gerber, 347–373. Ann Arbor: University of Michigan Press, 2012.

Gibson, James William. *The Perfect War: Technowar in Vietnam*. Boston: Atlantic Monthly Press, 1986.

Giguere, Joy M. *Characteristically American: Memorial Architecture, National Identity, and the Egyptian Revival.* Knoxville: University of Tennessee Press, 2014.

Ginsberg, Allen. "Demonstration or Spectacle as Example, as Communication, or How to Make a March/Spectacle." In *Deliberate Prose: Selected Essays 1952–1995*, edited by Bill Morgan, 9–13. New York: Harper Perennial, 2001.

Glassberg, David. *American Historical Pageantry: The Uses of Tradition in the Early Twentieth Century.* Chapel Hill: University of North Carolina Press, 1990.

Gross, Robert A. "The Celestial Village: Transcendentalism and Tourism in Concord." In *Transient and Permanent: The Transcendentalist Movement and Its Contexts*, edited by Charles Capper and Conrad Edick Wright, 251–281. Boston: Massachusetts Historical Society, 1999.

———. "Commemorating Concord." *Common-Place* 4, no. 1 (October 2003). http://commonplace.online/article/commemorating-concord/ (accessed July 7, 2020).

———. *The Minutemen and Their World.* 1976. Reprint, New York: Hill and Wang, 2001.

Grossman, Jerome. *Relentless Liberal.* New York: Vantage, 1996.

Hagopian, Patrick. "The Korean War Veterans Memorial and Problems of Representation." *Public Art Dialogue* 2, no. 2 (September 2012): 215–253.

———. *The Vietnam War in American Memory: Veterans, Memorials, and the Politics of Healing.* Amherst: University of Massachusetts Press, 2009.

Hall, Dennis. "Civil War Reenactors and the Postmodern Sense of History." *Journal of American Culture* 17, no. 3 (September 1994): 7–11.

Hall, Frank. "Rowing Toward Ithaka (The Uses of Poetry in Ministry)," Spring 2002. https://uuwestport.org/sermons/rev-frank-hall-minister-emeritus/frank-hall/rowing-toward-ithaka-the-uses-of-poetry-in-ministry-by-frank-hall-prepared-for-the-greenfield-group-spring-2002/ (accessed June 21, 2019).

Hall, Simon. "'Guerrilla Theater . . . in the Guise of Red, White, and Blue Bunting': The People's Bicentennial Commission and the Politics of (Un-) Americanism." *Journal of American Studies* 52, no. 1 (2016): 1–23.

Hammer, Richard. *The Court-Martial of Lt. Calley.* New York: Coward, McCann & Geoghegan, 1971.

Handler, Richard, and William Saxton. "Dyssimulation: Reflexivity, Narrative, and the Quest for Authenticity in 'Living History.'" *Cultural Anthropology* 3, no. 3 (1988): 242–260.

Hatuka, Tali. *The Design of Protest: Choreographing Political Demonstrations in Public Space.* Austin: University of Texas Press, 2018.

Hersh, Seymour M. "Looking for Calley: How a Young Journalist Untangled the Riddle of My Lai." *Harper's Magazine*, June 26, 2019. https://harpers.org/archive/2018/06/looking-for-calley/ (accessed June 26, 2019).

Horwitz, Allan V. *PTSD: A Short History.* Baltimore: Johns Hopkins University Press, 2018.

How Far Home: Veterans After Vietnam, directed by Bestor Cram. Boston, MA: Northern Light Production, 1988. VHS.

Huebner, Andrew J. *The Warrior Image: Soldiers in American Culture from the Second World War to the Vietnam Era.* Chapel Hill: University of North Carolina Press, 2008.

Hunt, Andrew E. *The Turning: A History of Vietnam Veterans Against the War.* New York: New York University Press, 1999.

Hunt, Michael H., and Steven I. Levine. *Arc of Empire: America's Wars in Asia from the Philippines to Vietnam.* Chapel Hill: University of North Carolina Press, 2012.

Hurd, Duane Hamilton. *History of Middlesex County, Massachusetts.* Philadelphia: J. W. Lewis & Co., 1890.

Jarvis, Gary E. *Young Blood: A History of the 1st Battalion, 27th Marines, 1968.* Jacksonville, FL: G. E. Jarvis, 1999.

Kaledin, Eugenia. "Vietnam Comes to Lexington: Memorial Day 1971." In *Against the Vietnam War: Writings by Activists,* edited by Mary Susannah Robbins, 147–156. Syracuse, NY: Syracuse University Press, 1999.

Kammen, Michael G. *Digging Up the Dead: A History of Notable American Reburials.* Chicago: University of Chicago Press, 2010.

———. *Mystic Chords of Memory: The Transformation of Tradition in American Culture.* New York: Vintage, 1991.

———. *A Season of Youth: The American Revolution and the Historical Imagination.* New York: Knopf, 1978.

Kehoe, Vincent J.-R. *"We Were There!": April 19th 1775.* Lowell, MA: Society for the Preservation of Colonial Culture, 1974.

Kerry, John, and Vietnam Veterans Against the War, eds. *The New Soldier.* New York: Macmillan, 1971.

Ketchum, Richard M. *Decisive Day: The Battle for Bunker Hill.* New York: Anchor, 1974.

Kiernan, Ben, and Taylor Owen. "Making More Enemies Than We Kill? Calculating U.S. Bomb Tonnages Dropped in Laos and Cambodia, and Weighing Their Implications." *Asia-Pacific Journal* 13, no. 7.3 (April 27, 2016). https://apjjf.org/Ben-Kiernan/4313.html (accessed August 14, 2018).

King, David. "Paul Revere Had a Horse: The Veterans' March to Boston." *New Republic,* June 12, 1971, 11–13.

King, Martin Luther Jr. "'I Have a Dream,' Address Delivered at the March on Washington for Jobs and Freedom," August 28, 1963. https://kinginstitute.stanford.edu/king-papers/documents/i-have-dream-address-delivered-march-washington-jobs-and-freedom (accessed February 6, 2020).

Kovic, Ron. *Born on the Fourth of July.* 1976. New York: Akashic, 2016.

Kranish, Michael, Brian C. Mooney, and Nina Easton. *John F. Kerry: The Complete Biography by the* Boston Globe *Reporters Who Know Him Best.* New York: PublicAffairs, 2004.

Kulik, Gary. *"War Stories": False Atrocity Tales, Swift Boaters, and Winter Soldiers—What Really Happened in Vietnam.* Dulles, VA: Potomac Books, 2009.

Lawrence, Jerome, and Robert Edwin Lee. *The Night Thoreau Spent in Jail: A Play.* New York: Hill & Wang, 2001. Print.

Leed, Eric J. "Violence, Death and Masculinity." *Vietnam Generation* 1, no. 3 (1989): 168–189.

Lembcke, Jerry. *The Spitting Image: Myth, Memory, and the Legacy of Vietnam.* New York: New York University Press, 1998.

Leslie, Stuart W. *The Cold War and American Science: The Military-Industrial-Academic Complex at MIT and Stanford*. New York: Columbia University Press, 1993.

Lifton, Robert Jay. *Home from the War: Vietnam Veterans: Neither Victims nor Executioners*. New York: Simon & Schuster, 1973.

Lindgren, James M. *Preserving Historic New England: Preservation, Progressivism, and the Remaking of Memory*. New York: Oxford University Press, 1995.

Linenthal, Edward Tabor. *Sacred Ground: Americans and Their Battlefields*. Urbana: University of Illinois Press, 1991.

———. "Sacred Ground: Martial Landscape in American Culture." In *Places of Commemoration: Search for Identity and Landscape Design*, edited by Joachim Wolschke-Buhlmann, 301–310. Cambridge, MA: Harvard University Press, 2001.

Longfellow, Henry Wadsworth, "Paul Revere's Ride." In *Longfellow: Poems and Other Writings*, edited by J. D. McClatchy, 362–365. New York: Library of America, 2000.

Lubow, Arthur H. "Veteran at Harvard Opposes War." *Harvard Crimson*, March 1, 1971. https://www.thecrimson.com/article/1971/3/1/veteran-at-harvard-opposes-war-pi/ (accessed January 2, 2020).

Lyons, David. "Moral Judgement, Historical Reality, and Civil Disobedience." *Philosophy and Public Affairs* 27, no. 1 (1998): 31–49.

MacLeish, Archibald. "The Young Dead Soldiers Do Not Speak." In *Archibald MacLeish: Reflections*, edited by Bernard A. Draback and Helen E. Ellis, 172. Amherst: University of Massachusetts Press, 1986.

Martucci, David B. "Flag and Symbol Usage in Early New England." *Raven: A Journal of Vexillology* 13 (2006): 1–40.

Massachusetts Advisory Committee to the U.S. Commission on Civil Rights and the Massachusetts Commission Against Discrimination. *Route 128: Boston's Road to Segregation*. [Washington, DC]: [U.S. Commission on Civil Rights,] 1975.

McKibben, Bill. "Patriotic Acts." In *The Bill McKibben Reader: Pieces from an Active Life*, 330–338. New York: Henry Holt, 2008.

Miller, Perry. *Errand into the Wilderness*. Cambridge, MA: Harvard University Press, 1958.

Moser, Richard R. *The New Winter Soldiers: GI and Veteran Dissent During the Vietnam Era*. New Brunswick, NJ: Rutgers University Press, 1996.

Mosse, George Lachmann. *Fallen Soldiers: Reshaping the Memory of the World Wars*. Oxford: Oxford University Press, 1991.

Nicosia, Gerald. *Home to War: A History of the Vietnam Veterans' Movement*. New York: Three Rivers Press, 2001.

O'Brien, Tim. "Ambush!" *Boston Magazine*, April 1993, 63–67, 101–106.

———. *In the Lake of the Woods*. New York: Mariner Books, 1994.

Oliver, Kendrick. *The My Lai Massacre in American History and Memory*. Manchester: Manchester University Press, 2006.

O'Mara, Margaret Pugh. *Cities of Knowledge: Cold War Science and the Search for the Next Silicon Valley*. Princeton, NJ: Princeton University Press, 2005.

O'Neill, John E. *Unfit for Command: Swift Boat Veterans Speak Out Against John Kerry*. Washington, DC: Regnery Publishing, 2004.

The Opium Trail: Heroin and Imperialism. Boston, MA: New England Free Press, 1972.

Paine, Thomas. "The Crisis" (1776). www.ushistory.org/paine/crisis/c-01.htm (accessed December 20, 2017)

"Peace, Protest, Patriotism," Lexington Panel Discussion, November 21, 2010. DVD.

People's Century. "Young Blood (1968)," dir. Mark J. Davis, June 14, 1999. VHS.

Philbrick, Nathaniel. *Bunker Hill: A City, a Siege, a Revolution*. New York: Viking, 2013.

Phinney, Elias. *History of the Battle at Lexington*. Boston: Phelps and Farnham, 1825.

Prados, John. *Vietnam: The History of an Unwinnable War, 1945–1975*. Lawrence: University of Kansas Press, 2009.

Pullen, Doris L., and Donald B. Cobb. *The Celebration of April the Nineteenth from 1776 to 1960 in Lexington, Massachusetts*. Lexington, MA: Lexington Press, 1960.

Purcell, Sarah J. "Commemoration, Public Art, and the Changing Meaning of the Bunker Hill Monument." *Public Historian* 25, no. 2 (2003): 55–71.

Rand, Christopher. *Cambridge, U.S.A.: Hub of a New World*. New York: Oxford University Press, 1964.

Raskin, Jonah. *For the Hell of It: The Life and Times of Abbie Hoffman*. Berkeley: University of California Press, 1998.

Rawson, Michael. *Eden on the Charles: The Making of Boston*. Cambridge, MA: Harvard University Press, 2010.

Robbins, Roland Wells. *The Story of the Minute Man*. Boston, MA: G.R. Barnstead & Son, 1945.

Rodiger, David R. "Gook: The Short History of an Americanism." *Monthly Review* 43, no. 10 (March 1992). http://www.davidroediger.org/articles/gook-the-short-history-of-americanism.html (accessed January 21, 2020).

Rosaldo, Renato. "Grief and a Headhunter's Rage." In *Violence in War and Peace: An Anthology*, edited by Nancy Scheper-Hughes and Philippe I. Bourgois, 150–156. Hoboken, NJ: Blackwell, 2004.

Rosegrant, Susan, and David Lampe. *Route 128: Lessons from Boston's High-Tech Community*. New York: Basic Books, 1992.

Rothweiller, Robert, Maurice Miller, and Teresa Urbanowski. *General Management Plan: Minute Man National Historical Park, Massachusetts*. Denver, CO: U.S. Department of the Interior, National Park Service, 1989.

Ryan, D. Michael. "White Cockade: A Jacobite Air at the North Bridge?" www2.bc.edu/donald-hafner/lmm/music-articles/white_cockade_ryan.html (accessed January 6, 2019).

Sauerwein, Leigh, ed. *J'ai vecu: La Guerre du Vietnam, 1961–1975*. Paris: Bayard, 2006.

Saunders, Nancy Miller. *Combat by Trial: An Odyssey with 20th Century Winter Soldiers*. New York: iUniverse, 2008.

Saxenian, Annalee. *Regional Advantage: Culture and Competition in Silicon Valley and Route 128*. Cambridge, MA: Harvard University Press, 2000.

Scarry, Elaine. *The Body in Pain: The Making and Unmaking of the World*. New York: Oxford University Press, 1987.

Schechner, Richard. "Guerrilla Theatre: May 1970." *Drama Review* 14, no. 3 (1970): 163–168.

Schiffrin, Andre, ed. *The Cold War and the University: Toward an Intellectual History of the Post War Years*. New York: New Press, 1997.

Sharp, Gene. *The Politics of Nonviolent Action*. 3 vols. Boston: Porter Sargent, 2000.

Shattuck, Lemuel. *History of the Town of Concord*. Boston: Russell, Odiorne, and Company, 1835.

Shay, Jonathan. *Achilles in Vietnam: Combat Trauma and the Undoing of Character*. New York: Scribner, 2003.

Sorby, Angela. *Schoolroom Poets: Childhood and the Place of American Poetry, 1865–1917*. Durham: University of New Hampshire Press, 2005.

Steinitz, Carl. *Alternative Futures for Minute Man National Historical Park. Harvard University Graduate School of Design*. Cambridge, MA: Harvard University Graduate School of Design, 1985.

Swikes, Frances, et al. *Minute Man National Historical Park: Alternative Transportation Evaluation*. Scotts Valley, CA: CreateSpace Independent Publishing Platform, 2005.

Taylor, Sandra C. *Vietnamese Women at War: Fighting for Ho Chi Minh and the Revolution*. Lawrence: University Press of Kansas, 1999.

Teachout, Woden. *Capture the Flag: A Political History of American Patriotism*. New York: Basic Books, 2009.

Thoreau, Henry David. "The Duty of Civil Disobedience." https://www.gutenberg.org/files/71/71-h/71-h.htm (accessed August 19, 2018).

Tourtellot, Arthur. *William Diamond's Drum: The Beginning of the War of the American Revolution*. Garden City, NY: Doubleday, 1959.

Tracey, Jack. "Memorial Day 1971, an Anti-War Journey." *Daily Kos*, May 20, 2011.

Tsipis, Yanni Kosta, and David Kruh. *Building Route 128*. Charleston, SC: Arcadia, 2005.

Turner, Rory. "Bloodless Battles: The Civil War Reenacted." *Drama Review* 34, no. 4 (1990): 123–136.

Turse, Nick. *Kill Anything That Moves: The Real American War in Vietnam*. New York: Picador, 2014.

Unfinished Symphony: Democracy and Dissent, directed by Bestor Cram and Mike Majoros. Boston: Northern Light Productions, 2001. DVD.

Veterans Against the War, directed by Hart Perry, 1971. DVD.

Vietnam Veterans Against the War. *FBI Files*. Beverly Hills, CA: BACM Research, 2004. CDs.

———. "An Interview with a Veteran: 'Nobody Buys Meat Anymore.'" *Winter Soldier: A Publication of Vietnam Veterans Against the War* 3, no. 3 (May 1973): 6. www.vvaw.org/veteran/article/?id=985 (accessed February 17, 2020).

Wagner-Pacifici, Robin, and Barry Schwartz. "The Vietnam Veterans Memorial: Commemorating a Difficult Past." *American Journal of Sociology* 97, no. 2 (September 1991): 376–420.

Warner, Lloyd W. *American Life: Dream and Reality*. Chicago: University of Chicago Press, 1953.

Webster, Daniel. *An Address Delivered at the Completion of the Bunker Hill Monument, June 17, 1843*. Boston: Tappan and Dennet, 1843.

Winter Soldier. Produced by the Winterfilm Cooperative, 1972. DVD.

Winter Soldier Investigation Transcript. www2.iath.virginia.edu/sixties/HTML_docs/Resources/Primary/Winter_Soldier/WS_02_opening html (accessed February 6, 2020).

Young, Marilyn B. *The Vietnam Wars 1945–1990.* New York: HarperPerennial, 1992.

Zenzen, Joan, and National Park Service U.S. Department of the Interior. *Bridging the Past: An Administrative History of Minute Man National Historical Park.* [Washington, DC]: National Park Service, U.S. Department of the Interior, 2010.

Zinn, Howard. *Disobedience and Democracy: Nine Fallacies on Law and Order.* Chicago: Haymarket, 1968.

INDEX

ACKNOWLEDGMENTS

In 1990, a group of Lexington residents joined forces to create the Lexington Oral History Project (LOHP) with the intent of interviewing veterans, civilians, and local officials who had participated in or organized against Operation POW, the protest staged by the New England chapter of Vietnam Veterans Against the War and recounted in these pages. Over the next four years, Eugenia Kaledin, Robert (Dick) Robbat, Eva Gordon, Lenore Fenn, Norma McGavern-Norland, Bonnie Jones, Nancy Earsy, and Kay Bell interviewed sixty-six people on video and deposited the results at Lexington's Cary Memorial Library. LOHP also transcribed and made available to the public on their website thirty-seven of these interviews. When I told Eugenia and Dick I wanted to write a book about the march, both kindly agreed to talk to me. In addition to sitting for an interview with me about his experiences as a longtime Lexington resident, a local high school history teacher, and a veteran of the Vietnam War era, Dick came to my parents' home in nearby Lincoln with the wonderful Faith Ferguson, who was a teenager in Lexington in 1971, and showed me all of the invaluable photographs he took of the veterans as they came through town, one of which he has kindly allowed to appear here. Both of them shared their memories of the march and the subsequent mass arrest. Eugenia, a PhD in American studies with an unwavering faith in the importance of dissent, invited me over to her Lexington apartment and, after several lengthy conversations, gave me her LOHP files, which include VVAW-NE materials not otherwise available in the archives. I am indebted to these dedicated citizens for preserving their town's past and making books like mine possible.

After reading all of the LOHP interviews, I wanted to talk to more veterans in order to get the most comprehensive view possible of why they chose to participate in the march and what the experience was like for them. I'm grateful to Peter Wilson, Bestor Cram (who sat down for an interview with me even though he had already completed an LOHP interview), Don Carrico, Ross Fenton, Joseph Baratta, and Rusty Sachs for sharing the stories that became the focal points of each of this book's six chapters. Ross and Rand Martin, another Vietnam veteran I was fortunate enough to interview and who has allowed me to use his 1971 photograph of Bestor in the VVAW-NE Cambridge office, have kept in touch with me over the years. Without their encouragement, this book would not have been completed.

My one regret is that I had to make the same choice Henry Wadsworth Longfellow did in "Paul Revere's Ride." Just as, for the sake of narrative economy, he left out the many other riders and signalers who helped spread the alarm on the night of April 18, 1775, I have consigned all of the other Operation POW organizers and participants to the footnotes. While I regret that the personal contributions of Christopher Gregory, Lenny Rotman, Howard Baker, Richard Colton, Gordon Fletcher-Howell, Bill Homans, Dale Reese, and others are not featured in this book, their collective efforts are on every page. I feel particularly bad about leaving out the herculean efforts of Arthur Johnson, the co-coordinator of the VVAW-NE office and a principal organizer of the march, if not the person who dreamed up the idea of reversing Paul Revere's ride. He is this book's William Dawes, having valiantly carried a message to the people only to be written out of this telling of it.

I'm sad, too, that Jennifer Levin did not live to see this book published. Jen played the role of the historical Paul Revere for the veterans and, being an avid fan of both the Grateful Dead and Disney World, proved to be a delightful person to interview. She was in her early teens and I was six years old when the antiwar veterans marched through our hometown of Lincoln on their way from Concord to the Lexington Battle Green, and it was instructive to compare notes on what we remembered from those days. Other Lincoln-area folks who helped me with this project include Jen's mother Betty Levin, who so many of the march organizers still remember fondly and who also kindly sat for an interview; Jane Brayton (then Williams), one of only two Lincoln women who got arrested on the Green with the veterans and whose agreement to sit for the very first interview I conducted for this book is only one of many times she has been an important presence in my life; Nyna Polumbaum, who generously forewent much of the permission fees the Newseum would have otherwise collected for her so that I could include six of her acclaimed husband Ted's photographs; Steve Bowden, who tracked down a couple of key leads for me; Victor Curren, who has unstintingly shared his prodigious knowledge of Concord and Lexington history with me and who gave me a tour of Buckman's Tavern on the edge of Lexington Green; Richard Frese, who took me on a tour of

Monument Square both through his written work and on foot; and, of course, my parents, who love Lincoln, the surrounding towns, and their role in history as much as I do and who helped with this project by walking part of the veterans' march route with me and, when I needed time in the archives, babysitting.

Like Nyna, Paul Szep, former chief editorial cartoonist for the *Boston Globe*, and filmmaker Hart Perry have waived permission fees so that I can include their work here. While a graduate student at Columbia University, Hart organized a platoon of filmmakers whose hours and hours of footage of the march proved invaluable in helping me understand the dissenting veterans' methods and the public's varied responses. The largest number of photographs in the book come from Cary Wolinsky, who in 1971 was as entranced as Hart, Dick, and Ted by the way in which the antiwar veterans repurposed the memorialized Revolutionary War landscape. Their still and moving images convey the same love and respect for these men that I have tried to show them in prose.

A very hearty thank you to cartographer Jeff Mathison for his artistry and patience. It was no easy task to figure out what kinds of maps would best help those readers not familiar with Massachusetts and its history to understand how the veterans moved through space and time.

I have also benefited enormously from the indefatigable assistance of many librarians and curators. At Cary Memorial Library in Lexington, reference librarian Linda Carroll helped me work through all of the LOHP interviews that have not been transcribed and mounted on the LOHP website. Terrie Wallace, curator at Minute Man National Historical Park, helped me pour through the park's archives. The staff at the Wisconsin Historical Society helped me access and read through the VVAW archives housed there. Kristin Parker, lead curator of the arts at the Boston Public Library, found several of the images in this book that I thought had been lost forever. David Brubaker, who serves on the Board of Directors of the Kansas Museum of Military History, kindly identified all of the different kinds of fatigues and weaponry the veterans used for their mock search-and-destroy mission in Concord's Monument Square. And finally, Carrie Marten and Kristen Heinrich at the Purchase College (SUNY) Library ordered more books, articles, and microfilm through interlibrary loan for me than either they or I probably care to remember.

Also at Purchase College, Nancy Kane and Nancy Diaz provided much-needed technical support with creating screenshots from the film Hart Perry made of the march. They and Aviva Taubenfeld, Gaura Narayan, Dolores Obuch, Louise Yelin, and my other colleagues in the School of Humanities continue to inspire me every day and make coming to work a joy. The financial support of the college has also been tremendously important. Research for this book was funded in part by the Purchase College Doris and Carl Kempner Distinguished Professorship, which I was fortunate to hold from 2011 to 2013. And a recent grant from New York State/United University Professions (UUP), made possible by our college's UUP chapter, helped to offset the cost of the maps.

I count myself incredibly fortunate to have been able to work with Jerry Singerman at Penn Press for three different book projects. This one has finally come to fruition thanks to his ability to ask the right questions, provide astute suggestions and edits, and find the best-suited external reviewers. Ed Linenthal did me the great favor of reading the manuscript during the review stage not once but twice, the second time after a major revision his comments rightly prompted. His books and articles on battlefields and memorials, many of which are referenced here, played a key role in creating the field of memory studies to which this book attempts to make a contribution. My thanks also to historian Lily Geismer for her suggestions during the review stage and for her book on the Route 128 suburbs, which was critically important in helping me figure out why the veterans had so much success in rallying Lexington-area residents to their side. I am also grateful to Randall Mason, who teaches in UPenn's Graduate Program in Historic Preservation and who is currently serving a term on the Penn Press Faculty Advisory Board. Randy's enthusiasm for the project and his insistence that the book needed a good set of maps got the project over the finish line. All remaining errors and issues are solely my own.

My dear friend Audrey Fisch has been an amazing writing partner since our time in graduate school together. She has read and commented upon every page of this book countless times while never failing to be an enthusiastic cheerleader. Now that we are empty nesters, I look forward to many more writing and other adventures. Thanks as well to my incredible tennis friends (Carrie Kaplan, Adrienne Concra, Aleksandra Chancy, Melissa Shumer, and so many others), my fearless travel partners (Jane Buchan and Inger Pols), and to the EBC for being so much more than a neighborhood book club.

This project was fueled by my husband's cooking, good humor, and steadfast love. Jim grew up on an American military base in Okinawa while his father served in Vietnam. Researching this book was a way for me to learn about a war that was very much a part of his family's life while my own childhood was completely sheltered from its reach.

Finally, this book is dedicated to the person I love to blame for it taking so long to finish. Of course, watching Eli become a young adult has been the greatest joy of my life, and neither Jim nor I regret a minute spent being part of his journey.

CPSIA information can be obtained
at www.ICGtesting.com
Printed in the USA
BVHW030006260321
603495BV00001B/1/J

9 780812 252972